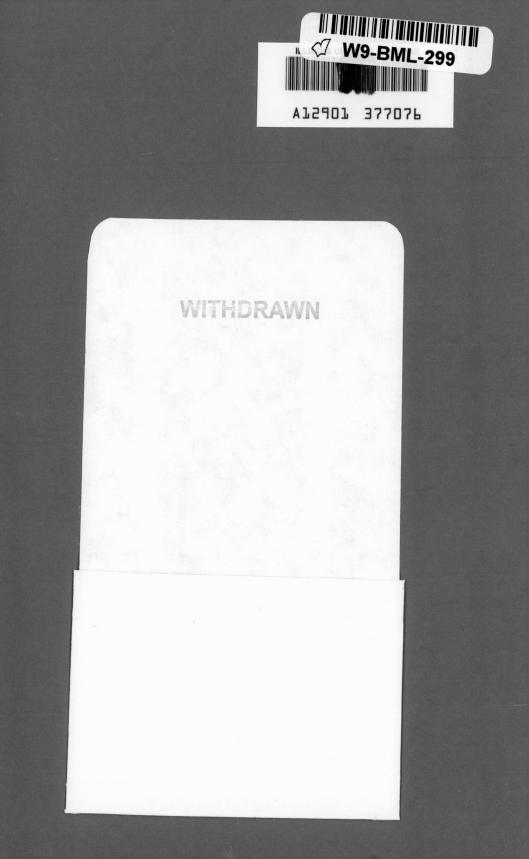

THE BOOTLEGGER

$\mathscr{A}$ STORY OF
SMALL-TOWN AMERICA

University of Illinois Press
Urbana and Chicago

The
Bootlegger

JOHN E. HALLWAS

© 1998 by the Board of Trustees of the
University of Illinois
Manufactured in the United States of America
C 5 4 3 2 1

This book is printed on acid-free paper.

Unless otherwise noted, the photographs in this
book appear courtesy of the Archives and Special
Collections, Western Illinois University Library.

Library of Congress Cataloging-in-Publication Data

Hallwas, John E.
The bootlegger : a story of small-town America /
John E. Hallwas.
      p.   cm.
Includes bibliographical references.
ISBN 0-252-02395-1 (acid-free paper)
1. Wagle, Thomas Henry, 1886–1929. 2. Prohibition—
Illinois—Colchester—History. 3. Liquor industry—
Illinois—Colchester—History. 4. Colchester (Ill.)—
History. I. Title
HV5090.I3H35   1998
364.1'33—dc21   97-45253
   [B]   CIP

To the people of Colchester
and McDonough County
who shared with me their
memories and stories

CONTENTS

PREFACE

The Bootlegger is a literary-historical hybrid combining several kinds of nonfiction. In large measure, the information that it provides, the truth that it tells, and the impact that it makes result from that combination.

First of all, it is a biography devoted to a small-town criminal who flourished in the Prohibition era. Like most biographies, it portrays a life in process and tries to reveal the character and motivations of a unique individual who became, in his time and place, a notable figure. No aspect of the book was more challenging, especially because the bootlegger left no written records and those around him left very few, and because his illegal occupation prompted him to be secretive. Beyond that, he was a legendary figure who was often recalled differently by the various people who had known him or had heard about him. For that reason the book also had to become an account of the town where he was, and still is, the most controversial aspect of local history.

Because Kelly Wagle's life ended with an unsolved murder that greatly troubled the town, his death seemed like an ideal point at which to begin *The Bootlegger*. It also became, then, a true crime story, a sort of nonfictional whodunit. Like so many works of that kind, it opens with a disturbing dead body and a complex public response to the killing. The focus of the story is not on the murderer, however, but on the victim, whose life was the deepest mystery of the town. Although the book finally explains who was responsible for the crime, the main purpose of

The Bootlegger is to reveal the context—the entire small-town cultural milieu—in which it occurred as the story behind the dead man unfolds.

As that suggests, *The Bootlegger* is also a community history. Encompassing the life of Kelly Wagle, it depicts the rise and decline of an Illinois coal town, with special attention to his family's experience there. Of course, many aspects of the town's history had to be omitted, or passed over lightly, because their inclusion would have resulted in a huge compilation of details that no one outside of Colchester, and perhaps few within it, would ever want to read. And in fact, the omission of many things is precisely what gave shape to the town's story, creating a symbolic structure of the people and events, values and conflicts, that were included. That's how meaning always emerges from the past.

Like any effective community history, this one portrays a unique place and reveals how, and to some extent why, it changed and developed over the years. In the process, however, the book also reflects the ideals and anxieties, dreams and disappointments, of the townspeople, who appear as a kind of composite character as well as individuals, and whose deepest struggle, perhaps, was not to survive and succeed but to find meaning in a world of chance and change, sudden death and gradual decline. As that suggests, the town's story has a kind of ironic plot, for much that was hoped for remains unrealized, and the bootlegger himself epitomizes the erosion of traditional values in the twentieth century.

Hopefully, readers of *The Bootlegger* will recognize that the history of Colchester and the story of Kelly Wagle are deeply interrelated. The town's enormous conflict over drinking was, after all, the issue that provided him with opportunity and framed his identity. And it is surely no accident that a lawbreaker who became legendary emerged when his community was troubled by economic decline and social discord.

As the double narrative approach, focused on both the town and the man, suggests, *The Bootlegger* is also an account of the two great American dreams, of community and self-realization, as they were pursued in one place over several generations. It is a case study of powerful and sometimes contradictory forces in American society—forces clearly reflected in the life and legend of Kelly Wagle, who symbolized neighborly concern to some and heroic individualism to others.

Of course, *The Bootlegger* also reflects the social history of small-town America, especially in the Midwest. Although early Colchester was a distinctive place in some respects, its losing struggle against decline was paralleled in thousands of other small towns during the late nineteenth and early twentieth centuries. The midwestern landscape, in particular, is filled with faded communities that used to have a vibrant social life and real promise. Until we have better histories of at least some of them, our knowledge of the past in that part of the country will remain strikingly incomplete.

Also, in our increasingly urban, impersonal, and atomistic society, we need to recognize that the small town of generations ago was not just a locality with a limited population; it was a way of life, a form of human experience. Like a tribal culture, it was characterized by close relationships in a thoroughly familiar, semi-isolated setting where the landscape and buildings, people and activities had deep meaning for the residents, and where disappointment was often muted and discord was controlled through the customs and rituals of community life. Early Colchester was a version of the America that we have lost.

Finally, it is well to remember that any good biography or community history is a composite of factual information cemented together by the author's insight to create a reconstruction of that life or that town and, in the process, reveal its significance. Interpretation is not only unavoidable; it is essential if the assembled information is to have any meaning. *The Bootlegger* tends toward the documentary because it includes many newspaper articles and editorials, in an effort to reflect local perspectives and values, but as the preceding comments reveal, it is still an interpretation of the man and the town. In fact, because it relies heavily on recollections and stories by the townspeople, as well as on newspaper materials, the book is to some extent an interpretation of Colchester's interpretation of the local past. More clearly than most works, *The Bootlegger* reveals the subjective, multilayered nature of our historical understanding.

As these final comments suggest, the author is well aware that differing views of Kelly Wagle will remain, that his story will change as long as people tell it, and that much more might be said about the history of Colchester.

THE BOOTLEGGER

The Bootlegger's Funeral

On April 8, 1929, shortly after nine o'clock in the evening, in the quiet little town of Colchester, Illinois, a man named Henry Wagle, whom everyone called "Kelly," was shot dead on the street a few hundred feet from his front door. It was a gangland-style slaying, and his killer was never caught.

Wagle had expected it, had told everyone it was coming, but no one saw anything except his perforated body lying in a pool of blood on the sidewalk, illuminated by the dim glow of the streetlight, and a new Ford roadster heading out of town.

Wagle was a bootlegger. Alive, he had been the most notorious man in McDonough County. Dead, he was a communal memory that the people of Colchester (population 1,350) had to wrestle with.

Two days later they held his funeral.

The dusty old mining town was strangely quiet that Wednesday morning, poised in a kind of unnatural stillness that perhaps symbolized the future of the community. The small brick stores were closed along the Chicago, Burlington, and Quincy Railroad tracks that divided the central business district into the North Side, or Depot Street, and the South Side, or Market Street. A very important resident, a man of consequence, was dead, and the town was showing its respect.

The schools were open, but most students did not attend on that day. They knew they didn't have to. The youngsters who did show up gathered in small groups at recess and talked about the bootlegger. He had been a fascinating figure to many of them—friendly and generous, exciting and mysterious.

In a certain sense the townspeople looked forward to the funeral. The killing had challenged their social consciousness, raising a host of uncomfortable questions about their community, so a great deal needed to be remembered, considered, and reconstructed.

By early afternoon the traffic was increasing on the hard road (nobody ever called it Route 9) that extended east and west of town along the railroad tracks. All of it was coming to Colchester.

Soon there was a steady stream of cars from the east, where the county seat lay six miles distant. A college town of about 8,000 people, Macomb had the only first-rate hotel in McDonough County, so travelers to the funeral who had come a long distance—from Chicago, especially—were staying there. Others who had driven from Galesburg, Peoria, Springfield, and smaller downstate towns had to pass through the county seat on their way.

As they drove to Colchester, the outsiders could see off to the north the still-bare trees, budding but not green, that covered the steep banks of Crooked Creek. To the south they could see rows of faded corn stubble and patches of new green weeds in fields that stretched away under a cloudy sky to distant farmsteads and small stands of timber. The weather had been unseasonably warm, well into the eighties, during the previous week, creating a kind of premature summer that had left the fields uncommonly dry. But the temperature was dropping and rain was expected.

A mile east of town the line of cars rumbled past the Cottonwood Inn, a roadhouse that catered to the growing horde of motorists who ventured onto the hard roads, especially on the weekends. People could get whatever they wanted there. It was one of the many places that did business with the bootlegger.

Close to town the vast empty fields were disfigured here and there by huge mounds of clay and rock, sprinkled with chips of coal. They were "gob piles," heaps of tailings—all that remained of the dozens of played-out shaft mines that had once flourished there. Traces of iron ore gave many of the piles a rich red color, so they looked like sores in the dark brown earth. One local newspaper editor said they reminded him of "the ruins of Old Troy." Perhaps he viewed the old-time coal mining as a kind of heroic struggle, and in a certain sense, that's what it was.

On the east edge of town there was a sign along the right side of the road pointing to the "Northwestern Terra Cotta Company," a small clay-mining operation. That mine was part of Colchester's only remaining industry, clay and clay products. There were also two clay mines west of town, a fire clay company south of town, and an old brickyard north of town. None of them was a large operation. In the past a paving brick company and a pottery had also operated in Colchester, but the clay industry too had started to decline.

The colorful incoming cars were a marvelous sight in Colchester, where black, squarish Model Ts were as common as buggies and farm wagons had been a generation earlier. The old Ford advertisements were right: the Model T was "sturdy, long-lived, and adapted to all conditions of roads and weather," so two years after Henry Ford had stopped production, it remained the universal car in rural America, including Colchester. Everybody seemed to have one. Some wagons and buggies were still around, too, and were apt to be used by farmers when the roads were bad, so the old white-painted hitching rails had not yet been removed from Depot and Market Streets.

But the 1920s had brought an explosion of automobile makes and models, and "motoring" had become a kind of self-expression, so that by the spring of 1929 shoppers at Macomb could buy not only a Model A Ford but also a Chevrolet, a Plymouth, a Whippet, an Overland, a Pontiac, a Dodge, a Nash, an Oldsmobile, a Studebaker, a Hudson, an Essex, a Buick, a Hupmobile, or a Packard—if they had the money. Most people in Colchester didn't.

On the day of Kelly Wagle's funeral, the townspeople also got their first look at some of the big new touring cars—Cadillacs, Lincolns, and Pierce Arrows—which were not even sold in McDonough County. Sleek and powerful, with chrome-plated radiators, wire-spoke wheels, and swept-back fenders, they came in colors like "Harbor Blue," "Forest Green," "Mansion White," and "Boulevard Red," as advertisements for them pointed out.

The line of cars coming into town that day was like a revelation from another world.

At the edge of town the westbound drivers slowed to observe the speed limit, fifteen miles per hour, and then drove past the small white houses that lined the road—and symbolized the modest hopes of the miners who had built them. Some were in bad repair, for hard times had come to Colchester with the decline of the coal mines, and the town had never recovered its economic momentum.

At the corner of Hun Street, where the hard road jogged to the right, a few elegant Victorian homes revealed a heritage of grander hopes and greater achievements. They reflected the success of nineteenth-century merchants.

On the left stood a pair of identical two-story homes with cross-gabled roofs, side porches, and fancy trim. They were built in 1882 by Albert J. Smith, a Canadian immigrant who had come to Colchester as a railroad agent during the Civil War and had made a small fortune as a coal shipper. He started a successful general store in the 1870s, later established the town's biggest clothing store, and afterward built the largest brick building on Market Street. One of the splendid houses was for him; the other was for his twenty-three-year-old son and new business partner, H. Walter Smith. The look-alike homes said much about the advantages and obligations of having money in the family and revealed the importance of social status in an age of heroic self-realization.

Built long before the hard road had been dreamed of, the Smith homes faced away from it, looking south toward the railroad tracks that had been the lifeblood of the community since the 1850s. By 1929 the elder Smith had been dead for twenty years, and another family owned his house. They had bought it for the taxes that were owed against it. Walter still lived next door, and he still operated the big Smith Clothing Store, but his business too was slowly declining.

Directly across the hard road was another imposing two-story house, adorned with a lovely front porch and scalloped siding in the gables, and to the townspeople it called to mind the ultimate success story in the history of Colchester. It had been built in 1884 by James W. Stevens, one of the six Stevens brothers. Born into a struggling pioneer family, he and his brother Edward became important local merchants and the town's first bankers. In 1890 they left for Chicago, where another brother had established a great silk emporium on State Street, and they took their younger brothers with them. The Stevens brothers soon invested in other ventures and became enormously wealthy. In 1927 the richest of them, James W., and his two sons built the largest hotel in the world, on Michigan Avenue, at a cost of $27 million. On a typical business day the Stevens Hotel had twice as many guests as the entire population of Colchester.

The Stevens house had changed hands a few times since 1890, and sections of the three-hundred-foot lot, as well as the cross-gabled carriage house, had been sold off. By 1929 there was a large sign hanging from the front porch:

Frank Williams, Jr.
FUNERAL HOME

The bootlegger's funeral wasn't being held there, but across the intersection from the old Stevens place was a more recent, one-story brick building with a similar sign:

WILLIAMS FUNERAL HOME

It was owned by Frank Williams, Sr. The town's undertakers, father and son, did not get along, and they had become intense competitors in the grim business of handling the local dead.

The elder Williams was in charge of the arrangements for the big funeral. A slim, balding man with a black mustache, he had practiced his somber trade in Colchester for almost thirty years. He had started as a carpenter back when the town was booming, but like many others who remained, he had adapted to the slow withering of local hopes.

On the previous day he had managed to embalm the bootlegger's body, despite the thirty-six new holes in it, and he had signed the death certificate. Some of the townspeople had stopped by his place later that day, to view the remains of their old friend and neighbor, but the funeral wasn't being held there either.

As the incoming cars jogged to the right, they proceeded past the dead man's house, a neat-looking forest green bungalow with white trim around the windows and a front porch with a rose trellis at one end. It sat on three lots and was surrounded by shrubs and flower gardens. On the funeral day nothing was in bloom. Much of the house was hidden from the passing motorists by more than two dozen parked cars owned by friends and relatives of the deceased.

In back of the house was a shallow ravine with a small gray horse barn standing on the far side. The bootlegger had always loved horses, and in recent years he had raced his thoroughbreds as far away as Louisville and New Orleans. He was a betting man—until his luck finally ran out.

Directly across the hard road from his house was an extension of the business district called Macomb Street. Running only two blocks before it blended in with the hard road at the curve, it had a service station on one end and the massive, three-story Fraternity Building on the other. All the stores and other buildings on that short unpaved stretch faced away from the hard road and looked south, into the rear of the stores on Depot Street. One might suppose that the merchants didn't care much about the people who drove to Colchester from other places, but they had in fact been busily, if not desperately, promoting the town as a place for outsiders to shop. It was just that Macomb Street, like the rest of the business district, had been developed in the early days, when everything depended on the railroad.

In the middle of that two-block business section, right next to the Carsten Paint Store, was a corrugated-tin coal shed riddled with small holes.

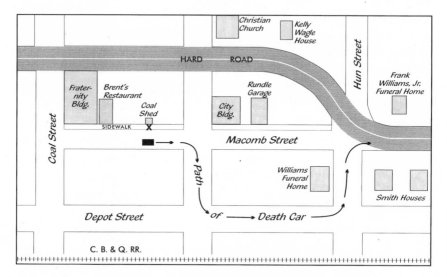

Map 1. The Colchester Street Where Kelly Wagle Was Murdered

Many of the outsiders gawked and whispered as their cars passed between the place where the bootlegger had lived and the place where he had died. Some even turned left onto Coal Street—the main road going north and south—and then left again onto Macomb Street to drive past the tin shed. Most people knew where to look for it because a map of the murder scene had already appeared on the front page of the *Macomb Journal.*

One block farther along the hard road was Elizabeth Street, where the drivers turned right and tried to approach the Methodist Church. The small parking lot was filled before 2:00, and people began putting their cars along the streets and in the alleys, wherever they could find a space. The number of cars reached 100, then 150, and continued to grow. Soon that part of town was a confusion of people with cars trying to find a place for themselves.

The Methodist Church was an old brick building that had been erected in 1862, just seven years after the town had been founded. For a long time it was the only church in Colchester, and it was hallowed by countless crusades against the evils of the town, especially drinking, gambling, and fighting. It symbolized one side of the local mind as surely as the bootlegger himself symbolized the other.

The old church had been remodeled three times. In 1885, when the mines were booming, it had been enlarged to handle the Sunday morning crowds, and a tall white-frame belfry had been added. In 1902 it had been modernized inside, with the inclusion of electric lights, to reflect the progressive spirit of the new century. During the last remodeling, in 1925, the wooden belfry had been removed, a heavy Romanesque side steeple had been added, and the old red bricks had been covered by gray stucco. So, although the townspeople regarded it as the same church their grandparents had attended, those early settlers would not have recognized it.

Inside there was a vaulted ceiling and white-painted plaster walls with radiant stained-glass windows. The floor sloped down toward the sanctuary, which was separated from the rest of the church by three carpeted steps and an old wooden communion rail. Behind that was an altar of dark polished wood and, to the right, a pulpit.

No other place in Colchester had a more traditional feel to it, and some of the townspeople could experience a deep sense of community, if not communion, just by sitting there. The church was a cherished link with the past.

In front of the communion rail was a mahogany casket that held the bootlegger's body. Several dozen floral pieces were banked around it—the most extensive display of flowers that local people had ever seen. Rumor had it that some of the more elaborate arrangements had been sent by Chicago people, the bootlegger's "business associates." One floral design that commanded attention stood directly behind the casket. It was a large horseshoe-shaped arrangement of blood-red roses with a purple ribbon that said, "Good luck on your journey."

The bootlegger had been a rather handsome man, with blondish-brown hair that was starting to recede, a wide, clear forehead, deep-set blue eyes, a Roman nose, and a square jaw. Fortunately the gunshots that killed him had completely missed his face. He was dressed in a dark suit and striped tie, with a white carnation in his lapel, and he looked very respectable.

Except that his eyes were shut and his thin lips were drawn tightly together, the dead bootlegger looked just like the photograph that had been stolen from his mother's living room table for use in the newspapers.

An hour before the funeral began, the oak pews were filled, except for a few up in front that were reserved for Wagle's family and close relatives. Perhaps three hundred people were seated for the service. Dozens who came later were allowed to stand in the rear of the church, and some two hundred others were taken downstairs and seated on wooden folding chairs in the basement, where they could at least hear the service through the open doors to the floor above.

By 2:15 several hundred more people, which the old church could not accommodate, stood on the lawn and in the street. Some were dressed in elegant, fashionable clothes, and there was an air about them, a worldliness that marked them as city people, for whom the drab little mining town was as strange as Chicago was to the people of Colchester.

Kelly Wagle's funeral was the largest gathering for the death of a local man since the early 1890s, when the townspeople had held the rites for William Egerton, James Roberts, and Thomas Terrill, wealthy mine operators who were the most admired men of their time.

Inside the church everyone sat in a dead hush, waiting for the service to begin. The townspeople were ill at ease because so many outsiders had come, making it difficult to relate the bootlegger's life to the pattern of things in Colchester. He had been one of them, connected like everyone else to the common experience of the town—born there, raised there, recognized and discussed there—but he was also strangely different, separated from the rest of them by the mysterious doings that had led to his death.

Some of the older townspeople had always known his family, and they recalled him as a towheaded boy in short pants who followed his mother to church on Sunday mornings and tagged along with his brother Joe on schooldays. Others remembered when he was a youth shooting marbles on his knees in the dirt street or playing baseball at the grounds near the old pottery. Many had known him when he worked at the brickyard or, later, for the railroad—a likable young man with a reputation for getting into trouble. By the time he was a bootlegger, when his cars, his women, his racehorses, and his scrapes with the law were the talk of Colchester, the whole town knew him or knew about him. And now he was dead at forty-three, lying in front of them like a stone.

Shortly before the service the casket was closed, and an immense blanket of red roses was draped over it, extending almost to the floor on every side. Then the bootlegger's family and close relatives were brought in to fill the reserved pews in front. Among them were his widow, Blanche, a tall, blue-eyed blond whom the townspeople regarded as strikingly beautiful; his fifteen-year-old stepdaughter, Elinora Loop; his white-haired mother, Alice Terrill, who had remarried after the death of her first husband; his brothers, Joe and Glenn; and his sister, Geneva. Also among the family mourners were two whom the townspeople did not recognize: Archer G. Wagle, the dead man's twenty-four-year-old son, who lived in Chicago, and the young man's mother, Ruth Ewing, who had divorced Kelly Wagle and left town long before he had become a bootlegger.

At precisely 2:30 Rev. Earl Fahnestock suddenly appeared in the sanctuary. He was a short stocky man whose red hair was starting to turn gray, and he was immensely popular with his parishioners. Forty-eight years old, he had held several other small-town appointments before coming to Colchester two years before. Since the early years of the century, he had held revivals in many churches and schoolhouses in the region, and he loved to exhort sinners to seek the Lord.

Pastor Fahnestock opened the funeral service with a prayer, and then, at his direction, the organist played and a local quartet sang "Sometime We'll Understand," a hymn that had been requested by the family. Considering the questions on everyone's mind, the choice could not have been more appropriate:

> Not now, but in the coming years,
> It may be in a better land,
> We'll read the meaning of our tears,
> And then, sometime, we'll understand.
>
> We'll catch the broken thread again
> And finish what we here began;
> Heav'n will the mysteries explain,
> And then, ah then, we'll understand.

The reverend then read a brief obituary about "Thomas Henry Wagle," the well-known resident of Colchester—but it omitted everything that might have suggested the unique identity of Kelly Wagle, the bootlegger. Still, sobs of anguish were heard around the church as he read it. By the time he finished, Geneva Wagle was crying hysterically and had to be comforted by her family. She was a small, attractive, thirty-two-year-old woman with light brown hair, and in many ways she resembled her dead brother. More than anyone else in the family, she knew what lay behind the mysterious but not unexpected murder, and better than anyone else, she knew the man responsible for it.

Perhaps from a sense of prudence, Pastor Fahnestock avoided any direct reference to the killing or the notorious events that had led to it. But in his funeral sermon he condemned the wickedness of the entire modern generation and appealed to God for help in reshaping his wayward spiritual community. The reverend's exact words have been long forgotten, but his text was Isaiah 64:6–9:

> But we are all as an unclean thing, and all our righteousnesses
> are as filthy rags; and we all do fade as a leaf; and our iniquities,
> like the wind, have taken us away.

And there is none that calleth upon thy name, that stirreth up himself to take hold of thee; for thou hast hid thy face from us, and hast consumed us, because of our iniquities.

But now, O Lord, thou art our father; we are the clay, and thou our potter; and we are all the work of thy hand.

Be not wroth very sore, O Lord, nor remember our iniquities forever.

That the reader of this ancient plea was thinking of the iniquities of Colchester, in particular, was certainly not lost on the local people, in a town where clay mining and clay ware manufacturing were the chief industrial activities.

The sermon ended with the promise of the Lord's protection for those who turn to him, as Pastor Fahnestock raised his voice to quote from the Ninety-first Psalm:

Thou shalt not be afraid for the terror by night; nor for the arrow that flieth by day;

Nor for the pestilence that walketh in darkness; nor for the destruction that wasteth at noonday.

A thousand shall fall at thy side, and ten thousand at thy right hand; but it shall not come nigh thee.

Only with thine eyes shalt thou behold and see the reward of the wicked.

As he spoke to the tense and perspiring crowd, thunder rumbled in the background, and by the close of his sermon rain was beating against the windows of the little church. The people outside ran for their cars.

At the end of the service, just before the closing prayer, the quartet sang the first and final verses of "The Church in the Wildwood." That hymn, too, had been requested by the family. It had been one of the bootlegger's favorites, and perhaps the sense of meaningful place it conveyed and the nostalgic pleading of the lines did reflect something essential about him:

There's a church in the valley by the wildwood,
No lovelier spot in the dale;
No place is so dear to my child-hood
As the little brown church in the vale.

Come to the church in the wildwood,
Oh, come to the church in the vale.
No spot is so dear to my child-hood
As the little brown church in the vale.

From the church in the valley of the wildwood,
When the day fades away into night,
I would fain from this spot of my child-hood
Wing my way to the mansions of light.

Oh, come, come, come, come, come to the
church in the wildwood,
Oh, come to the church in the vale;
No spot is so dear to my child-hood
As the little brown church in the vale.

As the mourners filed from the church, the pallbearers set the floral arrangements aside, lifted the casket, and carried it out into the rain.

Waiting beside the church was a new limousine-type hearse, an elegant Silver Knightstown funeral coach. It was not black, but a modern-looking gray—perhaps just the right color for the occasion. As the attendant opened the rear doors, people could see the blue mohair upholstery and walnut trim. It was the most impressive car of any kind in McDonough County, and Frank Williams had bought it just in time. Although he had two assistants that day, he drove the new hearse himself, with the rain streaming down like bullets, and an enormous procession of cars followed.

Mt. Auburn was a small, parklike burying ground that had been established in 1881 and named for the famous cemetery in Boston. It had once been enclosed by a picket fence with a tall arched entrance gate, but by World War I that had been replaced by a modern chain-link fence that had a cold, impersonal look about it. The cemetery was only a half-mile away, on the north edge of town, so some cars had not yet left the church when the hearse stopped beside the open grave and the bootlegger's casket was placed on a lowering device for the burial ceremony.

Twenty minutes later, hundreds of mourners stood quietly under their umbrellas with a stricken look on their faces, like people who had come to the end of something, as Pastor Fahnestock repeated the familiar words for the burial of the dead:

Man, that is born of a woman, hath but a short time to live, and is full of misery. He cometh up, and is cut down, like a flower; he fleeth as it were a shadow, and never continueth in one stay.

In the midst of life we are in death. . . .

As his voice droned on, the mourners could see scattered around them the graves of hundreds of people who had once belonged to Colchester—and who still did, in a certain sense, for the cemetery kept them like relics in a vault, and the townspeople retained them carefully in the mosaic of local memory. The names on the headstones were familiar: Baird, Carson, Cooper, Cowan, Egerton, Fentem, Foster, Greenbank, Hoar, Hocker, Hulson, Jones, King, Kipling, Martin, Moon, Myers, Newland, Pearson, Rippetoe, Roberts, Rundle, Smith, Stevens, Stookey, Terrill, Wagle, Wayland, Williams, and others.

The town was a huge and complex family. Kelly Wagle had quarreled with it—at least, whenever it tried to assert any authority in his life—but he had never rejected it, so even in death he continued to belong. That is a kind of consolation known only to those who spend their lives in a small town with a strong sense of community.

As the ceremony ended and the bootlegger's casket was slowly lowered into the ground, the rain began to dissipate. The outsiders climbed into their cars and headed back to the hard road that took them quickly out of town. Undoubtedly they had seen all they wanted to see of Colchester.

The townspeople slowly went home, and many had a strange, depressed feeling they could hardly describe, for something had vanished from their lives—some sense of promise, perhaps, that had been bound up with the bootlegger's presence among them. Whatever it was, it was surely symbolized by the enormous heap of funeral flowers—two truckloads of them—that covered his grave, spilling over onto several others, and quickly faded as the days passed.

When it was all over, the people of Colchester had another memory to keep, the last of their memories about the bootlegger, and they could only try to make a meaningful whole from a town-mind full of contradictory fragments. But notorious lawbreaking and renowned social commitment made a difficult mix, so the townspeople disagreed among themselves, and within themselves, about how they should finally regard him. As a writer for the *Quincy Herald Whig* soon remarked, "Wagle's own community isn't quite sure he is a hero."

On the next day, in an article entitled "1,000 Attend Henry Wagle Funeral," editor Harry Todd of the *Colchester Independent,* well aware of the community's psychological struggle, made a determined effort to suppress the dark reality of the dead man's career as he emphasized what many in town wanted to remember:

> During his entire life Henry Wagle was known for his generosity and kind deeds. He was ever anxious and willing to lend whatever aid was at his command to acquaintances and strangers alike, and he always derived a great deal of pleasure from doing someone a kind deed. In time of sickness, no matter whether it was a contagious illness or not, Henry Wagle was the first to volunteer his services. If one or more cars were needed at a funeral, Henry Wagle always furnished them. If some person in the community found it necessary to make a hurried trip to some point, Henry Wagle always offered to drive, no matter how distant the destination. And he was never known to accept pay for any of his services. No bigger hearted man ever lived than Henry Wagle, and we are proud to class him, not as a pleasing acquaintance, but as a friend.

That was the newspaper's only comment. The killing and what had led to it were ignored. To Todd, the bootlegger had been a model of neighborly commitment and generosity, an incarnation of the small-town spirit in an era of frightening social change. That was his importance to the community.

Many of the townspeople agreed. They recalled how warmly Kelly Wagle had greeted people, calling them by name and asking about their families, and how often he had done a good turn when someone, or some group, really needed help. It was Kelly who had saved little Edna Belle Clarke after a terrible accident north of town, and it was Kelly who had outfitted the entire Colchester High School football team when nobody else stepped forward to contribute.

Others in town had admired Kelly Wagle as an individualist, a man willing to go his own way, to take a chance, to do whatever was necessary to get ahead. They told a different set of stories—about the time he outwitted the police with two identical cars, or hid his liquor in the baptistery of the local church, or stood up to the Ku Klux Klan. In his later years the bootlegger had become a legend.

Still others had simply been afraid of him. They recalled the newspaper reports about his bootlegging, the stories about his fights with men who had crossed him, the rumors that he had killed his wife. Now that he was gone, they were relieved.

So were the authorities at the county seat. The editor of the *Macomb Journal* viewed Wagle's career as a perversion of the American rise-by-native-talent-to-success social pattern. In an editorial published shortly after the murder, he moralized about the notorious bootlegger, making an all-too-obvious point, but he also revealed a certain admiration for him.

A LIFE OF CRIME NEVER PROVES PROFITABLE

That Kelly Wagle was an outstanding success in his field cannot be disputed. He was the most notorious bootlegger in western Illinois, and he was also rated as a wealthy man. He had entered the game in its infancy, and he had made money.

His character was a combination of the dynamic force, natural shrewdness, and bold fearlessness that are necessary for great achievement in any walk of life. It is to be regretted that he did not turn his ability to legitimate channels.

Once again becomes apparent the great place that opportunity plays in our lives. Had opportunity placed Wagle in the employment of a big corporation, the characteristics for success which he possessed would have advanced him to a high place. Instead, he became the leading bootlegger of this section.

Although Wagle occupied the limelight, he lived under a constant strain. His last days were turbulent. He knew that he was doomed—that eventually his enemies would get him. He led a life that could but get on the nerves of the strongest man.

They say that the iron nerves of Jesse James finally broke before his death and he was as irascible as a maiden aunt. So, too, the strain of being hunted by relentless enemies was beginning to tell on Kelly Wagle. . . .

His assassination proves again that crime does not pay.

Editor Todd of the *Independent* did not approve of the bootlegger's career either, but he couldn't bring himself to say so. The implications for Colchester were too severe. Still, he knew that many people in town, especially young men, had an intense admiration for Wagle, so the next issue of his weekly newspaper displayed something new—a motto, set in bold type above the masthead:

"The road to success may be winding, but it is never crooked."

Todd wanted the people of Colchester to ponder the meaning of success in the light of Wagle's career in their community, and he gave them plenty of time to think it over. That motto remained at the top of every issue for two years, until he sold the newspaper and moved out of town.

And in truth, as the years went by, the townspeople thought and talked endlessly about the bootlegger, about why he had died and what he had done and how he had happened to come along in their town—Colchester, of all places.

Coal and Community in Colchester

The life of Kelly Wagle was tied up with the history of his town, with the complex forces that had lured, shaped, unified, and divided the people of Colchester from the beginning. Not that his career can be explained by depicting his community, but it cannot be understood without knowing about his community, for in the America that existed from the frontier period to the 1920s, each small town was a separate world, remote from every other town and focused intently on itself, and the townspeople deeply belonged to it.

Colchester was founded when the railroad came through McDonough County. On October 5, 1855, after several years of agitation, planning, and investment by early settlers, the Macomb newspaper made a joyous announcement:

THE CARS ARE COMING!

From reliable intelligence, just received, we are enabled to announce to our readers that the "iron horse" is expected to arrive at Colchester, a point some six miles west of Macomb, today. . . . This is glorious news and will, no doubt, be received as the harbinger of "the good time that's coming."

Later in the day dozens of pioneers gathered at that place, an unplatted stretch of prairie near the timbered ravines of Crooked Creek, just a mile southeast of Pleasant Valley Mill, to witness the arrival of the first locomotive. Finally they spotted it, off to the southwest, a small black engine chugging through the tall grass, pulling an open tender and a wooden passenger car, and belching a long dark cloud from its funnel-shaped smokestack. As it rolled into the would-be community, releasing blasts of steam and screeching its iron brakes, the crowd stared in awe at the high-wheeled contraption to which their destiny was harnessed.

The history of Colchester had begun. In the years that followed, the townspeople would reckon the age of their community from that event, which set the stage for their experience together.

Soon the Northern Cross Railroad constructed a small red-painted depot, made of vertical boards and roofed with wooden shingles. Standing alone by the tracks, with only a few log homes in sight, it was a shrine to the American promise.

The railroad had come there, and Colchester had been conceived, because of coal. In 1854 a small group of miners from New Castle, Pennsylvania, had opened a few drift mines, cut into the hillsides along Crooked Creek, and had started hauling wagonloads of coal by oxen to villages farther south that were already on the railroad. There it was shoveled into waiting freight cars. Three days after the first locomotive arrived, they began shipping coal from Colchester.

Their leader was James Roberts, a fair-complexioned, dark-haired Cornish immigrant who had come to the county in 1853. Answering an ad to work a drift mine near the Pleasant Valley Mill, he was impressed by the coal outcroppings in that vicinity. Soon he opened a mine of his own with his brother David, and he urged his friends back in New Castle to come and bring their families. First came the Pearsons, accompanied by James's brother Richard, who had married a Pearson daughter, and then the Brights, Cowans, Moons, Terrills, and others—families linked together by marriage, friendship, trust, and hope.

Ambitious and energetic, Roberts created the first mining company in Colchester, established a market for their coal at Quincy, and convinced the Northern Cross Railroad to locate the depot where it was, a mile or so from the mines along the creek. He didn't lay out the town, but he made it possible.

The men who did lay it out were not miners but young land speculators who had been born in New England and raised in McDonough County. Lewis Little and Charles Gilchrist were barely of legal age when they started selling lots for $20 to $50 apiece. Little, age twenty-two, had acquired most of the land from his father, who had settled there in 1836. Gilchrist, age twenty-one, had recently worked for the railroad and was the county surveyor, so it was he who created the town plat, with streets running parallel and perpendicular to the railroad tracks. It was dated November 21, 1855.

Colchester was named for the oldest community in England, which was not, however, a coal-mining town. Nevertheless, to the several dozen immigrants who were already living at the little mining camp near Crooked Creek, the name surely symbolized British tradition.

During the next year small wooden buildings went up near the depot, and a raw, dusty mining town emerged along the tracks. A woman named Mary Estella Garbet, who moved to Colchester with her widowed mother in 1857 to run a boarding house, later recalled the nascent community: "A few houses, mostly log ones, scattered over a big area, and all around was a big pond when it rained. No sidewalks, except [railroad] ties or slats laid lengthwise for short distances, and a few small shacks or buildings for stores. A typical new mining town, but building up rapidly after the railroad came, with miners. Not many cabins or houses, but each one was full of people. Our house was just being built and had no roof on it when we moved in." By the end of that year Colchester had several stores, dozens of log and frame houses, and 568 people.

In 1858 the first shaft mines were sunk just west of town, and railroad spurs were soon run out to them. James Roberts, in partnership with Quincy investors, also led that development, which started large-scale coal mining in Colchester.

Hard-working, forever-hoping men were drawn to the new community. Most of them were British immigrants, like the initial group from New Castle. In those days the men still called themselves "colliers"— the British term for coal miners—and back in "the old sod" their families had risen from peasant hopelessness to humble self-sufficiency through decades of hard and dangerous work done underground. They were American dreamers of a sort, even before they had come to America, and they were lured to McDonough County by the promise that Colchester held out to each of them and to their families.

As the years passed, a story grew up among them, a folktale. It seems that the Indians of that section had dug a secret mine from which they had extracted quantities of gold, or silver, or lead, depending on which version of the tale was being told. Abandoned when the whites came, the mine was supposedly located in the hills along the creek, waiting to be discovered and reopened, but of course, no one ever found it.

One of the few non-British residents of early Colchester was a certain Lewis Wagle, the bootlegger's grandfather. Like many other McDonough County pioneers, he came from Kentucky, where he was born in 1816. His family moved to Illinois in 1830, settling forty miles south of Macomb in what later became Brown County.

The Wagles were frontier farmers. They lived in a log cabin, raised some corn and a few hogs, suffered through the hard winters, and hoped for better days. Life was a continuous act of self-reliance.

Little is known about Lewis, but in general the men from Kentucky were hunters and storytellers, fighters and whisky drinkers. They revered President Jackson, the Old Hero, who had defeated the British at New Orleans, and they regarded themselves as tough, fearless individualists.

Lewis moved north to McDonough County in the late 1830s. He settled several miles south of Macomb near Camp Creek, in Bethel Township. That was a hilly, wooded area known locally as Gin Ridge, and it soon became legendary as the home of little-educated, self-assertive men who were prone to drinking and brawling. In one memorable five-handed fracas there, a boozer named "Dump" Jewel stabbed to death his own brother.

The law provided little restraint on the ridge, where some men cherished a dream of anarchic freedom until well after the Civil War.

In 1839 Lewis married eighteen-year-old Julia Venard, whose parents were among the earliest and most well known settlers in that area. During the 1840s the Wagles had three children: Margaret, William, and Jasper.

Lewis lived on his father-in-law's land. He never owned any property in Bethel Township, and like most of the Gin Ridgers, he was poor. Nothing else is known about his life there, except that he participated in the last countywide wolf hunt in 1843—and that he got one. He must have been good with a gun.

Family tragedy drove him to Colchester. On April 26, 1858, his wife died at age thirty-seven, and perhaps because he had not prospered or because of family problems, Lewis left the children with his in-laws and moved away. He never returned to Gin Ridge.

He probably came to Colchester because it was the one place in McDonough County where a poor man could easily find work and an unmarried man would be likely to fit in. Since Lewis was not a skilled miner, he probably worked at hauling coal—his later occupation—for which his farm experience with horses must have been useful.

Whatever the case, in September Lewis bought a lot on the west end of Depot Street, close to the mining area. Whether he built a house on it or simply remained a boarder is unknown, but he clearly had plans to stay.

In 1858 Colchester was at its wildest. Some of the early miners and haulers were temporary residents, or "floaters"—unmarried men who had little interest in the developing community. When they were not working, they hung out at the saloons, where they drank, gambled, and fought. Of course, some married men did the same, at least from time to time, and their families often suffered the consequences.

A woman named Paulina Vest, who moved to the town with her parents in 1858, later recalled the first clash over the saloons, which pitted the women against the men:

> We had been told that Colchester was a rough place and that saloons were opened in nearly every building in town. . . . Things had gotten so bad that on the day Father and Mother came over to buy the [Chester House] hotel, the women had concluded that they would clean up the town a little, so all of the better class of women got together and, with hatchets and axes, visited the saloons . . . and destroyed a vast amount of liquor. They didn't get all of it, however, for that night and the next day the men, many of them, got drunk and had a hilarious time in order to get even with the women.

That seriocomic episode foreshadowed much that came later in Colchester, for nothing divided the townspeople like the liquor issue.

Although Lewis Wagle may not have been involved, he was a heavy drinker, so he must have spent time at the saloons.

As it turned out, he himself was a floater. In February 1859 Lewis sold his property and moved to northern Missouri, to a hamlet called Willmathsville, set in the rolling hills of Adair County. He had relatives there and apparently worked as a farm hand. By then Lewis was forty-two years old.

During that winter or early spring he married a fifteen-year-old orphan girl named Martha J. Tompkins. She was his cousin, and she was probably the reason he had moved there. Because of her youth, their marriage was illegal, which perhaps explains why there is no record of it in Adair County. It may have been a common-law agreement.

Whatever the case, by April of that year Martha was already pregnant. Their first child, born on January 2, 1860, was Archibald A. Wagle, the bootlegger's father.

Back in Colchester mining operations were expanding. The fields west of town sported the first tipples, which stood like sentinels over the coal shafts. Each of the tall wooden structures housed a "cage," or open-sided elevator, that took the men down some ninety feet to the coal seam. And each cage was connected by cables to a steam-powered hoist located in an engine house nearby. The loud chugging of the engine could be heard all day long, together with the screeching and groaning of the cage as it was raised and lowered.

When a box of coal was brought up, it was lifted high in the tipple and dumped onto a big tilted screen made of iron rods, raising a cloud of black dust. As the lumps clattered against the rods, the screen eliminated the smallest ones, the "slack," which had no commercial value and for which the miners were not paid. The sizable coal tumbled off the screen into waiting railroad cars and was shipped out.

By the late 1850s the railroad itself had become a major consumer of coal, which had replaced wood as the fuel for locomotives, prompting the C. B. & Q. Railroad, the successor to the Northern Cross, to construct coal chutes one mile east of town. They were tall wooden storage bins, some thirty feet high, that had trapdoors and slides for dropping coal into the locomotive tenders. A separate shaft mine was operated nearby just to keep them filled, and all day long plodding workhorses pulled wagonloads of coal up a long ramp to dump it into the bins. The chutes became a landmark, a sign of Colchester's importance as a coal town.

The miners were proud of their independence: they worked for the bushel price of what they mined, not for a daily wage. (A bushel in this case was a measure of weight: eighty pounds.) Ability and effort made a difference. Yet there was a firm comradeship among them, as men who shared common skills and faced common problems. For most of them, coal mining was not just a job but a way of life. Their difficult work gave meaning to their lives, even as it knitted their families together through shared hopes, fears, and routines.

Economic adversity was a great promoter of mutual support, as illustrated by the strike of 1861–62. All the coal mined for the Roberts Company, in drift or shaft mines, was hauled in railroad cars to Quincy, where it was weighed, but the miners soon felt they were being cheated at the scale. They wanted their coal weighed in Colchester, but the company investors in Quincy refused to comply.

To make matters worse, in 1860 Hugh Roberts, a brother of James who had recently come to town, opened a general store on Macomb Street, and he expected the Roberts miners to trade there. But he charged 40 to 50 percent more than other stores did. The miners complained, but Hugh Roberts was hard to deal with, and James was spending most of his time in Quincy, concerned with the selling and shipping of coal.

Then, faced with low coal prices in 1861, the company suddenly dropped the bushel price from five and a half cents to three cents, cutting the miners' monthly income by almost 50 percent. The men responded by forming the Colchester Miners' Association, a local union, and in the late fall of 1861 they mounted the first strike in the history of McDonough County. Because the coal haulers stopped working, too, in support of their friends, even the accumulated coal piled outside the drift mines was not being shipped out.

In January 1862 the company responded by bringing in two teams and wagons driven by men from Quincy, and they began loading coal at the drift mines north of town. Before they had their wagons filled, however, the Colchester miners and haulers surrounded them, intimidated them, and convinced them to dump out the coal. As the wagons were emptied, the cheers of the striking men frightened one of the teams, which ran off into a ravine, overturning and smashing the wagon behind them.

When Hugh Roberts found out what had happened, he went to the county sheriff and filed a complaint. Dozens of men in Colchester were arrested. The *Macomb Journal* carried a brief, unsympathetic report:

A RIOT AT COLCHESTER

On Tuesday evening last, forty-six persons were brought to this city under arrest, charged with participating in a riot at Colchester. The coal miners at that place, it appears, are on strike, and have been interfering with those who are disposed to work for what they can get.

In the end only seven ringleaders were held on bail, and they managed to get the charges dropped later in the year. The strike was settled during the summer, when both parties agreed to a compromise price, and plans were made to weigh the coal in Colchester. As for the company store, the miners eventually killed it by not trading there.

The town grew little during the Civil War, when the coal market was depressed and many younger men were away fighting in the South, but afterward, as industrial demand rose and people increasingly burned coal in home furnaces, the market improved, and mining in Colchester started to expand. As a result, the railroad built a hand-operated turntable on the west side of town in 1868. Then a special locomotive came from Quincy every day, arriving at about four o'clock, and after being turned around by four stout men, it hauled a string of loaded coal cars back to the bustling river city. By the early 1870s local miners were shipping out more than 50,000 tons of coal every year, and the Roberts Company had been superseded by the Quincy Coal Company and the Colchester Coal Company, the latter operated by James Roberts and his sons.

One visitor to Colchester in the spring of 1872 was impressed by the town's industrial energy—and by one other thing: coal dust. As he put it in an article for the *Macomb Journal,* "Owing to the fact that its citizens dig coal, haul coal, trade in coal, ship coal, and burn coal, there is a grim sootiness about the place." Black dust coated the buildings, streets, wagons, teams, and miners, marking them as components of a distinctive culture, centered on coal.

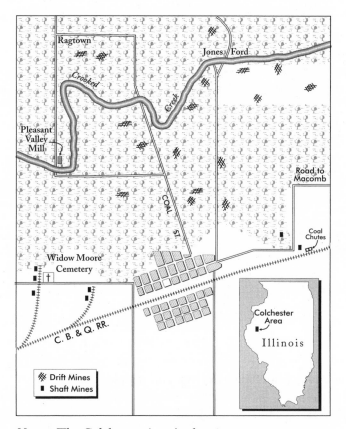

Map 2. The Colchester Area in the 1870s

By that time Colchester had indeed become a separate world. The little wooden town was still remote from the rest of America, despite the railroad—for people seldom traveled very far or very often—and local residents knew each other thoroughly and neighbored intensively. They shared a distinctive social context that gave them identity as well as opportunity, and they were pleased to be part of it. They had become the townspeople.

In those early years local issues were discussed and officials were elected at an annual town meeting held at the Chester House on the first Tuesday in April. Democracy was an extension of personal relationships.

Because Colchester had been incorporated in 1857, there were also monthly meetings of the village trustees, and at one of them soon after the Civil War, those leaders approved the new "Seal of the Town of Colchester," which symbolized the town's sense of identity. It was a circular emblem, centered on an American eagle perched on a railroad car filled with coal, and below that was an open book, the chronicle of their community. Above the image was a Latin motto, "Multum in Parvo" (much in little).

The words probably came from schoolteacher Socrates Stevens, who knew Latin, but the sentiment surely came from the townspeople. They were attached to their locality as to a sacred place where their lives had meaning and they shared a common destiny. They had developed a community consciousness that was bound up in a mystical way with the mining and shipping of coal. To live there was to acknowledge the mission of the town and to recognize the importance of coal production, even if one didn't contribute to it directly.

In fact, for the people of Colchester, coal was fate. In good times, when it brought five to six cents a bushel, coal was their link to the American promise, but when the market price of coal dropped, the bushel price for mining it also dropped, and the townspeople faced hard times. If the miners responded with a strike, as in 1861, their actions only made things worse in the short run, for mining families had little or no money to fall back on. And if those families suffered, so did everyone else.

After the Hugh Roberts episode, there was no company store, but all the merchants did business on credit, for the miners were paid just once a month. Each mining family had a passbook, and when a member of the family bought something, the transaction was entered there as well as in the store account book. Then on payday or shortly afterward, the miner went around and settled his accounts.

As that practice suggests, the mining families had a kind of organic relationship to the shops in town. They were dependent on the merchants, who in turn depended on them. It was an arrangement that fostered appreciation and trust. But if some miners couldn't pay what they owed, the merchants took heavy losses, and hard times hit the business district. In a long strike the very life of the town was at risk.

When a strike occurred in 1869, the Colchester correspondent for the *Macomb Journal* filed this blunt report:

> Colchester is dead. I just came from its funeral. It is defunct. It has bowed its head, passed in its checks, and given up the ghost. . . . The miners held a meeting this morning and resolved to stop work, *one and all.* It is now over six weeks since they commenced the strike in the shafts, but the bank men [drift miners] have worked more or less all the time until today. They have now joined the shaft men and will make a big strike of it. When work is resumed, business will be revived, and Colchester will be resurrected.

When the dispute was settled two months later, the town *was* resurrected, but no agreement was ever final. When the price of coal dropped again, during the depression of the mid-1870s, the miners responded with a longer strike, which was so hard on the town that the only clothing store was closed because of its massive debt and the only hardware store was taken over by its creditors. Later years brought other lessons in solidarity and suffering.

Consequently, most Colchester miners were relatively poor men who worked hard and remained poor. Their pay was often good—$40 to $50 per month—but their income was not steady. In the summers only one-fourth of the mines operated, so most miners were laid off for three or four months every year, and the periodic reductions in the bushel price of coal, as well as the occasional strikes, tended to wipe out any savings.

Although Colchester had no cracker-box, look-alike company houses, some of the residential streets had an unshakable look of poverty. The miners' houses were usually small one-story cottages that had only three or four rooms. Flat-roofed sheds (for tools, wagons, and horses) and folk-built outhouses stood in the backyards, along with occasional chicken coops and pig pens. Some people didn't even have a well. They carried water from a neighbor's pump. Living conditions were complicated by the number of children in a typical mining family—five or six, usually, and often more.

But despite their difficult circumstances, the coal miners seldom complained. Most people they knew were in the same situation, and besides, there were always reasons for optimism. The demand for coal was steadily rising, prices might go up next winter, Colchester was growing, and some miners had already escaped poverty—by digging coal for the railroad, becoming supervisors, or opening drift mines of their own. Clearly there was cause for hope, and that made all the difference.

Those who achieved real success in early Colchester usually did so by opening a store or becoming a shaft mine operator. One man who did both was Abram Newland, Jr., who was also the town's foremost Civil War hero.

Born in England's Durham County in 1838, he was the son of a coal miner, and by age eight he was already working in the mines. As a teenager he came to America with his parents, who settled at Colchester in 1856. Newland mined coal with his father and older brothers. A largely self-educated man who was popular and outspoken, he was one of the leaders of the so-called riot of 1862.

Later that year he joined the 124th Infantry Regiment and was named orderly sergeant. Fearless and patriotic, he was commended for his bravery at the battle of Raymond, Mississippi. Three days later he was shot in the face and reported killed.

Newland eventually recovered, but the bullet had taken out several teeth and damaged his vocal cords. Thereafter he made a peculiar clicking sound when he talked, like fingers snapping, and his voice was a constant reminder of his heroism. Loved by the men of his company, he was later commissioned as a captain, and by the war's end he had participated in some two dozen battles and skirmishes.

Back in Colchester he was referred to as "Captain" for the rest of his life, and like a tattered battle flag he symbolized the town's commitment to and sacrifice for America. He also became a Methodist minister, but he refused to accept a pastorate, preferring instead to stay in Colchester and preach wherever and whenever he was needed. He never tried to make a living as a clergyman.

In his business career Newland achieved success by providing what the townspeople needed and wanted. Because the Hugh Roberts company store had closed during the war, the young veteran opened his own general store on Depot Street, where he sold "dry goods, groceries, queensware, clothing, hats, caps, boots, shoes, and notions." Building his business on friendship and understanding, fair prices and honest dealing, Newland soon had the biggest store in town, a two-story frame building with a gable roof and large display windows stretching across the front. Later he sold out to become a mine owner, employing dozens of men and boys in an operation known for its interest in the welfare of the miners.

In the small world of post–Civil War Colchester, Abram Newland had made it, and no one more clearly symbolized the town's social ideals or a poor man's possibilities there.

Among the poorest of local families were the Wagles. They remained in Missouri for a few years, until after the Civil War was well under way, and during that time Lewis and Martha had another son, Frank, who was born at a hamlet called Coffeyville. Then they returned to Colchester, Lewis bringing his young family in a covered wagon.

The Wagles slowly put down roots in the little mining town, sharing the hard work and long hopes that characterized the community, but like many other families, they never really prospered. Lewis hauled coal from the mines to the railroad, driving teams that pulled heavily loaded wagons onto a raised platform by the tracks, where they could be emptied into the waiting freight cars. From time to time he probably also hauled coal to nearby towns like Fandon and Blandinsville, which were not on the railroad and where people bought directly from the drift mine operators.

Lewis made only about $30 a month, so he and Martha must have known hard times, especially since over the years they had six more children.

As a boy Arch did the many jobs that fell to the oldest son in a poor family—such as cutting wood for the stove and carrying water from the well—and he undoubtedly worked with his father, too. He attended school of course, and in 1867 Colchester had a new four-room brick school building on North Street. Later he and his brother Frank went into the mines, like dozens of other Colchester boys, including the three Bailey brothers, the four Kipling brothers, the five Terrill brothers, and the six Rhodes brothers. Families were units of economic production, and sons were expected to contribute until they left home. The Wagle boys worked for the Quincy Coal Company, the largest mining operation in town.

It was the filling and moving of small wooden railroad cars that brought boys like them to work in the mines. The cars—always called "boxes" by the miners—were shoveled full of coal and then "wheeled" out to the cage that hoisted them up the shaft. Because most of the tunnels were only three or four feet high, except near the shaft, mules were not used in Colchester mines. Instead, the cars were often hitched to a big dog, which pulled at the command of a coal-begrimed boy who pushed from behind. It was a hard life for a youngster, but it fostered enormous self-discipline, respect for the miners, and a capacity for relentless toil.

By their late teens Arch and Frank were digging coal, wielding a miner's pick, a sledgehammer, and a scoop shovel by the light of a carbide lamp, and they no doubt counted themselves among the men of the community. For Colchester boys, that was the ultimate rite of passage: learning to do a man's work in the mines.

By that time Lewis was in his sixties, and the habit of heavy drinking had taken its toll. He worked less and less effectively and less frequently, and his two older sons increasingly supported the family.

The bootlegger's other grandfather was no more successful than Lewis Wagle. Born in England in 1836, Henry Walley lost his mother a few years later. In 1840 he came to St. Louis with his father, and shortly afterward they moved to the Mormon community of Nauvoo, where Henry grew up.

In 1860 he married a widow named Jane King, who already had four children. They soon had two more: John, born in 1861, who later became the bootlegger's favorite uncle, and Alice, born in 1864, who became his mother.

Jane Walley died when Alice was a year old, so just as Lewis Wagle had done in a similar situation, Henry Walley left his children with relatives and moved away. He eventually married again and homesteaded in Montana before finally returning to Colchester late in the century. John and Alice were taken in by an uncle and aunt, Joseph and Alice Booth, who were childless. Mrs. Booth, for whom Alice had been named, was Henry's sister. Like the Walleys, the Booths were Mormons.

In 1867 they moved to Colchester, where Joseph worked as a brickmaker. His employer was Abraham Horrocks, a British immigrant who had recently started a brickyard a half-mile north of town, on Coal Street. When the business changed hands in 1874, Joseph worked for the new owners, John and Moses King, who were also British immigrants.

Like most people in town, the Booths were poor. They lived in an old log building near the park, and to get by they planted a big garden every year and raised a few chickens. Things got worse in the spring of 1879, when Joseph was run over by a loaded coal wagon. His leg was crushed, and he was unable to walk for a long time. To help support the family, young Alice worked as a dressmaker. Neighbors also pitched in to help them manage while Joseph was laid up.

Although poverty was sometimes hard to cope with, there was something far worse that hung over the town like a shadow: death. In Colchester it was more than a grim fact of life; it was an ever-threatening presence, a grisly phantom that relentlessly invaded the community and preyed on the townspeople. And more often than not, it came from the mines.

The first death of a local miner occurred before the coming of the railroad. The man's name was John Cooper, and he was killed in a drift mine during 1855 when an enormous rock fell on him, shattering his bones and squashing his insides.

His death set the pattern, for most of the miners who died were crushed under a slab of limestone that suddenly dropped from the "roof" (as the mine ceiling was called). It was that layer of unstable limestone just above the coal seam that also kept the tunnels so low, except near the cage in a shaft mine. Some miners' bodies were so flattened or disfigured by a ton or more of rock that a regular funeral was impossible. The remains were wrapped in a blanket and the coffin was sealed.

The earliest local mining death described in a newspaper was of that kind, and it occurred in 1872:

TERRIBLE ACCIDENT IN COLCHESTER

John Hood, one of the miners . . . had just started his box of coal up the shaft when a huge stone, weighing over a ton, dropped from the ceiling, eight feet above, upon him, killing him instantly. When the body was taken out [from beneath the rock], his neck and back were found to be broken and his head smashed to a perfect jelly.

In the 1870s Colchester still had no newspaper, so most mining deaths were not publicized. No doubt the *Macomb Journal* was moved to report this story because the dead miner was only fourteen years old.

The prevalence of death in the mines is illustrated by the case of the four Roberts brothers: James, David, Richard, and Hugh. Only James, who was primarily a manager, not a miner, lived to be an old man. The others died in the mines: David in 1875, Richard in 1878, and Hugh in 1881.

That was the way death always took the Colchester miners—one at a time. There was no town-shattering disaster, just a continual, grinding loss of life. Working in the mines was like participating in a grim lottery.

Each victim of a mining accident was a separate tragedy with a distinctive impact on the community, and the details surrounding a death were often shaped into a poignant story that drifted through the town like coal dust in the wind. In the summer of 1874 one such story reached the pages of the *Macomb Eagle:*

TERRIBLE ACCIDENT

The citizens of Colchester were startled on last Monday by another of those calamities which terminate in the loss of human life. The particulars of the accident, as we learn, are as follows:

William Stevens, a Scotchman, aged about 32 years, was employed in the coal bank owned by Mr. McIntosh. On Monday, Mr. Stevens, accompanied by his little boy, entered the drift mine to work. There was a loose rock over him, and as it was dangerous, the boy suggested to his father the propriety of propping it up. The father replied, in substance, "We'll not bother with it until we run out some coal." After this, Stevens went to digging, the result being, in a few minutes the rock fell upon him, crushing him badly, causing his death in a short time. After the rock fell upon him, Mr. Stevens called to his little son, as follows: "Johnnie, you and your mother take care of yourselves in this world. Come and kiss me." And then he died.

He was buried on Tuesday at the cemetery near Colchester. Mr. Stevens leaves a wife and seven small children in needy circumstances.

Illinois had an 1872 mine safety law, but its provisions were not enforced. Among other things, it provided for a mine inspector in each county, but throughout the nineteenth century McDonough County never had one. It also prohibited boys under fourteen from working in the mines, but they continued to do so, especially alongside their fathers. Johnnie Stevens, who saw his father crushed to death, was only ten years old.

The threat of unforeseen death did even more than the gnawing presence of poverty to foster a code of mutual concern and community-wide support. In November 1881, when the tragic story of Mike Mason's death appeared in the *Colchester Independent*, it reflected the operation of that code:

KILLED IN THE MINES

After supper a miner, Wallace Purdy, was on his way up town when he was met by a woman who was crying. She asked him if he knew "Mike Mason, a coal miner in Shaft No. 12," adding that he was her husband, he had left early in the morning, and he had not returned. She was fearful that something had happened to him.

Purdy did not work in No. 12, nor did he know Mason, but he immediately proffered his service to hunt up some of the miners of that shaft and find out about it. Soon the word was circulated, and hard-handed men, who were just beginning to enjoy a rest from their hard day's labor, in a moment forgot their tired limbs, in the thought that a comrade might be suffering in the shaft. A common danger makes the miners common friends in all that pertains to the business, and in less time than we can write it, a hundred men—prepared to work the night through, if need be, to save a fellow miner—were hurrying to the shaft a mile away.

Arriving there, a number were lowered to the bottom. They hurried to Mason's location, and . . . they saw all that they feared— their comrade lying dead and stiff underneath a heavy stone that had fallen upon him from the roof. . . . He leaves a wife and four children, who not only lose the loving protection of husband and father, but must feel keenly the pinchings of poverty.

As always, the miners and their wives offered sympathy and assistance to the devastated widow. They cared about her situation, and they showed it.

Although the code was strongest among the mining families, it pervaded the entire town. In any kind of emergency, misfortune, or difficulty, the townspeople were always willing to help.

The editor who wrote the Mike Mason story realized that his death, like all such tragedies, made the other mining families more conscious of the terrible threat that hung over them: "For a time, each miner will carefully examine 'the roof' [in his mine] and with a graver mind pursue his labor, and each wife will have forebodings, when her husband leaves in the morning, of a like fate for him and her."

Because of the constant danger in the mines, there was a great deal of repressed fear. In the early mornings many a coal miner bid good-bye to his wife in a very formal way before he went off to work, just in case it was their last moment together. Unable to avoid the source of their death anxiety, most miners became fatalistic. If a rockfall occurred in their mine and they were not injured, they often said things like "It just wasn't my time" or "My number wasn't up yet." But what they also meant was "Next time, it might be." Death was never far from their thoughts.

Of course, their wives shared that anxiety, not only out of love, but for a practical reason: a sudden death in the mines often left a family destitute. Many a Colchester widow was forced into a speedy second marriage—so many, in fact, that in 1874 the *Macomb Journal* regarded such marriages as a distinctive feature of the town:

CUPID IN COLCHESTER

For mining and marriage, lager and love, our neighbor, Colchester, "bangs the bush" of every city, town, and village in McDonough, and in any other county in the state. . . . A rock falls upon a miner; the light of his mining cap and his life go out at the same time; his disconsolate widow enters upon a second connubial voyage 'ere the sun sets twice; "the boys" at the saloon drink all 'round, and that's the end of it.

The satirical tone of this article reveals the tendency of folks at the county seat to criticize some aspects of life in Colchester. But they didn't live in a mining town, so they didn't really understand the people there.

As the *Macomb Journal* report also suggests, saloons had an important social function in Colchester, just like the pubs back in the British mining towns from which so many residents had come. The miners' hard and dangerous work promoted a sense of comradeship that could not be fully expressed in the dark rooms and tunnels underground, where they could barely see each other's face. The saloon, with its bright, jovial atmosphere, was in fact the opposite of the gloomy, tense world of the mines. Men could relate to each other there.

In 1892 a speaker in Quincy, whose lecture entitled "The Saloon" was printed in a local newspaper, made general comments on saloon life that characterized the situation in Colchester:

> The saloon is the poor man's club. It is not the love of liquor that primarily leads men and boys to frequent the saloon. It is the social life, the comradeship. A large number of the patrons have no cheerful homes. . . . Some of them have but one or two rooms to live in, with many beds and sleeping or fretful children in them. Some of them are boarding, with only sleeping accommodations. The day has been filled with dreary, wearying work. But the saloon is a room filled with light, comfortable and attractive, warmed in winter. . . .
>
> There is a welcome [for each man] the moment he opens the door. He is not talked to patronizingly. His independence is respected. For a nickel he sits there for hours enjoying himself.

In the saloons the miners joked together and told stories about their experiences—their hard jobs, sharp deals, good times, and close calls—the interplay of will and circumstance in their lives. And drinking with friends was a means of coping with the fear of death, the uncertainty about tomorrow, that haunted every man who went into the mines.

They sometimes sang in the saloons, too, as miners did in the old country. Every man in Colchester knew the British tune "Down in a Coal Mine," with its easily remembered, double-rhymed chorus:

> Down in a coal mine, underneath the ground,
> Where the gleam of sunshine never can be found,
> Digging dusky diamonds all the season round,
> Down in a coal mine underneath the ground.

In 1890 the Colchester newspaper printed a locally popular ballad called "Dan McGinty," about a hapless miner who "drank his whisky fast and wild," ran into hard luck, and killed himself—then reappeared as a ghost, "Dressed in his best suit of clothes." Songs like these fostered a sense of community among the men who struggled to make a living in the mines.

In the 1870s and 1880s Colchester commonly had four or five saloons, and some had names like The Soldier's Home and The Miner's Arms.

Most of them were located on Depot Street, in the middle of the business district, and passersby could smell the beer and hear the men talk and laugh inside. By the late 1870s three of them had pool tables in a back room or upstairs.

The most popular saloon was simply called "Hickey's." It was operated by James ("Slim Jim") Hickey and located just north of the depot, at what was then called "Hickey's Corner." It was a narrow, square-front, white-sided building, with small windows and a door that had two large panes of glass. Inside on the right was a bar of dark-stained wood, with rows of bottles and a beer keg behind it, and across from the bar were several wooden tables where the miners played cards and dominoes. Spittoons were scattered around the sawdust-covered floor. In the mid-1870s Hickey built a "ten-pin alley" next door, and on Saturday nights the sound of bowling balls crashing into pins could be heard along Depot Street until well after midnight.

But perhaps the chief attraction of the place was Hickey himself, a portly, outgoing Irishman from County Tipperary who had moved to Colchester with his parents at age fourteen and had worked for many years in the mines. He and his brothers opened the saloon in 1871, and he later bought them out. Hickey knew all the men in town and always had a cordial greeting for anyone who came in. He was also the confidant and counselor of his regular customers, as well as the only saloon owner who provided his daytime drinkers with a free lunch.

To many people in town, Hickey was the epitome of social concern, despite the fact that he was occasionally charged with violating a liquor law. When a man was sick or injured, Hickey often sent along a few bottles of his finest liquor, and when a miner died, he provided flowers for the funeral and took up a collection for the bereaved family. Even townspeople who disapproved of his business nevertheless liked him personally. In many respects he was a forerunner of the bootlegger.

But the saloons had another side too. They were rough places, especially on a Saturday night—or any night after the miners were paid (usually the tenth of the month). Drunken behavior was common, even expected, and it often led to fights, which usually started in a saloon and continued outside. Once in the street, two men could generally fight undisturbed, and they often got encouragement from their supporters. In a sense the fights were rituals of identity in a very masculine town that admired self-assertion and toughness. Some of the bloody contests became informal "ring fights" that drew sizable crowds and lasted until one of the men was too damaged to stand up.

Of course, the town had ordinances that prohibited fighting and drunken behavior, but the fines were generally small—$3 was common—so the drinkers and brawlers didn't restrain themselves on that account. And law enforcement was erratic at best. D. Wilson Campbell was the town marshal from 1858 to 1882, but he was a drinker himself and knew everyone in town (they all called him "Wilse"), so he tolerated a certain amount of wild behavior. In fact, he too sometimes got drunk and fought in the streets. No wonder an 1876 Colchester correspondent to the *Macomb Eagle* complained, "Our police failed again to effect any arrests for the pandemonium on our streets Saturday evening."

When Henry Stevens brought his newspaper to Colchester several years later, he was astounded at the lack of control over drunken behavior. As he said in an 1881 editorial, "Men come here, get drunk, parade the streets, use profane and obscene language, threaten to fight, do fight, and conduct themselves as no men should be allowed to conduct themselves in a civilized community, and go home without being arrested, fined, and punished as their offense deserves."

Stevens claimed that outsiders were responsible for much of the wild behavior, and he had a point. But as the lax law enforcement suggests, most of the townspeople were tolerant of drinking and fighting because local men had done the same since the 1850s.

On November 10, 1877, one such fight led to the killing of Charles Foster by William Vest. Both men were coal miners. They were in Frank White's saloon on Depot Street that Saturday night when they began exchanging insults. Finally Vest issued a challenge, yelling, "I'm the best God-damned man in this saloon!" Foster told him they would settle it outside, and when he stepped into the street, most of the crowd followed him, anxious to see the fight. Realizing that he was not supported, Vest decided that he didn't want to fight, but as soon as he left the saloon, Foster provoked him, "with his fists in a fighting attitude," according to the newspaper account. They sparred; then Vest suddenly drew a knife, stabbed Foster in the neck, and ran off. Stunned and bleeding, the wounded man pulled out the knife, turned slowly to the crowd, and said, "I'm a goner." Then he fell on his face in the street.

Vest was eventually arrested and charged with murder, but the jury decided that he had acted in self-defense. Apparently Foster had pulled a knife too, or so a few witnesses claimed. Anyway, Vest was a regular guy, well liked in the mines, and no one thought of him as a killer. Some of the townspeople also testified to his upright character. As his trial clearly demonstrated, to be well accepted in Colchester was to be included in a vast, irrevocable assumption of innocence.

There was no obituary for Charles Foster, but the *Macomb Journal* carried an article about the fight that summed up the human consequences in two sentences: "Charles Foster was a man about 35 years of age, an Englishman and a miner. He leaves a wife and five children, all girls, in destitute circumstances."

By the time Foster was killed, Colchester was often called "the toughest town in western Illinois."

Because the death or injury of a miner usually caused severe hardship for his family, in 1867 a group of local miners formed the most important organization in the town's history, the Miners' Friendly Society. It was a kind of insurance club, modeled on a similar one back in Cornwall, where several of the miners had been raised. The members paid one dollar per month into the treasury. From those funds a sick or injured miner was paid three dollars a week, and the family of a dead miner was paid a one-time benefit of one dollar for every member of the society. The group started with thirty-three charter members but soon had twice that many, and by the early 1880s there were over two hundred members.

Although the Miners' Friendly Society had a practical purpose, it also strengthened the social bonds in Colchester. The death of any miner became a tragedy shared by the townspeople, and the welfare of each family was regarded as a matter of common concern.

On the day of a miner's funeral, the coal banks and shafts were closed, and the members of the society attended the service as a group, sitting together like a stricken family to mourn the loss of one of their number. Their official presence made each mining death seem like a kind of sacrifice for the town. After the service they walked in solemn procession, dressed in their dark suits and derbies, behind the wagon carrying the coffin. Before Mt. Auburn was established on Coal Street, they went to the Bean Cemetery, east of town, or the Widow Moore Cemetery, west of town. The long line of somber coal miners, followed by an even longer line of townspeople, expressed the social dimension of a mining tragedy in a community that depended on those men for its existence and knew each one as a friend. Grieving was a communal affair.

A folk song called "The Miner's Doom," which was sung in Colchester a century ago, reflects just such a scene:

> At the day of his funeral the great crowds had gathered;
> He was loved by his friends, by his neighbors, by all.
> To the grave went his corpse, by his friends it was followed;
> The tears from our eyes like the rain they did fall.

The Miners' Friendly Society also developed the most important annual event in the town's history: the Miners' Picnic. It started in the late 1860s as a dinner for members only at the Chester House, but by 1875 it was a July picnic at Egerton's Grove, west of town, or Hume's Grove, south of town, to which all the townspeople and nearby farm families were invited.

Like the warriors of ancient city-states, the miners were the heroes of the town, the makers and sustainers of the community, and at an appointed hour of the morning they marched to the grove at the head of a long procession to begin the day's festivities. An 1882 *Macomb Journal* article vividly captured one such procession:

COLCHESTER'S MINERS' FRIENDLY SOCIETY

At 10 o'clock the Miners' Friendly Society, to the number of 150, in handsome regalia, formed, and to the music of the superb Colchester Band, marched to the grove, a half mile northwest of town. They were not members of a secret order from various avenues of trade and life out on a sort of recreation from office and counting room, but strong men, made iron-framed and sturdy of grip by the arduous labor they perform; men who go before sunrise down into the midnight of the coal shaft, who for days and weeks at a time know little of daylight; men who have spent their whole lives in coal mining, their sons having grown up in the same vocation; men bound together by a common danger and common dependence on each other—their mining clothes laid aside, the grime and soot washed away, arrayed in holiday attire, with their bodies erect and step as firm as soldiers on general review: such were the men who marched from Colchester to the grove Tuesday—such are the members of the Miners' Friendly Society.

Then the wagons went out, and for each miner's family went great baskets and tubs and pans of provisions, prepared by the skillful hands of the female portion of the household. And then the miners' wives and daughters and sons, down to the least toddlers, all marched to the grove, for it was the event of the season.

In the mid-1870s the wagons of food prepared by the mining families fed all who came. It was a meal that symbolized the sustenance that coal mining had brought to Colchester as it displayed the inclusive concern that characterized the community. As the annual crowds grew, it soon became impossible for the members to provide all the food, and people were expected to bring their own unless they were invited to share with some family.

The early picnics featured speeches, singing, and band music, but more central was the socializing among local families, who gathered around magnificent spreads of food set on snow-white sheets that were scattered throughout the grove and talked with their friends and neighbors through the long hot afternoon. As the *Macomb Journal* editor noted in 1883, "It is not an uncommon thing to see farmers' and miners' families grouped together and dining as one family, everybody enjoying themselves and wanting to contribute to the enjoyment of others."

The Miners' Picnic was a massive celebration of community that combined aspects of Thanksgiving and the Fourth of July, as well as perhaps the ancient British midsummer festival. It was the town's most important ritual, a yearly affirmation of Colchester itself as the "friendly society," a sort of superfamily to which everyone belonged. As the socializing continued, it renewed the vast complex of interrelationships that gave the townspeople their identity. Despite the hardship and tragedy that characterized the community, they were reassured that their lives were part of a meaningful pattern, stretching back to the early days that so many could still recall.

The speeches at the picnics commonly celebrated America and praised the workingman, so they reflected the most deeply held values of the townspeople, who listened intently, like believers at a camp meeting.

One of the most well received and widely reported speeches was delivered by the mayor of Macomb in 1878, at the close of the great depression that had marked the decade. Entitled "Men Who Have Risen," it was, according to the *Macomb Journal,* "a stirring, though short address, showing that in this free country men are untrammeled; that each has an equal chance in the great race of life; that labor is honorable; that our greatest and richest capitalists have risen from the ranks of working men." For the townspeople it was inspirational.

The Miners' Picnic continued to grow. By the early 1880s races, games, and rides were provided in the business district, and a hot air balloon ascension in the late afternoon usually drew everyone's attention. At that time the crowds often exceeded 10,000 people, drawn from all over western Illinois, and booths were erected to sell food and drinks on the railroad grounds between Depot and Market Streets. Cries of "Ice Cream!" "Candy!" and "Lemonade!" could be heard throughout the late morning and afternoon. The saloons were open too, and great masses of thirsty men and boys drained ninety or a hundred small kegs of beer before the day was over. At the end of it all, fireworks exploded in the dark sky, the country folks and other visitors departed, and the townspeople slowly walked home, no doubt satisfied that Colchester was at the center of things.

Boomtown and Saloon Town

The bootlegger was born in the 1880s, when Colchester was booming and it seemed that everyone's hopes were about to be realized. After years of small growth, the little mining town was steadily increasing in population. There were 1,067 townspeople in 1880 but 1,643 ten years later, a jump of more than fifty percent. In 1882 alone some forty new homes were built, including the two identical ones for Albert J. Smith and his son. Still, there was a housing shortage, and many people took in boarders.

Coal production was increasing, so most of the newcomers were mining families. By the mid-1880s more than four hundred men and boys worked in seven or eight shaft mines and forty drift mines. They produced about 80,000 tons of coal every year—enough to fill 4,000 railroad cars.

The miners all shared the same routine. Before dawn you could hear the sound of their hobnailed boots thudding on the wooden sidewalks and see the tiny yellow flames from the carbide lamps on their caps as they marched through the darkness toward the shadowy tipples beyond the west edge of town, or north to the drift mines along the creek. One by one they were swallowed by the low black tunnels that led nowhere except the coal face. Ten hours a day, six days a week, they worked bent over, squatted down, or lying on their sides, digging the clay and rock from beneath the coal seam, then shattering sections of it with a sledgehammer and wedges, and finally shoveling the fallen hunks into mining cars. In the late afternoon they trudged home, to bathe and eat and sleep and start again. Their willingness to do that day after day made everything else possible.

The miners were not well paid, but in the 1880s they were doing better than they had done for many years. The combined payroll of the three local shaft-mining companies alone often exceeded $20,000 a month, so there was money in town, and the merchants did very well.

By 1886, when the bootlegger was born, Colchester had a remarkably well developed business district, which the local newspaper once promoted in a seriocomic list of community assets and liabilities.

COLCHESTER HAS

No dudes,
One bank,
Two tailors,
One dentist,
Good schools,
Two churches,
Two jewelers,
No Chinamen,
A few loafers,
Two attorneys,
Honest officials,
Four physicians,
Two feed stores,
A few old fogies,
Two bookstores,
One grain buyer,
Two drug stores,
Two good hotels,
One undertaker,
A few meddlers,
One greenhouse,
One livery stable,
One harness shop,
A Salvation Army,
Two wagon shops,
Three restaurants,

Two lumber yards,
Two butcher shops,
Lots of pretty girls,
Three barber shops,
Two millinery stores,
Plenty of cheap fuel,
Three clothing stores,
Some chronic kickers,
Nearly 2,000 people,
A dozen dressmakers,
Three carpenter shops,
One implement dealer,
A bakery but no baker,
Two shoemaker's shops,
Three blacksmith shops,
One tile and brick yard,
Three insurance agents,
Two hardware merchants,
Too many scandal mongers,
An intelligent class of people,
One good job printing office,
A good stockyard with scales,
No thieves—that we know of—
The best stone coal in the state,
A genial class of businessmen,
Over $2,000 in the city treasury,
The best ball park in the county,
A Building and Loan Association,
Some worse than worthless curs,
And five saloons more than we need.

Connected with the saloons—which the editor wanted to close—were three billiard halls and a bowling alley, and the town also had an opera house and a roller-skating rink.

The variety of stores, shops, and entertainment places made Colchester an exceptional "Saturday night town." Rural people from several miles in every direction came to town on that night, and by six o'clock teams harnessed to wagons stood in two long rows at the hitching rails on Depot and Market Streets. It was not uncommon to see more than two hundred teams on a Saturday evening—and many people walked into town. The wooden sidewalks swarmed with shoppers, and most of the businesses stayed open late, until well after the lamplighter had made his rounds, lighting the few dozen gas lamps that held back the dark.

Colchester was an excellent market for farm products—especially cream, butter, and eggs—because the townspeople were nonproducers. They were miners and shopkeepers, not farmers, so rural folks knew that "trading" was always good at the Colchester grocery stores.

But Saturday night was not just an economic event; it was a ritual of community, a weekly renewal of the bonds between the townspeople and those farm families for whom Colchester was also a complex, personal reality. While the women shopped and visited, the men gathered in small groups along the sidewalks or went to the pool halls. Girls tagged along with their mothers; boys played in the street.

For men and women alike, the great entertainment was talk, and their easy sharing of rumor and experience wove them together and shaped their identities until Colchester was the axis of their spiritual lives.

Most of the stores and shops faced the great central area known as "the railroad grounds." There stood the depot, still reflecting the economic hope of the community that had grown up around it, and emblazoned with the word that said it all: COLCHESTER.

In truth, the town was just a gathering of small stores and modest houses along the railroad track, an uncomplicated symbol of the plain, hard-working people who lived there, but in the 1880s it seemed to be a place of real promise. In fact, during the summer of 1884 the *Chicago Times* featured Colchester as one of the up-and-coming towns of "The Rowdy West," primarily because it was noted for its high-quality coal and was linked by the railroad to the unfolding future of the country.

On any day of the week the depot was the busiest place in town. During the 1880s no fewer than twenty trains stopped in Colchester every day, ten going east and ten going west, and local residents often dropped by just to see them come in. The railroad had built a new depot in the early 1870s because the town had outgrown the first one, and just ten years later it had to be enlarged. The west end of the building was a passenger waiting room with bench-type seats and a pot-bellied stove; the east end was a storage room for freight; and in between was the station agent's office, complete with a telegraph and a ticket window. Like the several new brick buildings in town, the depot was a reflection of satisfying progress.

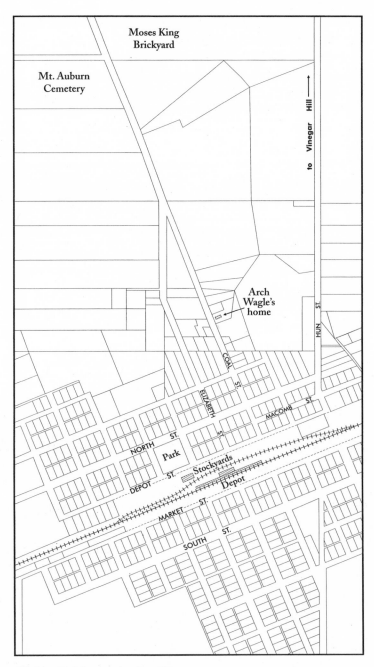

Map 3. Colchester in the 1880s

The C. B. & Q. also built stockyards across the tracks from the new depot, right in the middle of town, just like at Dodge City and Abilene, for livestock shipping had become a major activity. In the summer and fall especially, nearby farmers drove herds of cattle and hogs into town almost daily, raising billows of dust along the dirt roads. It was not uncommon to see ten or twelve carloads of livestock shipped to Chicago in a single week.

Flour was another major product. The old Pleasant Valley Mill, down by the creek, was still operating, but far more important was the modern Daisy Roller Mill, an imposing four-story structure located at the east end of Market Street. Inside it the rumbling grindstones and humming conveyor belts made an enormous, never-ending din, and fine white dust covered the chutes and bins, floors and walls, machinery and workers. Buying wheat from farmers throughout the county, the mill shipped out thousands of barrels of flour each year, packed in railroad cars bound for markets in St. Louis, Quincy, Davenport, and other cities. Before the decade was over, it was also selling flour to the British Isles.

Bricks were also shipped out by rail, for the King brickyard had grown into a sizable operation, with three round kilns and two long drying sheds that could turn out 100,000 bricks a week. It kept fifteen or sixteen men and boys busy from late March through November, when the weather was warm enough to dry the bricks. Two of the boys did little else day after day but stack bricks in freight cars.

But of course, the railroad's most important function was shipping coal, sometimes 150 carloads a week, for which the depot was the weighing office, counting house, and communications center.

The depot was also where the payroll was kept for the shaft-mining companies and where, once a month, the miners were paid. That arrangement led to the most disturbing crime of the decade.

On March 10, 1881, "the competent, accommodating, and most highly esteemed station agent of the C. B. & Q.," David H. Howell, stole the entire payroll of the Quincy Coal Company, some $9,500 that had been deposited in the depot's safe, and fled to Mexico. Like most others in town, he was thoroughly known and completely trusted, so the townspeople were incredulous: "What? Davie Howell? Impossible!" His crime was an assault on the town's cherished sense of innocence. That it occurred at the depot and victimized the coal company that employed almost half the miners made it all the more obviously a betrayal of the community.

The *Colchester Independent* accurately reflected the local view of Howell when it said, "His sudden fall is universally deplored." The townspeople were like a church congregation; their relationship to one another was spiritual. And they realized that Howell had broken the bonds of neighborly trust and mutual support that gave meaning to life in Colchester.

Eventually he realized it too. Although he worked hard and did well in Mexico, Howell suffered anxiety, alienation, and remorse. So, more than two years after his crime had shocked the town, he returned and gave back all the money. For the townspeople it was a vindication of their faith in the community.

Howell was never prosecuted.

Other problems were not so well resolved. In fact, many were not resolved at all, and chief among those was the frequency of death in the mines. Although no local accident records were kept, an 1884 article in the *Colchester Independent* estimated the number of mining deaths and expressed their continuing impact on the community:

KILLED IN THE MINES

Notwithstanding the fact that over fifty sons of toil have met death while underneath the ground in Colchester mines during the history of the town, and that a fatal accident in the mines is an occurrence of every few months, still, the same feeling of horror greets each new accident, and the same gloom overcasts the community as victim after victim is added to the long list.

The latest victim is William Carroll, who worked in a bank [drift mine] on the Hickey land, one-fourth mile northwest of town, and who was killed last Wednesday.

Perhaps the most pathetic mining tragedy of the decade was the death of young Oliver Foster, whose story appeared in the *Colchester Independent* in 1886:

FATAL MINE ACCIDENT

Just after noon last Tuesday there occurred another mine accident, which caused the death of Oliver Foster, aged between thirteen and fourteen years.

The boy was working with his father in the bank on Mr. Foster's place. He was mining, and his father was loading a box, when a piece of the roof, five feet long, three feet wide, and six inches thick, fell upon the boy. The father sprang to his assistance, and lifted the heavy stone, but owing to its heavy weight taxing his utmost strength, he could not hold it up and pull the boy out at the same time. The rock was of a soapstone nature, and, during his exertions, his handholds broke out twice and allowed the heavy rock to fall back upon the boy.

When his father first raised the rock, the boy was conscious, and said he was not frightened, but begged his father to hurry and take him out.

Finding that he could accomplish nothing, not even hold the weight from off his son, Foster ran to the outside, where Charlie Myers was, and together they succeeded in releasing the imprisoned body. But it was too late!

There being but slight marks upon the body, it is believed that death was due to suffocation, the heavy weight upon the body making it impossible for the boy to breathe.

At thirteen Oliver Foster was the youngest miner ever killed in the Colchester coal fields. After that heartrending tragedy, Newman Foster did not allow his younger sons to work in the mines, but dozens of other boys continued to do so, despite the danger.

During the 1880s the pressure of death on the tightly knit community became enormous. Aside from the continual mining accidents and a few deaths connected with the railroad, there were several epidemics. Early in 1880, for example, scarlet fever killed more than a dozen children, and the following fall typhoid fever killed several adults. Twice in a single year the town was filled with sorrow and fear.

Nevertheless, for carpenter and coffin maker Stephen D. Mills, death was good for business. He could finally afford to buy a hearse, the first ever in Colchester. It was an ornate, black, high-wheeled vehicle, polished like a piece of furniture and pulled by a team of magnificent black horses. Thereafter townspeople with money could be buried in style.

The multiple deaths also emphasized the need for a city cemetery, so Mt. Auburn was established in the fall of 1881, across from the King brickyard on north Coal Street.

That was just in time. A few months later, in the winter of 1882, small-pox ravaged the town. When the dread disease was identified and the word spread, both Macomb, to the east, and Tennessee, to the west, placed armed guards along the road to prevent Colchester residents from coming to those communities. Within the stricken town the schools, churches, and saloons were closed, and afflicted families were quarantined. Victims were buried in the night, to avoid crowds, and their wooden coffins were puttied shut so that the deadly disease couldn't get out. Still, more than twenty people died.

Shortly afterward, a local poet named Fanny Dunne wrote a poem for the Colchester newspaper that expressed the life-shattering experience of losing someone and the grief that pervaded the town:

DEAD HOPES

Plunged suddenly into the darkness,
    With never a ray of light
To lead us through pathless perils
    Out of the gloom and the night,
No wonder if we sometimes falter
    And fall by the wayside bare—
Hearts impregnated once with hope,
    Now filled with blank despair.

Alas for our fond illusions!
    Alas for the joys that die!
Alas for the grisly sepulchre,
    The place where our loved ones lie!
There is never a heart so happy,
    Nor a joy so perfect quite,
But what has a grave where some dead hope
    Lies buried away from sight.

On more than one level the townspeople struggled against despair. They prayed and consoled. They grieved and remembered. They made Mt. Auburn into a park, fronted by a white picket fence with an arched gate, where the unforgotten dead lay waiting for them in the sunshine.

The bootlegger's parents were married in 1882, that year of promise and despair, marked by the great building boom and the awful small-pox epidemic. By then Arch was a strong, capable, twenty-two-year-old miner, sporting a mustache. Ambitious and self-reliant, he made about $40 a month working for the Quincy Coal Company. Alice Walley was just eighteen and still working as a dressmaker. She was a tall, attractive young woman who wore her long brown hair pulled up in a bun, as the fashion was in those days. The Wagles were married at the Methodist Church on October 26.

Arch did not remain a coal miner for very long. Soon after his wedding, the shaft he was working in caught fire, trapping some thirty men and boys in the mine. It was No. 12, more than a mile east of town, which provided coal for the chutes that supplied the railroad. As the smoke billowed high into the air, people rushed to the scene, where the flames had already climbed up the shaft and ignited the tipple. It was soon engulfed by a crackling, swirling blaze and burned like a massive torch. Despair seized the crowd when they were told that the miners were not out.

Down below, the fire created a draft that drew bad air, called "the black damp," out of played-out rooms and into the main tunnel. It was loaded with carbon dioxide. The miners knew they were in grave danger when their carbide lamps flickered and went out, leaving them in total darkness, and it became harder and harder to breathe.

Fortunately one man remembered an abandoned tunnel that connected with an old shaft, No. 13, a quarter-mile away. The men slowly made their way to it, only to find that passage blocked by a heap of clay and other mine waste. With no other alternative and time running out, they worked desperately in the darkness to make an opening. Finally they entered the tunnel and crawled along, one after the other, to the main passageway of No. 13, which proved to be nearly full of water. There was just enough space for the men to keep their heads out, however, so they waded through, finally reaching the old shaft, where they climbed up a wooden ladder attached to the sidewall.

When the frightened and exhausted miners emerged, they hurried across the field to No. 12, where hundreds of the townspeople had gathered, and as the newspaper later put it, "They were received as men returned from the dead."

After that harrowing ordeal—as close to a mine disaster as Colchester ever had—Arch vowed to quit mining, and he soon did. By early 1883 he was a conductor for the C. B. & Q., punching tickets on the Lightning Express, the fastest run between Quincy and Chicago.

In 1884 the Wagles built a house just north of town on Coal Street. It was located within sight of Mt. Auburn Cemetery, on land purchased from brick maker Moses King. A narrow one-and-a-half-story frame building that Arch worked on himself, it was a plain but respectable home with white-painted siding, a small porch, and a big window on either side of the front door.

The bootlegger was born there, on January 14, 1886. He was the third of six children—Joseph L., John M., Thomas Henry, Charles L., Archibald Glenn, and Alice Geneva—who were added to the family between 1883 and 1897.

Some months before Henry was born, however, tragedy struck the Wagles. Their second son, John, died as an infant in 1885. The cause of his death is unknown. He was buried at the new city cemetery just down the street from their home. When Henry was born early the next year, he must have been a welcome addition to the bereaved family.

During the 1880s the talk in Colchester was often focused on how the widow of some dead miner or the mother of some dead child was getting along. People saw in those stricken figures a possible future for their own family, and they were reminded of the presence of death in the community. It is thus not surprising that the decade was marked by the first appearances of the Woman in Black, a ghost that haunted Colchester off and on for half a century.

As early as 1883 a young man who was out alone one night saw a woman dressed in black on the south side of town. As she brushed past him silently in the dark street, he glanced at her and saw that she had no face. Terrified, he ran to the depot like a demon was after him and, in a trembling voice, told the astonished railroad agent what he had seen. He refused to leave the dimly lit building until a sizable man who stopped by the depot agreed to walk him home.

As the story spread, others also began to see the strange figure, lurking in the shadows just beyond the edge of certainty, and frightened townspeople began to stay indoors after dark.

From time to time the Woman in Black returned, like an unshakable nightmare, to stalk through the dark streets. In September 1887 the local newspaper provided this striking account:

A GHOST STORY

Those residents of the south side who are supernaturally inclined were frightened by a ghostly apparition last Thursday evening. . . . People passing along Market Street saw a low, thick figure, enveloped in a sombre black dress, features concealed by a heavy black veil. No one got a close look at the strange form, for it was shy of human kind. When people hailed it, it went on its way in silence; when they followed it, it disappeared.

The always skeptical newspaper editor suggested that it was not the ghost but a certain woman who was involved in a local court case and had disguised herself to slip out of town. But many were not convinced.

Those who believed she was more than an image in the mind or a person in disguise began to recall the old stories about local women who had mysteriously died. Some of the old-timers linked her with the shocking death of Isabella Craig, a miner's wife of legendary strength and endurance who once had carried a cast-iron stove on her head all the way from Macomb. On a cold Christmas Eve back in the 1850s, she was found frozen stiff in the snow not far from her home, and her story, if not her ghost, haunted the town that holiday season. Others recalled the mysterious death of Jane Greenwood during the Civil War. Her abusive, alcoholic husband, blacksmith Sam Greenwood, was suspected of killing her, so the townspeople exhumed her body and held an inquest, which dragged on indecisively. Before the town could make up its mind, Greenwood himself suddenly died—and some wondered if she had come back to get him. There were other women, too, whose deaths had been disturbing.

In truth, the Woman in Black was an image of the town's deepest anxieties, so it is not surprising that she was seen from time to time as long as sudden death and apprehension about the future were part of life in Colchester. She came back again in 1893, and in 1898, and in the next century. Each time she appeared, as the newspaper put it in September 1898, "She excited no little apprehension in the breasts of scores of citizens . . . and made many a man look behind him when he had to go out in the dark."

During the 1880s the most profound expression of community life, aside from the Miners' Picnic, was the local newspaper, and Colchester waited a long time to get one—twenty-five years. Finally, on September 7, 1880, a slim, pale, bearded man named Henry H. Stevens brought to town the *Macomb Independent,* locating his printing office above Sam McGee's butcher shop on Coal Street. At the county seat his newspaper had supported the Greenback Labor Party, born in the hard economic times of the 1870s, and he continued to crusade for that cause with the renamed *Colchester Independent,* paying little attention to local matters. But the townspeople were not as interested in third-party agitation or national politics in general as Stevens had expected, so the newspaper struggled to remain solvent. In 1883 he leased the operation to his printer's devil, Van L. Hampton, who edited the *Independent* for one year on that arrangement and then bought it and moved it to the Union Hotel on Depot Street.

That was an ideal location. A two-story frame structure built in 1869, the hotel had a dining room, a sample room (for salesmen to display their goods), a dozen bedrooms, and a second-story verandah with a spindle railing. It had been the largest building in Colchester for ten years, and the townspeople viewed it as an expression of confidence in the future of their community. When Hampton moved the newspaper there, it was painted red with white trim and had a big blue-lettered sign saying "UNION HOTEL." The aptly named building was a kind of community center, second only to the depot as a structure of local significance, and people often came there, bringing the news or making it. The proprietor, J. D. Trew, was a plump, jovial immigrant from Wales, and he exemplified the ideal of civic commitment, serving as city councilman, school director, county supervisor, and justice of the peace. Under his management the hotel dining room was a popular gathering place, used over the years for weddings, parties, lodge meetings, political rallies, inquests, and even medical operations.

At twenty-two Van Hampton was the youngest newspaper editor in Illinois. Some thought he was too young to manage a newspaper, but he proved them wrong, and he soon became the foremost civic leader in the town. A short, chubby, but handsome young man with a dark brown mustache and a ready smile, Hampton loved Colchester and mixed well with the townspeople, even though he had been raised in

Macomb. Unmarried, he spent seven or eight hours a day at the tiresome task of setting type by hand, puffing on his pipe as he picked out the tiny metal slugs and placed them in tight columns that were a mirror image of the printed page. In the evenings he wrote articles and took care of business matters.

Hampton soon changed the political orientation of the *Independent* to Republican, but he was not primarily a party advocate. He viewed himself as the recorder of local life, the conscience of the community, and the chief promoter of the town. After he took over, the newspaper became intensely focused on Colchester and the nearby countryside. Local events were covered in detail, social life was carefully reflected, and obituaries appeared on the front page. Country correspondents reported from nearby hamlets and rural areas such as Argyle, Camp Creek, Fandon, Friendship, Gin Ridge, Gooseneck, Hills Grove, Horseshoe Bend, Troublesome Creek, and Vishnu Springs. The young editor also projected a concerned, sympathetic voice, and as he laughed, consoled, bragged, remembered, and called for action, the *Independent* became the heart of the community.

The townspeople started poring over the weekly issues, their reading a silent ritual of reconnection, and circulation jumped by more than two hundred the first year.

To Hampton, life in Colchester was both fascinating and significant— "Multum in Parvo," indeed—and he loved to chronicle it. Every issue carried a column of local items, mentioning who was coping with sickness or building a home, having children or switching jobs, visiting relatives or shipping livestock, buying a buggy or fishing in the creek. And sometimes he simply reported what he saw in town, as in this 1884 item: "On Friday afternoon . . . there was in front of this office at one time five sleighs, a wagon, one bobsled, eleven small boys, a tin bucket, two cows, seven dogs, a sack of flour, four mules, a bag of shot, twelve horses, a valise, and an old sow with three little pigs. Who says Colchester isn't a live town?"

Hampton's eagerness to report the local news got him into trouble once. In the summer of 1885 a heartrending suicide note found in a young woman's handbag near the Pleasant Valley Mill dam provided such a sensational story that Hampton brought out his weekly issue two days early, covering every aspect of the case. He urged the community to respond, and as the *Macomb Journal* later reported, "The miners ceased work, and the sympathetic village turned out *en masse,* and for two days an organized force of over a hundred divers searched for the unfortunate victim."

After a frustrating effort to locate her body, the townspeople realized that it was all a hoax. Hampton was briefly suspected because he had known so much about the apparent tragedy so soon and had scooped a short-lived rival newspaper with the story, but another man soon confessed—and left town one step ahead of a mob with tar and feathers.

In reality the cynical, alienated man who perpetrated the hoax was the spiritual opposite of Hampton, who encouraged and respected the sympathy and mutual concern of the townspeople.

A man of some literary pretensions, Hampton occasionally wrote lists of local assets or activities that were poems of a sort, characterized by the mixing of trivial and important matters in ever-longer lines that moved toward some key social insight. The 1886 piece called "Colchester Has" was one of them. Another, which appeared later that year, reflects small-town life in the fall:

IN SEASON:

Coal,
Dances,
Harvest,
Revivals,
Candidates,
Good roads,
Public sales,
Hickory nuts,
Pork sausage,
Coon hunting,
Fresh oysters,
Corn shucking,
New millinery,
Autumn leaves,
Fishing parties,
More weddings,
Apple gathering,
Church festivals,

Neighbors calling,
Moonlight nights,
Painting the town,
Chimney repairing,
Mushroom picking,
Serenading parties,
Leaves falling down,
Street corner politics,
Indian summer is coming,
Treats from the candidates:
Good business for the saloons until election.

Hampton's message was clear: life in Colchester was characterized by a stable economic and social cycle that peaked in the fall when the coal orders came in and common activities flourished. In the mid-1880s everything was in place and life was good.

The seasonal rhythm of community life was an assurance of continuity and meaning for the townspeople, and Hampton recorded a variety of social activities all year round. Christmas brought special programs at the schools and churches, where religion and education were deeply intertwined, and New Year's Eve was marked by townspeople calling at the homes of neighbors and friends, a tradition that renewed the community's social bonds, much like the Miners' Picnic. When it was cold enough, there was ice skating at Crooked Creek, where bonfires blazed in the frigid evenings, and if it snowed, there was coasting at Colchester Hill on North Coal Street, where sleds rushed down the white slope and across the iron bridge at the creek. On Friday and Saturday nights during the winter, there were dances at the Masonic Hall above Smith's clothing store and occasional plays at the opera house performed by the Home Dramatic Club. After 1884 there was roller skating, too, at Daisy Roller Rink, where skaters glided and tumbled for ten cents apiece.

In warm weather the townspeople returned to the creek, to fish for bass and catfish at the mill dam and to picnic at nearby Cedar Bluffs. On Sunday afternoons Hampton sometimes counted upward of two hundred people in Pleasant Valley, as they called that area north of town where the old mill sat in picturesque decay amid the huge oaks and hickories. No local place was more laden with memories.

The town park was important for community life too. After the city fathers built a two-story octagonal "parkorium" there, the Colchester Band played evening concerts once a week in the summertime, and Hampton always gave those hometown musicians extravagant praise. He realized that the performances contributed to a vital local culture. The park was also used for special events, such as the one reported in this notice printed by Hampton in July 1887:

LAWN FESTIVAL

Ladies of Colchester will give a lawn festival in the park Friday evening of this week, the proceeds going for the benefit of the Occident Baseball Club. Ice cream and cake will be served. The Colchester Band will be in attendance, and also the Serenade Band and the Colchester Glee Club. Everybody is welcome to attend and hear the music and singing.

As the purpose of that lawn festival suggests, there was one summer activity that had a level of importance quite beyond anything offered by the creek or the park. It was baseball.

Soldiers from Colchester had brought the game home after the Civil War, and by 1870 a group of local men, mostly coal miners, had put together a team called the Black Diamonds, which beat all the other nearby teams for three years straight. (Some of the men had played cricket back in England, so they already had baseball skills.) From that time on, baseball had a special importance in Colchester, and the ball field at Vinegar Hill, northeast of town, was crowded on Sunday afternoons. It is not surprising that a baseball game, or even a double header, became an important part of the annual Miners' Picnic.

Hampton occasionally managed the team, so his enthusiasm for the game was boundless. In 1887 he bragged that "Colchester has a ball team that can beat any Macomb nine composed exclusively of home talent," provoking a rivalry that lasted for decades. And like others in town, he regarded the best players as local heroes who somehow symbolized the spirit of Colchester.

But the town itself was Hampton's greatest hero. In his pages Colchester emerged as a kind of multifaceted competitor, able to beat its "opponents" and succeed in the struggle for prosperity, as suggested in this 1885 list of community assets:

COLCHESTER HAS

A population of 1800 . . .
The best mill for miles around,
The prettiest park in the county,
The finest band in our part of the state,
More gossip than there is any need for,
The champion baseball club in McDonough,
The best local newspaper in the county as well,
More civic societies than any other nearby towns,
A larger local trade than most other towns of its size,
The most energetic stock buyers in this part of the country,
A larger annual output of coal than any other town on the "Q,"
Once every year the most popular local celebration in this state,
And a more rapid and steady increase in population than any of its
    competitors.

With Hampton in charge, the *Independent* became widely and deep-ly read, and as he produced the weekly issues, like a bard slowly com-posing the epic of his people, Colchester achieved a kind of transcen-dent value. Setbacks and tragedies occurred, individuals passed away, but the town always continued, struggling to make it, supplying a mean-ingful place. And the townspeople felt they were part of a great venture.

Despite his love for the town, however, Van Hampton always quar-reled with it. In the entire history of Colchester, only the bootlegger himself was more controversial, and the notoriety of both men stemmed from the same issue: drinking. But the two stood on opposite sides. Hampton was the voice of temperance in a community where saloons had thrived for more than a generation.

Of course, there had always been some people in the community who opposed drinking. The women who had attacked the saloons in 1858 were among them, and members of the Methodist Church had also cru-saded against liquor since 1859, when they had founded a chapter of the Independent Order of Good Templars, Colchester's first temperance organization. After the Civil War that church, together with the newly established Christian Church, held a series of revivals that condemned the sins of the town, especially drinking, and some people gave up li-quor—at least for a while. By the early 1870s Colchester also had a La-dies' Temperance Society that distributed anti-liquor information and encouraged women to oppose "demon rum." But as long as temperance was voluntary, the reformers had little impact.

In the early 1880s, however, they changed their tactics. Instead of wearing red ribbons and asking people to sign the pledge, they started agitating to close the saloons, often referring to the most popular one as "Hickey's Hell." For such people, the saloons were the source of all social evil, the devil's foothold in the community, and their struggle to stamp them out was a holy crusade.

Van Hampton became their spokesman.

Colchester's proximity to Macomb made the drinking problem worse. Saloons were voted out at the county seat in the spring of 1883, and the town stayed dry for decades, but the people there who wanted to drink simply took the train to Colchester. As Hampton pointed out later that year, "The 'jug line' between this place and Macomb does a land office business on Saturday nights."

Temperance crusaders realized that they had to organize on a countywide basis, so a meeting announcement appeared in the *Independent* and other newspapers in November:

NOTICE

All citizens of McDonough County, both male and female, who are in favor of prohibiting the crime of liquor selling, are requested to meet at the Court House in Macomb, on Tuesday, November 27, at 2 o'clock p.m. to organize a county temperance union.

While that group was forming, the women of Colchester, supported by the only two churches in town, organized a local chapter of the Women's Christian Temperance Union, which started meeting in January 1884. The members committed themselves to "rescuing inebriates, caring for the fallen, and opposing the liquor traffic," and Hampton praised and encouraged them. He himself was a leader of the Good Templars, which by then had well over one hundred members.

Soon the liquor issue all but dominated the cultural life of the town. There were temperance speakers, temperance debates, temperance plays, and temperance revivals. Like the sound of a nagging spouse, the temperance crusader's voice was inescapable. And the big question before the voters every spring was "Will it be license or no license for the saloons?"

The temperance advocates finally succeeded in the spring of 1885. Saloons were voted out everywhere in the county. In Colchester on the Saturday night after the election, the defeated drinkers raised a black flag on the town flagpole. In big white letters it proclaimed, "Prohibition City—by 40." Strung up along with it, however, was an empty whisky bottle.

As that suggests, the millennium didn't come. Men continued to drink, and selling liquor simply became an illegal activity, carried on in restaurants, drug stores, club rooms, and other places. Hampton soon lamented: "It is unfortunately a fact, at least as shown by Colchester's experience, that the abolishment of the public saloon does not abolish the sale of liquor. The profits of the traffic are such, and the principles of the men who handle it are such, that it has been and probably will be sold diametrically at variance with the will of the people and the laws of the land."

What he and the other crusaders failed to recognize, of course, was that the will of the people was irrevocably split on the liquor issue. The matter went much deeper than politics, into the very soul of America, where an immense conflict between self and society was always smoldering. Alcohol simply made it flame and burn.

The defeated saloon supporters became more organized, and in the following spring they redoubled their efforts to secure votes. They even held bonfire rallies in the center of town, where they drank to show their determination and vowed to defeat those who were striving to control their lives. In April 1886 they overturned local prohibition. In that effort they were assisted by one important trend: business had declined after the saloons were closed.

Year after year the conflict over saloons was a pitched battle in Colchester. The anti-temperance side had no newspaper or formal organization, but among the men who drank whisky and beer, chewed tobacco, told stories, and talked politics at the saloons, temperance crusaders were continually criticized and ridiculed. And since the latter controlled the churches, drinkers felt less welcome at the Sunday services.

On the other side, Hampton stepped up his efforts to rid Colchester of "the saloon menace." Every spring brought strident temperance editorials prior to the election. In 1886 he proclaimed, "The record of whisky in Colchester is a bad one," and he referred to local accidents, crime, and poverty that could be associated with liquor. But the saloons were licensed again anyway. In 1887 he declared, "If saloons could be effectively got rid of, we might be sure of conquering the devil himself," thereby demonizing his opponents, and he provided a long list of rural people who had signed his petition stating, "We would much prefer to do business in a town where there are no saloons." But that approach failed too.

As one might expect, all the public pressure led to hypocrisy. In a comment published later that year, Hampton acknowledged that not all the crusaders were sincere:

COLCHESTER HAS

Some temperance men who drink whisky
The way Christians should pray—in secret.

Meanwhile the pro-license people, whom the young editor often called "saloonatics," viewed him as the voice of repression and refused to advertise in his newspaper. They pitted their will to survive against his, and one evening at a saloon rally they burned him in effigy on Depot Street.

As that act of symbolic violence suggests, the strident anti-liquor campaign damaged the social solidarity that had prevailed in Colchester since before the war. A town united by coal mining as a way of life and committed to mutual support was evolving into polarized factions that felt justified in forcing their values on hostile opponents. Among some of the temperance crusaders, dedication to the community was being replaced by dedication to a cause.

But Hampton, like so many others, never understood that change in the spiritual fabric of the town. In 1887 he predicted that "the *Independent* will still live when the saloon business in Colchester will be no more, because of the triumph of that great principle—Prohibition." He was right, but experience should have taught him that it would be a hollow victory.

Soon Hampton began to emphasize the domestic impact of drinking. In May 1888 the suicide of a nearby tenant farmer's wife provided him with a lurid example of the saloon's impact on the home, and he made the most of it. From the tragic story of nineteen-year-old Ida Wright he created unforgettable anti-saloon propaganda:

A WIFE SUICIDES:
Between Rum and a Rope, the Hapless Bride of a Few Weeks Chooses the Rope

In the extreme northwest corner of Tennessee Township . . . there stands on George Eakle's farm a neat, tidy, one-story farmhouse, situated pleasantly among shade trees and surrounded by an air of quietness and comfort wholly at variance with the tragedy about to be related. Here since their marriage on March 27 lived Silas Wright and his young wife.

Last Monday the husband came to Colchester for medicine for his wife. Wright is a drinking man and is addicted to sprees. He drank at the saloons Monday afternoon and did not go home. The spree continued Tuesday, and it was not until Wednesday forenoon that he departed for home. He arrived there at six o'clock. In the house he found a note signed by his wife:

May 14th, 1888

Dear Husband Silas:

It is with pleasure that I write these few lines. I am as happy as I can be and hope you are the same. I am going to hang myself today. . . . Please send my trunk and things to my mother. Bury me in my wedding clothes.

I am as happy as I can be. I haven't shed a tear since you left, for I was too happy to cry. I am going to die believing in God, but if I don't go to heaven, I will still be happier than to live with a drunkard.

Good-bye forever,
Ida M. Wright

To the smokehouse the husband went, and there DANGLING LIFELESS from a rafter was the body of his wife. . . . The woman had climbed a ladder that was in the building, and with a rope around her neck in an ordinary slip noose, she had deliberately LEAPED INTO ETERNITY.

Although Hampton did not realize it, the Wright tragedy revealed more about the mounting psychological stress associated with the temperance cause than it did about the evils of drink. Like many women,

Ida Wright was a temperance crusader, and before her marriage she had pressured Silas Wright to stop drinking. When he relapsed afterward, she must have felt the weight of her own failure to redeem him as well as the disgrace of living with one of the devil's own "saloonatics." So, despite the fact that he never abused her, she was desperate to escape her situation.

A year later, in a long article called "The Saloon vs. the Home," Hampton referred to saloons as "schools of financial, physical, social, and moral disorganization and corruption," and he hit hard at the impact of drinking in Colchester: "We see men beat the women they promised to cherish and protect. . . . We see men squander their earnings in drink while mothers economize. . . . We see men fined in police court for misdemeanors, the result of drunken sprees. . . . We see an old man bent with age, once a proud citizen of this city, now living at the county almshouse, whose gray hairs would now be honored but for that devilish compound—drink."

The old man Hampton was referring to was apparently Lewis Wagle. Several years earlier he and his young wife were separated. The exact reasons are unknown, but his drinking and failure to support the family were surely important factors. When their youngest child, Arthur, died of croup in 1884, Martha was living with relatives in Chicago. She brought the child's body back to Colchester on the train, and he was buried in a cemetery plot supplied by Arch. Then she returned to Chicago. Lewis was not present at the burial of his son.

In 1888 he was taken to the McDonough County Almshouse, not by his family, but by a local farmer named B. F. Myers, who took an interest in old and indigent people. The facility was a three-story brick building two miles south of Macomb, and for that time it was well operated. Still, it was "the poorhouse," and the stigma of failure was attached to everyone who ended up there. That Lewis was still separated from his wife is apparent from the reason he gave for entering the institution, which the director wrote in the almshouse register: "He wanted a home."

The register also refers to his occupation as being a "coal hauler," and it mentions just one word about his condition: "intemperance." Perhaps for that reason, he was also estranged from their seven remaining sons and daughters, who might have taken him in but didn't.

In the late 1880s Hampton also started printing lists of men who were fined in the local court for "intoxication and disorderly conduct," and he played up liquor-related brawls—like this one from early 1889:

A WHISKY ROW

The railroad track just inside the eastern limits of the city was the scene of a six-handed drunken fight last Thursday afternoon, which by the narrowest possible margin missed terminating in murder. Con Murphy of Macomb, Sam Stuart of Augusta, James McIntire and Robert Masterson of Industry, and Harry Mikesell and James Walker of Monmouth were the parties of the melee. It originated in a saloon.

At the time this fight occurred, Colchester was the only saloon town in McDonough County and the only one on the C. B. & Q. Railroad between Galesburg and Quincy, a distance of one hundred miles. Men were coming from all over the region to drink there. Supplying them with liquor, despite increasing pressure from the forces of prohibition, was regarded by some as a great opportunity.

Hard Times
and the
Marshal

The decade of Henry Wagle's boyhood was a traumatic period for the townspeople, whose dreams were destroyed by harsh economic reality. When hard times had come before, in the 1860s and 1870s, the community had maintained an unflagging optimism. Setbacks were viewed as temporary; the future—"the good time that's coming"—seemed as certain as the afternoon coal train. But this time it was different. In Colchester, it was the end of an era.

By 1890 forty-three local mines had been worked to capacity and abandoned, so when coal shipments declined and the miners started working only a few days a week, rumors circulated that Colchester was running out of coal. But in fact, less than one-fourth of the black seam that ran under and around the community had been mined.

The problem was not the amount of coal but the cost of extracting it. Mechanical equipment such as the pneumatic drill was starting to have an impact on mining, but it was not useful where the coal seam was narrow. At Colchester the seam was quite narrow, only twenty-four to thirty inches thick. So, local mining remained labor intensive, and Colchester coal became more expensive than other kinds. Production declined as local companies found it more and more difficult to market their coal.

Van Hampton realized that the town's future was at stake, so early in 1890 he spearheaded the formation of the Colchester Businessmen's

Improvement Association, an organization to encourage economic development. Most of the members were self-made men who had come to Colchester with little or nothing and had achieved success, especially in the boom period of the 1880s. Among them were Albert J. Smith, the former railroad agent who was then erecting a huge clothing store on Market Street; Thomas Terrill, who had worked as a coal miner for many years and eventually became superintendent of the Quincy Coal Company and principal owner of Terrill and Sons general store; Stephen D. Mills, a carpenter who had started the first lumber yard, built many homes and stores, and eventually organized the Building and Loan Association; and Edward and James Stevens, who had been raised in a log cabin south of town and had prospered in dry goods, banking, and other ventures.

For them and others in the association, Colchester had brought the better life that it had held out as a hope for everyone since the coming of the railroad.

With the wealthy and dynamic Edward Stevens as president, the association strove to develop manufacturing, and within six months Colchester had a second brickyard, owned by James Underhill, as well as a new harness company, a cigar factory, a broom factory, and a pottery. Other small towns took note, and Colchester was widely praised for its "enterprise and progressive spirit."

The economic development effort received a setback later in the year, however, when Edward and James Stevens sold their local assets and moved to Chicago, taking two younger brothers with them. Their eventual success in the big city made the Stevens brothers legendary among the townspeople they had left behind—the supreme example of what Colchester men could accomplish—but still, they were gone.

That was when Chicago emerged as a reality in the minds of local people, although many of them never saw it for themselves until the great Columbian Exposition opened there in 1893. For decades, starting in about 1890, the townspeople derided the great city for its crime and corruption, but they admired it too, for no other place so readily symbolized the promise that was fading around them.

Despite the loss of leadership and declining coal production, Colchester managed to maintain a certain economic vitality in the early 1890s. Some miners moved away, but others continued to toil in the shafts and banks, or they worked in the new brickyard north of town or in the pottery east of the business district. The town's new industrial base seemed to be in clay products and other small-scale manufacturing, as well as in more limited coal production, which prompted a reporter for the *Quincy Journal* to comment in an 1892 article that "Colchester has a very bright future."

As if to symbolize that perennial hope, a group of local investors had formed the Colchester Electric Light Company during the previous year, and by the fall of 1892, when the Quincy reporter came to visit, the streets were lit by electric lights. Unfortunately the town's power plant was inadequate, so the streetlights were often very dim—"like lightning bugs on a night in June," as the newspaper later put it. And sometimes all the lights in town went out. It would be many years before Colchester had an adequate power supply.

The decline of coal mining became a psychological reality, an inescapable conviction, during 1892 when two men died who had spearheaded the local industry. One was William Egerton, a British immigrant who had come to Colchester as a miner in 1856, walking all the way from Galesburg, and had risen to become the wealthiest independent coal operator in town, employing some sixty men at three shafts during the 1880s. By that time he was often referred to as "Uncle Billy" Egerton, for he was in his seventies and had become a widely admired elder in the community. He died on January 14 and was buried at Mt. Auburn, following funeral rites that were massively attended.

Two months later, on March 23, 1892, Colchester lost the most important man who ever lived there, James Roberts. Without him there would have been no town. If anyone embodied the promise of the community, it was he.

Everyone knew his story—about a poor Cornish lad who dropped out of school at age ten to work in the copper mines, later immigrated to America and dug coal at New Castle, came west and started the mining camp that became Colchester, secured railroad connections and opened the first shaft mines, and eventually headed the Colchester Coal Company, which employed some 150 men and boys during the 1880s.

His remarkable life story, about a man whose "indomitable pluck and energy" led him from "a very humble beginning" to "great success," was written for all to read in the 1878 *History of McDonough County,* but that was not how the townspeople knew it. They possessed it as a collection of shared memories and tales that illuminated their own experience in Colchester. He had dug coal, hauled coal, weighed coal, and shipped coal; he had opened mines, built tipples, formed companies, and hired men and boys. No wonder his life epitomized the industrial venture that lay at the heart of the community.

On the day of his funeral the stores were closed and the mines were shut down. The bell tolled slowly at the Methodist Church, which Roberts had helped to found back in the early days, as the townspeople drew together to honor him and reflect on their loss. The church could not accommodate many of those who came, but they waited and joined the funeral procession, which stretched all the way to the cemetery, as if the whole town were marching out to bury him. James Roberts had been so important to the townspeople for so long that it must have been hard to maintain their hopes without him.

Mortality was deeply felt in other ways as well. In the fall of 1889 Colchester was struck by a diphtheria epidemic. The *Independent* said little about it, to avoid frightening nearby people who might then stay out of town, but a newspaper in another county mentioned that forty cases had been recently identified in Colchester, where ten children were already dead and there was "no check to the disease." The final death toll was not reported, but diphtheria returned the following fall and killed several more children, who died as the earlier victims had, by slow strangulation.

One of the dead children was Charles L. Wagle, the third son of Arch and Alice, who was always called by his middle name, Leonard. He died in November 1890, at the age of two, and was buried next to his brother.

By that time Henry was almost five years old, but his brother's death again made him the baby of the family. He was a lovely blond-haired boy whose mother doted on him while his surviving brother, Joe, was in school all day. It would be several years before the two younger children came along. Henry too had contracted diphtheria, but he was lucky. His number would not be up for a long time.

During that period of anxiety, loss, and uncertainty, the temperance conflict continued. In the spring of 1889 Hampton and his supporters again succeeded in voting out the saloons.

This time they had the help of a colorful figure named Gilbert ("Gib") Miller, who had emigrated from Scotland in 1875, when he was twenty-five years old. Miller was a huge man, six feet, eight inches tall, with broad shoulders and long arms, and he was a notorious drinker and saloon fighter. On one memorable occasion in 1886 he fought two opponents at the same time, and according to the newspaper, "one lost several teeth and the other was badly disfigured." But after his first wife died, leaving him with six children to care for, he married a much younger woman for whom he gave up his drinking and brawling. His efforts in the 1889 anti-saloon campaign were praised by Hampton: "Gilbert Miller deserves special credit for the work he did at the polls, and before, against the saloons. Formerly a drinking man, Mr. Miller has not drank for a long time and is not slow to express his convictions." When the saloons were voted out, Miller leased one of the vacant buildings on Depot Street and opened a restaurant and pool hall.

Nevertheless, despite the temperance victory, Hampton soon reported the inevitable: "Illicit liquor selling is carried on with impunity." Nothing much had changed.

Of course, Colchester had a marshal who was supposed to enforce the law, but his job was difficult because the townspeople remained so deeply divided on the liquor issue. When Marshal Lewis Underhill resigned late in 1889, he cited "the failure of city authorities to prosecute illicit sellers of intoxicants upon information supplied by him on several different occasions."

In the following year Arch Wagle quit his railroad job and went into law enforcement. He was appointed city policeman and made $35 a month helping Marshal Benjamin F. Barrett, a former coal miner, and his successor, Marshal George Agnew, a former blacksmith. Neither Barrett nor Agnew stayed on the job very long. The pay was modest and the pressure was awful.

In the spring of 1891 Arch was elected marshal, for despite the saloon controversy, he liked police work and was good at it. The election also ended two years of local prohibition—by a one-vote margin. Although it could not have been more deeply split on the liquor issue, Colchester was again a saloon town.

Arch, then thirty-one years old, was an ideal man to enforce the laws governing liquor sales and drunken behavior because he himself was not a drinker. His mother had seen to that. So there was some social distance between him and the saloon crowd, even though he had many friends who drank.

After the vote was in, Arch went over to the local photography studio and had his picture taken—with a five-pointed badge on his double-breasted blue coat, a policeman's cap on his head, and a nightstick in his hand.

The marshal's office was on Macomb Street, in a two-story, tan-brick building constructed in 1887 to house the town government. The part-time mayor worked there, and the city officials met there every month. The marshal's office was in the north end of the building, on the first floor, where the jail, or "calaboose," was located. From there Arch went forth to make his rounds—walking the streets, stopping at the depot, checking the saloons.

Things were usually pretty quiet in Colchester, except on Saturday nights. Most of the lawbreaking was vice—drunken behavior, fighting, gambling, and prostitution—which flourished on the weekends. Because the townspeople were closely knit, there was little crime that victimized the innocent.

Arch made frequent arrests for drunken and disorderly conduct, and he occasionally encountered opposition, as revealed in this account from the summer of 1891:

POLICE COURT

Ralph McConnell was arrested at about dark Saturday evening on a charge of profanity, he having taken a position in the middle of a principal street and rendered his opinion of various real and imaginary grievances in a blasphemous vocabulary that can be attained only by long practice. . . .

"Don't you know me?" shouted the drunken man. "I'm one of the McConnells of Hancock County, and they're bad men. But I'm twenty times worse than the worst one!"

Nevertheless, Marshal Wagle gathered him in. . . . As they walked to the jail, passing Hendel's corner, the prisoner cried, "Oh, boys!" to a small crowd standing in the dark. There was a rush of men, a drawn revolver in the hands of the marshal, and a frustrated attempt to rescue the prisoner. . . .

There is a very tough crowd that now has it in for Marshal Wagle.

As a result of that episode and others like it, Arch gained a reputation for being tougher than the boozers and fighters he had to deal with, and the townspeople respected him. Still, they did not always support him when it came to arresting and prosecuting local people.

One case that did result in a conviction dramatized the conflict over liquor, and it occurred in November 1892. A burly saloonkeeper named Homer Bond, seeing Van Hampton loitering in front of his saloon, came out and argued with him, went back inside for a fireplace poker, and reemerged to hit him on the head with it. The two men fought on the sidewalk, and another joined in, until onlookers pulled them apart. Arch arrested Bond, who was charged with "assault with a deadly weapon." He eventually pleaded guilty and paid a $500 fine, but the episode only increased the animosity on both sides of the liquor issue.

Gambling was also hard to suppress because, like drinking, it had always been part of community life. Coal miners were great believers in luck. Trapped in poverty, they often gambled in the hopes of getting enough money to gain control over their lives. And the intensity of the contest was an escape from the grim realities they faced. Poker dens were common in back rooms and private homes, and crap games were not hard to find on payday. The miners also bet while playing dominoes and quoits (a British ring-toss game similar to horseshoes). The stakes often exceeded a week's income.

By the 1890s the anti-saloon campaign had grown into a broadly focused crusade against vice, so there was mounting pressure to eliminate gambling, whether or not it was connected with a saloon. Van Hampton railed against "gambling dives" in the *Independent,* and Arch Wagle occasionally raided the most notorious ones and made arrests, but the problem continued.

Early in 1893 Arch gathered evidence that led to twenty-three grand jury indictments for gambling. It was the biggest strike against vice in the history of Colchester. But that enormous effort made him unpopular with some townspeople, including one city official who was arrested.

Among the indicted men was Gib Miller. The brawny, outspoken giant had allowed poker playing in his restaurant, which had become a popular hangout for local men. Miller often played right along with them. When the saloons were voted in again, he simply changed his restaurant to a saloon—although he still didn't drink—and the gambling continued. By that time he had a new nickname: "Gib the Sport." Like the others who were indicted, he resented the authorities who had cracked down, including Arch Wagle.

Prostitution was also prevalent, as one might expect in a town where men came to carouse, and it was just as hard to stop. Much of it was itinerant. As Hampton pointed out as early as 1883, "It is a noticeable fact that a certain class of the 'fair but frail' make this town one of their special rendezvous." Commonly two or more prostitutes would come by wagon with a male companion to the edge of town, often camping in the woods near the creek, like Gypsies. The man would then go to the saloons and drum up business. For a few days or weeks the camp would become "the center of attraction for lewd men and boys," as Hampton put it following one such episode in 1897, and many a marriage vow was broken for no more than fifty cents. By the time local authorities found out what was going on, the group was usually gone.

Local prostitution was also difficult to eradicate, and the trial of Mary Wiley is a case in point. Arch arrested her in 1891 for running a bawdy house on Coal Street. Although many townspeople, especially women, wanted her sent to prison, the case was difficult because the men who knew the most were not anxious to testify, and the all-male jury wanted to protect local reputations. As a result, she was acquitted. In a short, sarcastic article Van Hampton expressed his frustration—and no doubt Arch Wagle's as well:

POLICE COURT RECORD

Last Thursday night 'Squire Richards and a jury tried Mary Wiley on the charge of maintaining a house of ill-fame. But the jury decided that said house was pure and spotless—as white as snow. Business will therefore be conducted at the old stand, to the gratification of various sympathizers.

Previous to the trial there was an exodus of sundry male citizens, who were fearful of being put on the witness rack. So far as heard from, they are all home again.

As the Wiley trial suggests, Arch was in a difficult situation. If he did not make enough arrests, reformers complained, but if he tried to clean up the gambling and prostitution, people he had known for years, people that everybody knew, were apt to be implicated, embarrassed, and resentful—and prosecution would probably fail. The townspeople would not convict the townspeople.

Despite Arch's efforts to clean up the town, impatient reformers organized a chapter of "The Mystic Brotherhood of Justice," a secret society dedicated to "the detection, arrest, and conviction of lawbreakers." Thriving on rumor and self-righteousness, they met every month to share information, and they pressured the young marshal to make more arrests.

By the fall of 1893 Arch was the most controversial figure in town. In October the city council suddenly discharged him from the office of marshal, supposedly for not arresting two women who were running a bawdy house. The mayor supported him, however, and so did Van Hampton, who criticized the council and reminded his readers that it takes solid evidence to convict a woman of prostitution, as the Wiley case had demonstrated. He also called Arch "the best marshal and policeman that Colchester has had in many years." Many townspeople agreed, and two weeks later the council reinstated him.

Arch's only recorded comment as the Colchester marshal was made shortly afterward. "The town's cussedness comes in streaks," he said, but whether he was referring to the local lawbreakers or to the townspeople in general is an open question.

While Arch was embroiled in controversy, his father died at the almshouse on October 2. The old settler had lived to be seventy-six. The *Independent* did not carry an obituary, a most unusual omission, especially in an era when pioneers were celebrated and idealized. The only notice was a single line in the *Macomb Journal*: "Old Mr. Wagle died at the county [poor] house on Monday and was buried Tuesday at the Oakwood Cemetery in Macomb." As that suggests, there was no funeral for Lewis Wagle and no interest in burying him at Mt. Auburn, where Arch and Alice owned several lots.

Whatever the bootlegger's grandfather had done to alienate himself from his family and his community, the result was everlasting. Long before he died, Lewis Wagle was a man without meaningful social relationships.

By the fall of 1893 the townspeople had something new to worry about. The crash of the stock market and the failure of hundreds of banks in the spring and summer had brought on a depression marked by widespread layoffs and bankruptcies. By October more than half of the American labor force was out of work.

In Colchester Hampton at first tried to rally the townspeople, urging them to face an even greater economic struggle with unwavering optimism. Referring to his own rise from printer's devil to successful newspaper editor and businessman as an example, he reaffirmed the collective faith of the community, concluding that "Colchester is the best town on earth for people who can hang on and hustle."

But he was wrong. As the economy spiraled downward, coal consumption declined dramatically, and the winter was mild that year, further reducing the demand. By January 1894 the bushel price for coal was below five cents, and the miners in Colchester were working only two or three days a week. Even Hampton had to admit that "the conditions are bad and the prospects discouraging."

Similar circumstances across the country prompted the United Mine Workers of America, then a new force in the labor movement, to call a nationwide strike for April 21. Some 125,000 men responded immediately, and another 45,000 soon joined them, including the miners at Colchester, who were not even in the UMW until after the strike began.

As striking miners pressured others to stop working, violence erupted in several states, including Illinois. Men were shot, tipples were burned, and coal trains were dynamited. By mid-June the strike had lost public support, and the UMW was forced to accept terms that accomplished nothing for the miners.

There was no violence in Colchester, but the strike had a devastating impact on the town. Dire poverty engulfed many families, and when the UMW settled, the Quincy Coal Company refused to hire back 105 men, who then continued to picket the mines until September. Those who were eventually rehired worked just two or three days a week and received only four cents a bushel for their coal.

For that price it was hardly worth crawling around in the low, dark tunnels that stunk of urine and feces, struggling to shatter the coal face one section at a time. The miners' usual stoicism gave way to grumbling and despair, expressed in a little folk poem of the period:

Now some people say
There ain't no hell—
But they never mined coal,
So how can they tell?

For many of the mining families, life became a struggle for mere existence. Some of them left town, following others who had already moved out in 1892 and 1893. The most popular destination was Mystic, Iowa, a newer coal town that had perhaps 200 former Colchester residents by the end of 1894.

Others in town suffered too. Stores that extended credit to the miners took severe losses. In 1895 the Terrill and Sons general store, which was the largest business of any kind in McDonough County, went bankrupt, shocking the town. (It eventually reopened, however, under a strict arrangement with its creditors.)

Among the businessmen who left Colchester for more promising places was J. D. Trew, the smiling Welshman who had operated the Union Hotel for twenty years and had founded the most popular lodge in town, the Knights of Pythias. The townspeople would miss his sunny disposition and civic leadership. No one in the town's forty-year history had done more to make the business district a social center.

Worse than that, Van Hampton leased the *Independent* to his two assistants, giving them generous terms, and moved to the county seat, where he and his father bought the *Macomb By-Stander*. Colchester's foremost civic leader and most outspoken booster was gone.

The Wagles were affected too. Arch lost the support of some town leaders, who either blamed him for the rise in burglary that accompanied the depression or feared that his crackdown on vice would lead to an even greater business decline, so he did not run for marshal again in the spring of 1894.

Instead he opened a restaurant on Depot Street, not far from Hickey's Corner. Unfortunately, that was just before the big strike began. Putting in long, anxious days, Arch struggled to make the new business go, but it was never very successful. He sold it the next year.

Reluctantly, he went back to the drudgery and danger of mining. Working with his brother Frank in a bank northeast of town, he supplied coal for the local market.

But through it all Arch continued to love police work, so to help make ends meet he swallowed his pride and agreed to occasionally assist the new marshal, John Riggs, who was more sympathetic to the saloon owners and gamblers.

By that time young Henry was almost ten, old enough to realize that his father's efforts at law enforcement had aroused the animosity of some townspeople. In fact, during the mid-1890s Arch was being sued by one resident, saloonkeeper Gib Miller, on complaints relating to his work as marshal. It was a tense and troubled time for the family.

Not much is known about the bootlegger's childhood, yet some things can be stated with certainty.

During the spring of 1886 he was baptized into the Methodist Church by the Reverend T. J. Wood. The ritual took place in Crooked Creek near the old Pleasant Valley Mill. It was a lovely spot where a dirt road that had once been a pioneer trail led down between steep limestone bluffs to a ford. Since before the Civil War that place had been hallowed by countless baptisms, prayer meetings, and Sunday school picnics. In the years that followed, Alice took Joe and Henry to church every Sunday. Arch did not attend, but he apparently didn't discourage his wife from taking the boys, who were enrolled in Sunday school.

In those days it would have been impossible for anyone, even a child, to attend that church without being exposed to sermons and lessons about the evils of drinking. The Methodists knew how the devil worked, and they were ardent social reformers.

At an early age Henry also participated in the rituals of the town, including the Miners' Picnic, with its games and rides for children and its spectacular fireworks display. The much more solemn Memorial Day ceremony started with a long procession that filed past the Wagle home to Mt. Auburn, where the band played, a local speaker recalled the war, the old veterans stood at attention, and young girls placed armloads of flowers on the soldiers' graves. Among the honored dead was Uncle Joseph Booth, who had been like a father to Alice Wagle.

For several years Henry attended the old North Side School, built in 1869 and located just two blocks from his home. It was a two-story brick building with tall windows and a massive cupola. The front yard had a pump; the backyard had two outhouses, one for boys and the other for girls. Inside the building were four classrooms. The lower-grade classes were held downstairs and high school classes were conducted upstairs. When he was ten years old, Henry started going to an older, white-painted frame schoolhouse on the south side of town, which held the intermediate grades.

The two schools not only educated the town's children but also fostered a sense of community among them. Long before they finished the eighth grade, youngsters of roughly the same age knew each other well and had a vast experience in common. Like brothers and sisters in a big family, they felt emotionally connected.

When not in school, boys were free to roam the town unsupervised. However, relatives, neighbors, shopkeepers, and others knew who they were and took an interest in them, reinforcing the notion that their lives and their behavior were important to the community.

Henry and his friends were naturally drawn to Crooked Creek, where they went fishing and swimming in the summertime. Big Rock and Flat Rock were the two skinny-dipping sites that every boy knew. They also played baseball at a field west of the railroad turntable. No one loved the game more than Henry Wagle, who was a good hitter and a fast base runner.

Another game they all played was marbles, which had come to town with the British mining families. In March 1881, not long after he had brought his newspaper to town, Henry Stevens remarked, "Colchester boys are marble players, they are. There have been but few days this winter too cold or too stormy to check their games." The boys loved to play "keeps," in which the winner got to keep his opponent's marbles—whatever he had knocked out of the circle. Marble playing was in fact a form of gambling as well as a game of skill. Perhaps for that reason men often played too. On a Saturday afternoon it was not uncommon to see a dozen games being played simultaneously along the edge of the dirt street or in the finely ground cinders by the railroad track.

Decades later some of the old men in town recalled that Henry Wagle had been a skillful marble shooter who played with fierce intensity and hated to lose.

Most boys also learned to handle horses, and Henry Wagle was no exception. Arch always kept a horse in the shed in back of their house on Coal Street, and he taught Joe and Henry how to hitch it and drive the buggy. Like his father before him, Arch was interested in horses throughout his life, and he never failed to show up at any horse show, stakes race, or exhibition of bronco riding near Colchester.

The Walley family was good with horses too. In about 1890 Alice's father, Henry Walley, left his second wife and returned from Montana to Colchester, where he worked as a teamster, hauling coal from the mines and goods from the depot, so he was constantly handling horses. His son, John, made a living in exactly the same way, but he also owned a pair of mules. The Wagle boys learned to drive those too.

In the summer of 1897 a family accident occurred when Joe was driving the mules, and it got into the newspaper:

A RUNAWAY

Last Sunday Arch Wagle's son Joe hitched up John Walley's mule team to a hack and started to take the folks to visit Jake Myers, at the old Pleasant Valley Mill. When north of the Widow Moore Cemetery the mules took fright, turned short around, and threw the entire party out. In the vehicle at the time were Mrs. Arch Wagle, Mrs. Alice Booth, Joe Wagle, and one or two children. All were bruised considerably, Mrs. Wagle being the most severely injured. . . . Immediately after accomplishing all this havoc, the mules stopped. They did not want to run away—only thought they did.

Henry was among the bruised and battered, but that didn't dampen his enthusiasm for handling horses and mules.

Unfortunately Henry admired his Uncle John, a brawny, long-legged man with a mustache who was in many ways the opposite of his father. Arch was self-disciplined and serious, although apt to be indulgent with his children. He centered his life on his family and his work, and like most men in town, he felt morally accountable to the community. But John Walley liked to carouse with his friends and resented the impact of authority in his life. In fact, the rough-talking teamster was a boozer and a fighter. One time, in 1886, he was arrested because he took money for a wagon-load of coal that he never delivered, and the essence of his defense in court was that he had been drunk that day, so a friend delivered the coal—to the wrong address. He also got into a number of saloon brawls and was arrested more than once for disorderly behavior. On one memorable occasion a desperate opponent bit off the end of his left thumb.

Uncle John also fought with his wife, Rosa, whom he married when she was just seventeen. He was arrested once for beating her, which led to a short-term separation during the early 1890s. Nevertheless, they eventually had nine children.

He was also an eager storyteller who had a vast repertory of colorful tales from the town's past, such as the time outlaw John Tuggle shot two men on Depot Street, jumped on his horse, and galloped out of town with his guns blazing, pursued by a posse that never caught him; or the time miner Erhard Walter hanged himself in the boiler room of Shaft No. 16 and his ghost was seen in town for three nights afterward, making some men fearful of working in that mine. Of course, those and other stories were the common property of the townspeople; John Walley just knew them better than most.

It was Uncle John Walley who gave the bootlegger his nickname, or at least the early version of it.

In a small, relatively isolated town like Colchester, one's identity came easily, almost automatically, as a product of growing up in a very personal world. And a man's or boy's identity was usually acknowledged by a nickname. Having one meant knowing that you belonged. Henry Wagle's generation sported names like "Frog-leg" Mills and "Cat" Kipling, "Wink" Valentine and "Chock" Rippetoe, "Turk" Stephens and "Pus" Tones, "Dummy" Martin and "Fatty" Nelson, "Punk" Averill and "Bumps" Moon, "Mush" Carson and "Joke" Park, "Heydad" Stookey and "Fizzer" Wayland, "Goosie" Goldsberry and "Flunk" Webster.

Anyone with a pretentious given name was sure to get a nickname that deflated his parents' hopes. The oldest of the Carson boys, Rella Vespucia, was always called "Jerk."

Henry Wagle's nickname came from his habit of fighting with the boys his age, and he himself told the story to a reporter for the *Macomb By-Stander* the year before he died: "When I was a youngster in Colchester we used to go to the park every day and fight things out. Well, I used to be a pretty good battler, and my uncle, John Walley, started calling me 'Johnny Kilrain.' Kilrain was one of the best prize fighters in those days. The boys shortened that name to 'Killie,' and that's how I got my name. Later, when that 'Kelly' song came out, the 'Killie' was changed to 'Kelly.'"

His Uncle John had wrongly recalled the illustrious boxing match between John L. Sullivan and Jake Kilrain that took place outside of New Orleans on July 8, 1889, for he mixed the two famous names. The last bare-knuckle heavyweight championship in American history, that fight lasted an incredible seventy-five rounds in 105-degree heat and became the most famous sporting event of the nineteenth century. Kilrain was a great prizefighter all right, but he lost.

The "Kelly" song that Wagle mentioned was C. W. Murphy's 1909 hit, "Has Anybody Here Seen Kelly?" In the years before World War I everybody knew at least the opening lines:

> Has anybody here seen Kelly?
> K, E, double-L, Y.
> Has anybody here seen Kelly?

Despite the song, however, Henry at first spelled his nickname "Kellie"—just one letter different from the "Killie" of his youth—but in the 1920s the press always spelled it with a *y*, so that's what he eventually adopted.

In any case, after 1895 or so, Wagle was never called "Henry" by his friends, although his mother vehemently and continually insisted on that name (her father's), as if she were fighting for his soul. Among his pals he was "Killie"—named for a tough guy and probably proud of it. The strange, suggestive nickname was not inappropriate for a scrappy, hot-tempered boy, and it was, in a dark sense, prophetic.

Still, most of the townspeople simply knew him as "Henry," the likable second son of Arch and Alice Wagle, and surely no one suspected that he would become the most well known figure who ever lived in Colchester. The only public reference to him in the 1890s is a newspaper comment on his health, for in July 1896 an inflammation led to edema, and he almost died: "Henry Wagle, dangerously ill last week with dropsy, is much better." He was ten years old then, so he must have been aware of the public interest in him. In later years that interest would assume extraordinary proportions.

Early in 1896 Arch Wagle plunged back into the thick of local controversy when Mayor John Hoar suddenly fired Marshal Riggs for "general neglect of duty" and reappointed Arch as the town's main law officer. Anxious to make a good impression, Arch lost no time in clamping down on saloon-based gambling dens that had operated with the tacit approval of Riggs, who was a poker player himself. The mayor went so far as to join in some of the raids, including this one in early May:

POKER GAME RAIDED

Mayor Hoar has decreed that gambling dens shall not run in this city, so a raid was made last Saturday night on a poker game over William Rundle's saloon, and eleven festive sports were gathered into the toils of the police. . . .

On Saturday night policeman Wagle noticed the maneuvering of the sports about Rundle's place, and at about half past ten o'clock came to the conclusion that a game was going on. He notified Mayor Hoar. . . .

Wagle forced the door open, and he and Mayor Hoar led the way up the dark stairway, followed by two special policemen. The sports were there, and the game was going on when the officers entered. . . .

The men surrendered. 'Twas all they could do. And when they were safely bound and lined up, a march began to the police court. . . .

They all pled guilty to the charge of gambling and were fined $10 and costs.

Part of the moral support for Arch's vigorous law enforcement came from women. They could not vote, but by the 1890s they wanted to, and prohibition advocates were agitating for women's suffrage. The Colchester Young Women's Christian Temperance Union, of which Alice Wagle was an outspoken member, even presented the city council with a petition, signed by sympathetic male voters, that requested for women "the privilege of voting on the Saloon License Question." Arch had been one of the first to sign it.

But the measure was rejected. Everyone knew which way the women would vote, and most council members were deeply concerned about the business impact of closing the saloons. Like other mining towns across the country, Colchester was still in a depression, even though the nation's economy had started to improve. Beyond that, some men resented the growing influence of women in the community and didn't want them to vote on anything.

It is hard to say why Arch Wagle's career as a lawman finally came to an end, but it did in the spring of 1897. He did not enter the race for marshal, nor was he appointed to serve as city policeman. The fact that his staunchest supporter, Mayor John Hoar, did not run for reelection may have had something to do with it. In any case, the town was still deeply split over the saloons—which were licensed by less than ten votes in 1895, 1896, and 1897—causing the animosity between their supporters and their opponents to continue. Moreover, Arch had been threatened as well as sued, so he may have simply decided that the job wasn't worth the stress.

Whatever the case, in the spring and summer of 1897 Arch was unemployed, except for occasional police work in other towns, and the Wagles began to feel the pinch of hard times. For Arch, who had always prided himself on being a good supporter, joblessness threatened his identity. Alice was doing some work as a seamstress, but little Glenn still needed her attention, and to make matters worse, she was pregnant. Like so many others in town, the Wagles worried about their future, which had never looked so bleak.

Unfortunately coal mining could no longer provide a decent alternative income. At that time the miners in town were getting only three and a half cents per bushel for their coal, a record low price.

Across the country the income of coal miners had reached the lowest level since the Civil War, so the UMW called another nationwide strike, which began on the Fourth of July 1897. In Illinois some 40,000 miners quit work by the end of the month.

But the Colchester miners did not join them. By that time there were fewer than 200 miners left in town—perhaps no more than 150—and they were resigned to the hard times. Some recalled that the great strike of 1894 had accomplished nothing, while others felt that local companies were paying what they could, considering the cost of mining operations in Colchester.

Of course, as the strike continued, Colchester coal found a ready market, but the miners knew that would be only temporary. And the bushel price never rose above four and a half cents anyway.

That year was also marked by the death of the last great pioneer of the coal industry in Colchester. He was Thomas Terrill, a stocky, bearded man whose impoverished childhood in Cornwall and subsequent immigration to America made him akin to the legendary James Roberts.

An orphan at fourteen, he had later come west with the initial group from New Castle, and without a single day of formal education, he had risen to become superintendent of the Quincy Coal Company, Colchester's largest mining operation during the 1880s and 1890s. Following the death of Roberts he became the most admired man in town. People told stories about his hard work, intelligence, and generosity.

When Terrill died in September, the townspeople honored him by closing the stores, shops, and factories, dismissing the public schools, and turning out in huge numbers for his funeral at the Methodist Church and his burial at Mt. Auburn.

Terrill's obituary presented him as a heroic, self-made man who had triumphed over adversity by sheer force of character—"infallible judgment," "dauntless courage," and the like. Clearly his success was intended to inspire a town that was all but overwhelmed by hard times. But coal had given him an opportunity that it no longer provided for anyone in Colchester, and many of the grieving townspeople must have wondered whether that kind of self-transcendence, or even a secure future, was still possible in their community.

Arch and Alice Wagle had already considered that question and had made up their minds. Not long before Terrill's funeral they had decided to leave town.

Arch felt that his chances would be better in Galesburg, fifty miles northeast of Colchester. It was a rapidly growing railroad and factory town of about 18,000 people, and he had friends there from his days as a C. B. & Q. conductor. Probably through them he had gotten a job working as a night clerk in the railroad's huge freight depot, located at the switchyard in the southwest part of the city. It wasn't very challenging work—a matter of moving goods and keeping records—but it was a steady job.

Because Alice was pregnant, she and the boys stayed behind. Joe was an eighth-grader, almost at the end of his schooling, and Henry was a fifth-grader. Glenn was only two. Aunt Alice Booth, who had been a widow since 1883, came to live with them, and the plan was for her to remain in the house on Coal Street, at least for a time, after the Wagles left. Arch was not in a hurry to sell the place, which turned out to be a fortunate decision.

Geneva, the last of the Wagle children, was born on November 9. A few days later Arch came down from Galesburg on the train to see his new daughter.

After the fall school term was over in December, Arch came again to help get everything packed up, and they all left on the train for their new home, bringing Aunt Alice along to stay through the holidays.

Arch had rented a one-story frame house on the southwest side of the city, in a working-class neighborhood that looked much like Colchester. The houses were close together, and the fenced-in backyards were cluttered with sheds, outhouses, and woodpiles.

But Galesburg itself had much to offer, including a long and busy main street, dozens of brick business places, good public schools, two small colleges, an array of churches and social groups, and streetcar transportation. To a family from a still-isolated mining village, it must have seemed like a metropolis.

One special feature of the town was the Williams racetrack, located in the southeast part of the city. It featured a dead-level, one-mile track and a huge 250-foot-long grandstand, not to mention several horse barns and office buildings. In 1894 a mare named Alix had set the world's trotting record there, and every summer massive crowds came to watch the outstanding trotters and pacers. The magnificent track was only several blocks from the Wagle home, and Arch must have been drawn to it, like a baseball fan to a ballpark.

Despite the town's appeal, however, the Wagles' stay in Galesburg was short. For some reason the depot job ended after about a year, and Arch couldn't find other promising work. By the winter of 1899 Alice and the children were again staying in Colchester with Aunt Alice Booth while Arch got started in another town.

This time it was Galena, Kansas, located along the Kansas-Missouri border just west of Joplin. Exactly what Arch did there is unknown, but it must have been associated with mining, for in the 1890s Galena was a boomtown focused on the mining of zinc and lead. Founded in 1877, it already had 10,000 people by the time Arch arrived. Some forty companies operated scores of mines with names like the "Cripple Creek," the "Tin Horn," and the "Yukon," and in 1898 alone they produced $2 million worth of zinc ore (called "jack") and $350,000 worth of lead ore (known as "galena").

Mining wages were two dollars a day—about what they had been in

Colchester before the hard times set in—and for those who leased a piece of land and worked their own mines, the potential was astounding. The local newspaper bragged that "any Galena man can reel you off a yard of names of those who walked in with a 'grub stake' and who now ride in Pullman cars and can't keep their bank accounts down to reasonable proportions." The town was full of miners hoping to make it big.

Arch came with his brother-in-law, John Walley, to look the place over. What they found was a vast mining camp where tipples and smokestacks dotted the horizon outside of town. Aside from the mines, there were sixty ore crushers, two smelters, and three sludge mills. Scattered near the residential areas were a half-dozen lumber yards and more than thirty grocery stores.

Like many other boomtowns, Galena had a raw, impermanent look, and the main thoroughfare, called Red Hot Street, was lined with hotels, dry goods stores, and saloons. Houses, which were hard to come by, were often nothing more than two-room shacks with loose-swinging doors and single-pane windows. But the two men must have found a place by spring, when Alice and the children left Colchester to join them.

Galena was a wild place then. Drinking and fighting were even more common than in Colchester, and there wasn't a very strong sense of community. Making money was the only reason for being there.

Henry attended school in Galena, as he had in Galesburg, but it couldn't have been the same without his pals, and he must have been homesick for Colchester. He was thirteen then, so he probably also worked from time to time with his father, uncle, and brother, perhaps at mining or hauling.

By the summer of 1900, however, the boom in the Galena-Joplin area was over, and some of the mines were closing down. People began to leave town, discouraged by the collapse of their hopes, and the Wagles were among them.

They drifted north to Windsor, Missouri, a town of almost two thousand people, twenty miles southwest of Sedalia. Why they went there is unknown, but the community was similar in some ways to Colchester. There was coal mining in the area, and the town had good railroad connections. Brick making and livestock shipping were important too.

In 1900 the newest venture was a tomato-canning factory, which badly needed workers—men, women, and children—in the late summer.

The Wagles moved to Windsor in July, but again, they didn't stay long. If any of them were employed at the canning factory, the work would have run out in October, which was about the time they left.

By that fall Arch knew the bitterness of repeated failure. Three times he had struck out for a better life but had gotten nowhere, and the frequent moving had been hard on everyone in the family. The Wagles were small-town people whose identities had been shaped in Colchester, and nowhere else seemed very meaningful. If they were going to keep on struggling, they might as well do it there. Before the weather became too cold, they headed back home.

For Henry it was the end of an ordeal of struggle and insecurity that deeply affected his character. For the rest of his life he had an enormous longing for success and a profound attachment to Colchester.

Depot Street in Colchester, ca. 1890. On the right is the Abram Newland
general store, built in the 1860s.

Members of the Colchester Miners' Friendly Society, ca. 1890s.

The J. D. Trew grocery store and, on the right, the Union Hotel in 1889. Arch Wagle is holding the team of horses at the left.

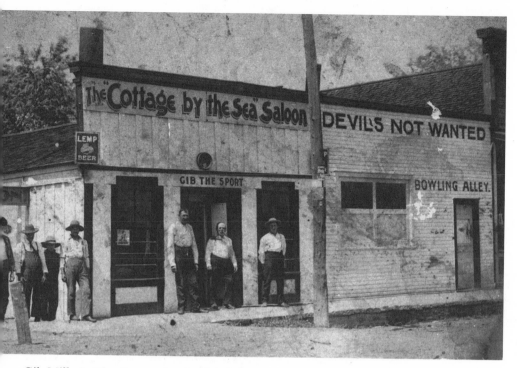

Gib Miller's The Cottage by the Sea Saloon, ca. 1900. Miller is the huge
man by the doorway.

The busiest place in town, the C. B. & Q. Depot, ca. 1910.

Mt. Auburn Cemetery, from a turn-of-the-century postcard.

Miners with carbide lamps at the Baird clay mine early in the twentieth century. Owner Jackson Baird is standing next to the mule.

Miners wheeling a "box" of coal from a drift mine near Crooked Creek.

Below: Workers at the King brickyard in 1894. At the right, holding his hat, is owner Moses King.

Arch Wagle, shortly after he became the Colchester marshal in 1891.
(Photograph courtesy of Marilyn Richey.)

Van Hampton, editor of the *Colchester Independent*, ca. 1895. (Photograph courtesy of the *Colchester Chronicle*.)

The pride of Colchester in 1901, the Fraternity Building, from a postcard.

The first day of Rural Free Delivery at Colchester in March 1903. Arch Wagle is the second carrier from the right. (Photograph courtesy of Marilyn Richey.)

Kelly Wagle in his early teen
at the turn of the century.
(Photograph courtesy
of Pat Irish.)

Ruth (Jones) Wagle and her
brother Clyde, shortly after her
divorce from Kelly. (Photograph
courtesy of Elsie Carnahan.)

The Colchester Fraternal Picnic, looking across the railroad grounds to Depot Street, ca. 1912. (Photograph courtesy of Larry Carson.)

Struggling into the New Century

While the Wagles were gone, the people back in Colchester battled against despair, the inevitable result of a sharp decline in the industry that had fostered the town. Coal mining continued, but the market remained in a slump, and the approaching turn of the century held little hope that the economic situation would change. Forces beyond the control of local people seemed to be shaping their lives, and they found it hard to believe in the future.

In an 1899 article the editor of the *Colchester Democrat,* a short-lived newspaper of that era, revealed the spiritual condition of the town as he tried to rally his disheartened readers:

A TIRED COMMUNITY

Those of us who have listened day after day to the disgruntled lamentations of discontent, have almost grown into the belief that there is no hope—no future for Colchester. As a community we are weak and debilitated, and every little blow sets us howling louder. Instead of striving for new life the people of this city are hunting for a soft place to lay down and die. These are hard words, but they are true. . . . If we can't drum up some enthusiasm, we move that the city float a bond to erect a scarecrow over the town, to keep off the birds of carrion.

Unfortunately things got worse. In the spring of 1900 the last Egerton mine was worked out, and the company said it could not afford to sink another shaft. The market price of coal was too low. The federal census for that year listed only 142 coal miners in the community, fewer than the Quincy Coal Company alone had employed a dozen years earlier. Many former miners worked as day laborers, making much less than they once had earned, while others continued to dig coal for only a few days a week.

Contributing to the general market decline, the railroad ceased to be an important customer for Colchester coal, and in 1901 the local newspaper explained why: "In late years large tenders have come into service, trains make better time, and it is possible for enough coal to be taken on at either end of the division [Galesburg or Quincy] for most engines to make the run." That summer the C. B. & Q. tore down the great coal chutes that had stood along the tracks east of town since before the Civil War.

Then, early in 1902, the miners working for the Quincy Coal Company were asked to accept a half-cent reduction in the bushel price of their coal. The *Independent* commented on the impact it would have on the struggling town:

WANT TO REDUCE THE SCALE OF WAGES;
Colchester Miners Will Quit.

In the past several years the miners of Colchester have not grown wealthy from the proceeds of their toil. In fact, coal mining in Colchester is pretty much of a farce. The miners who still linger and go through the comedy of toil are those who own little homes here, and young men who are averse to breaking the home ties. Each year our coal industry has been on the decline, and one by one our citizens depending upon the occupation for a livelihood have drifted into other camps. At present our miners are afforded but a hand-to-mouth existence. During the past month they were employed nine days, the average pay being $1.50 per day. Most of them have large families to support, and manage to do this only by making a few extra dimes digging fire coal in the hillsides around Colchester.

We are not prepared to say whether the coal industry in Colchester could be improved to any great extent under different management, but it is an evident fact that coal will never again be produced, in the vein worked here, in sufficient quantity to make the industry one of any great advantage to the commercial interest of our city. The request for a reduction sounds like a joke, and it would be very amusing were it not so serious. If the company insists on the reduction, the mines will close, and our miners will be forced from the town.

The reduction was eventually avoided, but the outlook remained bleak. This article was in fact a requiem for large-scale coal mining in Colchester. Within a few years the Quincy Coal Company too was out of business.

When the Wagles returned to Colchester, they moved back into their house on Coal Street, which was occupied by Aunt Alice Booth. Arch, then forty years old, went back to the hard, dark toil of a drift mine. He hated the dangerous work, but it was a living. He soon rejoined the Miners' Friendly Society, which then had scarcely more than one hundred members.

However, he had plans to do something else. People in the countryside were talking about an innovation that would surely improve their lives: Rural Free Delivery. No longer would they be cut off from the world for days at a time. They could send and receive mail and packages at their homes, regardless of the weather. In the fall of 1900 Arch circulated a petition for operating a rural route, which was supposed to start in a year or so. A lover of horses, he was excited about the prospect of earning a living by driving a mail wagon.

Little is known about the Wagle children, but Henry did not attend school again. He was then fourteen, the age at which many boys ended their education and started working. He apparently worked from time to time as a drayman, helping his uncle John and his grandfather, Henry Walley. As the youngest contributor to the Wagle family income, he must have been deeply affected by their struggle against hard times.

The best money he made as a youth was on Miners' Picnic day in July. For many years John Walley had driven a hack between the depot and the grove, carrying people back and forth for ten cents apiece. In those days more than a dozen hacks ran all day long, raising dust so thick that it was impossible to see the road. Starting in 1901 Henry Wagle did the same, often driving the empty carriage back to town in the morning, and back to the grove in the evening, with the horse at a gallop, so that he could make as many dimes as possible.

The Wagles didn't stay long in the small crowded house on Coal Street. In 1901, with a bank loan and financial help from his mother, who had remarried in Chicago, Arch was able to buy a house with twenty acres of land at a place north of town called Vinegar Hill (later known as Vinegar Knob). It was a wooded elevation in the back country near the creek, where several of the earliest drift mines had been located.

According to local legend, the hill got its name because some early whisky makers dumped the leavings of their mash there. Although that is probably folklore created by a town with whisky on its mind, Vinegar Hill had been the home of Irish saloonkeeper Jim Hickey until his death in 1894. And that points to another, more likely origin of the name, for Vinegar Hill in County Wexford, Ireland, was the site of the decisive battle in the Irish Rising of 1798, much celebrated since then in Irish story and song. So, the colorful name was probably Hickey's way of reminding himself of home and the cause of Ireland.

The two-story frame house that stood at Colchester's Vinegar Hill was old, narrow, and not much bigger than the Wagle home on Coal Street, but Arch eventually enlarged it so that it had six rooms. Just to the north of it was an unpainted barn with a sliding door and stalls for several horses. That was probably the reason Arch bought the place. When his rural route started, he would need his own horses and a place to store and repair the mail wagon. The Vinegar Hill property also had a woodshed, a smokehouse, a chicken coop, a vegetable garden, and a few acres of apple trees. It was a kind of miniature farm. There was coal on the property, too, so Arch worked in his own bank and later leased the mine to someone else.

In the spring of 1901, while fixing up the new place and waiting for Rural Free Delivery to begin, Arch ran for "constable," as the marshal's job was then called, but he lost. The election was not close.

Meanwhile the townspeople struggled mightily against decline. While miners were seeking other jobs, local leaders were promoting business development of all kinds. In 1896, for example, the faltering Daisy Roller Mill was purchased by three local investors who modernized it over the next two years and renamed it the "Colchester Milling Company." Although the Underhill brickyard closed in 1898, Moses King's Colchester Brick and Tile Company increased production by adding a fourth kiln and a second drying shed. Meanwhile two other men started a quarry north of town, producing flagstone for sidewalks.

The most promising industrial development was clay mining. In 1894 an energetic farmer and entrepreneur named Benjamin Franklin Myers had started a clay pit on his farm northwest of town, chiefly to supply the Colchester Pottery, which he managed. The pottery had economic troubles and soon passed into other hands, but within a few years Myers employed fourteen men at his clay mine. They stripped off twenty feet of dirt and stone, exposing a vein of fine gray clay sixteen feet thick, which they dug out and hauled by mule teams and wagons to the railroad. For the first several years they shipped one carload every day, but by the end of the century they were shipping three times as much, and the stripping operation had given way to drift mines. At that time most of the clay went to a pottery in Monmouth, thirty-five miles away, although some went to the still struggling Colchester Pottery.

By 1900 B. F. Myers was the mayor, and the townspeople were beginning to see a future in the production of clay and clay products.

Unfortunately workers at the pottery were paid only a dollar a day—about two-thirds of what a good coal miner could make when the price of coal was reasonable. The King brickyard paid better, about $1.50 a day, but it operated only eight months of the year. Myers's clay mine was the best-paying industrial employer, but it was still a small operation.

Although the boom years were over, the merchants still did fairly well, and one of them achieved real success. In 1898 A. M. Walty built a huge, two-story brick hardware store at the corner of Market and Coal Streets. With plate glass display windows and two recessed entrances, it was the most impressive store in town, and it sold everything but clothes, including wagons, buggies, harnesses, farm implements, furniture, stoves, tools, furnaces, plumbing supplies, rugs, dishes, guns, toys, and books. Walty was a talented promoter who advertised widely, decorated lavishly for the Christmas season, and held a big clearance sale every spring that drew hundreds of shoppers. The big Walty Hardware Store was soon known in several counties.

Two other well-known merchants were Henry and Ed Terrill, who bought out their brothers in 1904 and improved the old Terrill and Sons general store, known afterward as Terrill Brothers. They did an enormous business in clothes and groceries, employing more than a dozen workers in the big building on Depot Street that had been constructed for the family enterprise in 1887. It was the largest and busiest general store in McDonough County.

The saloons did well too. After being voted out in 1899, they were relicensed again in 1900, and since they were the only saloons in the county at that time, they did help bring money into the community. There were six of them, and none was more popular than Gib Miller's place. He bought the old Jim Hickey saloon north of the depot, fixed it up, and renamed it The Cottage by the Sea. Next door he remodeled and reopened the bowling alley that had not operated since 1890. Both . places had a large clientele.

Concerned about the influence of temperance crusaders, saloon owners tried to give their business a new respectability. In a 1904 newspaper commentary designed to promote local trade, a businessman named P. F. Campbell referred to one saloon as "an ideal place to while away leisure moments in pleasant recreation or to meet a friend and be one of the boys," and he claimed that "a select patronage, made up of the town's most progressive element, visits this resort, where cheerful surroundings and good order are at all times maintained." In similar remarks on another saloon, he asserted that such places were an immense social benefit: "There is no place where the capitalist and laborer can meet upon such friendly terms as they can at a bar, and no other thing does so much to unite all social classes as a place like this, where the rich and poor stand side by side and tip the social glass."

Despite that effort, the anti-saloon and anti-liquor agitation continued. Van Hampton had returned and reassumed control of the faltering *Colchester Independent,* so in the early years of the century readers were confronted with editorials like "Stop the Liquor Traffic" and "The Saloon vs. Civilization." Local ministers still railed against the evils of drinking, and Sunday school teachers still propagandized the town's youngsters. In October 1903 the *Independent* proudly reported that Mrs. Bert Oldham, a teacher at the Methodist Church, had persuaded all twelve boys in her class to sign the pledge. Soon afterward the Christian Church Sunday school put on a temperance cantata called *King Alcohol,* which was laced with songs that linked drinking with all kinds of misery.

At that time the local WCTU had more than 200 members, and the Good Templars, still around after more than forty years, was the largest lodge of its kind in Illinois, with 130 members. In Colchester the temperance crusaders were well organized, and soon men were running for local office on the Prohibition ticket.

In general the first decade of the century was the high tide of membership in social organizations. The largest and most important structure of the era was in fact the Fraternity Building, financed by the two most prominent lodges in town, the Knights of Pythias and the Odd Fellows. A three-story brick edifice with turrets at the corners, it covered the entire block between Macomb Street and the main road (later called Route 9). The first floor, with tall plate glass windows, three sets of double doors, and fancy trim, was soon occupied by the Colchester State Bank. The third floor was designed for use by the two lodges, which together had 400 members, and the second floor provided accommodations for smaller fraternal groups, such as the Red Men, Royal Neighbors, and Modern Woodmen.

Dedicated in March 1901, the building symbolized the town's determination to succeed in the new century despite the decline of coal mining, and it soon appeared on a popular photographic postcard. Not since the Union Hotel had gone up after the Civil War had a building so clearly represented the hopes of the community. But the Fraternity Building also emphasized the growing importance of secret societies, which thrived on status and exclusivity, in a town no longer centered on one occupation or sure of its identity.

If anyone characterized the era of secret societies, it was the boyishly handsome, socially prominent Henry Terrill, who had been elected county treasurer in 1898 and was the foremost planner of the new building. A politically ambitious man who was later elected to the state legislature, he was a member of the Odd Fellows, the Knights of Pythias, the Elks, the Modern Woodmen, the Rebekahs, and the Royal Neighbors. As that list suggests, "brotherhood" connections were both socially desirable and politically useful in turn-of-the-century Colchester.

Ironically, the last spurt of coal-mining prosperity came to Colchester in the midst of a national crisis: the great coal famine of 1903. A cold December, followed by sub-zero January weather in the Northeast and

Midwest, led to a fuel shortage that some mine owners and shippers aggravated by withholding coal to drive up prices. Soon the newspapers reported "unspeakable suffering" in the northern cities, with "thousands of people . . . sick and at the point of freezing." The death rate began to climb.

By mid-January Colchester coal was worth twelve to fifteen cents a bushel—a record high price—and haulers started camping out at the mines and waiting their turn for a wagonload. The *Independent* reported that "every mine is being worked and every miner is employed." Even after spring came, the demand for coal remained high as frightened consumers stockpiled it for the next winter.

During that year several new mines were opened at Colchester, bringing the total in operation to forty-two. All but a few were banks that employed one to four men. The era of large-scale shaft mining was drawing to a close, and a strike against the Quincy Coal Company in the spring of 1903 hastened the process. Still, the temporary prosperity caused by the coal famine reduced the immediate impact on the townspeople.

By 1903 the town also had three more clay-mining companies, and a fourth, started by Abram Newland, was about five miles away in the countryside near the village of Tennessee. The busiest of those mines was operated by the Weir Pottery of Monmouth, the largest stoneware factory in the world. To move the clay from that mine to the railroad with less mule power, the company built a mile-long tramway of steel tracks on which a small open clay car could be pulled by a single mule. Soon a half-dozen mule cars were operating on those tracks.

That summer the *Independent* proclaimed, "Colchester is rapidly becoming a great clay mining center," and one optimistic leader even predicted that "Colchester is soon to become a booming town through the clay industry, greater than it ever was on account of the coal industry." The townspeople were beginning to hope so.

The good economic times provided a positive context for the last Miners' Picnic, held in August. In keeping with their long tradition, the miners assembled on Macomb Street in their bright regalia, and with people watching and the local band playing, they marched to the city park, where the day's festivities began. Although more than a hundred men took part, Van Hampton noted that the group was changing: "One thing about the society's parade is becoming more noticeable every year. The ranks are composed of old men and middle-aged men. Few young men are members of the society."

Colchester was no longer a young man's town, as it had been so obviously when the picnics began. Because the future of coal was so uncertain, fewer young men were going into the mines. Those who did lacked the strong communal bond that once united the local men.

The older ones, too, had changed. They were no longer the heroes of the town, the makers of the local future, and they knew it. Some, like Arch Wagle, who marched with his old friends, were not even involved in coal mining any more. They were links to a time that seemed increasingly remote from twentieth-century Colchester, and their appearance on the street symbolized the town's nostalgia.

Still, the group organized a successful day. After the speeches and music in the park, there were sports and amusements in the business district: mule racing, bicycle riding, team driving, and more. One of the heroes of the day was twenty-year-old Joe Wagle, who won the mule race—the spectators laughing and cheering as he crossed the finish line.

The previous March had also marked the start of Rural Free Delivery at Colchester, after several long delays, and Arch Wagle was assigned Route 2, running west of town. When the service began, the frost had just come out of the ground and the dirt roads were long troughs of mud. Arch had more than his share of troubles, some of which were reported in the newspaper:

THE RURAL MAIL DELIVERY

Rural free delivery of mail from Colchester has been carried on successfully for ten days. . . . In spite of as bad March roads as we have ever had, not one of the carriers has failed to make the delivery of his entire route. . . .

With the exception of one or two days, the mails have been carried on horseback, the roads being too muddy for any kind of a vehicle on the twenty-five-mile drive.

The heaviest mails are on routes 1 and 2. Carrier Wagle has the Joetta pouch . . . besides his rural delivery. Two days last week it was necessary for him to use two horses to carry his mail.

Arch took advantage of the opportunity to break a new broncho into service for Uncle Sam. The critter was firmly bound and

loaded with one of the heaviest sacks. When he was turned loose,
there were scenes which outstripped any in the history of Buffalo
Bill's pony express. . . . On the return trip the broncho finally
succeeded in kicking the mail sack off its back, within a block and
a half of the post office.

Like the other carriers, Arch had to buy his own specially built mail
wagon. It was a tall, boxlike enclosure on a buggy frame, with a narrow
door on each side and an opening in the front through which he drove
the horse or the team. (Two-horse teams were used in the winter, when
there was snow, and in the early spring, when the roads were muddy.)
Because he liked to buy horses from the West and break them into service himself, Arch continued to have occasional difficulties on the route.
During the first few years of his work he was twice injured in mail wagon accidents caused by runaway teams.

Delivering the rural mail was a steady, six-days-a-week job that paid
$500 a year, but most people thought it was easier than it actually was,
so Arch turned poet in 1905 and told readers of the *Independent* all
about it:

THE TRIALS OF AN R.F.D. CARRIER

You may talk about Sheridan's ride,
    Or the midnight ride of Paul Revere,
But listen, my friends, to an R.F.D.
    Who rides and struggles here.

You think that he
    Has got a snap—
No work to be found
    In a job like that:
Drives to a box
    And drops the mail,
Clucks to his horse
    And away they sail.

Or writes a receipt
    Once in awhile,
To the farmer chats
    In good old style—
Tells him the price
    Of taters and wheat,

The current news
    And the latest cheat.

But in sleet and hail,
    And rain and snow,
Don't envy his job
    As you see him go—
Through mud and mire,
    Over logs and stones,
And sticks and roots
    That shake his bones.

It's a ceaseless round
    Of toil each day,
With fingers cold
    And bills to pay,
For coal and wood,
    For feed and hay—
And the blacksmith too
    Most every day.

These are the "joys"
    Of an R.F.D.
If you don't think so
    Just watch and see.
I've done it two years,
    And I know full well
There is just one step
    Between him and _____.

Despite what this lively poetic complaint suggests, Arch loved the job. He greatly enjoyed driving horses and chatting with the people on his route. In fact, he was the central figure of a new kind of community, composed of hitherto isolated country people who knew their mail carrier well and were linked to each other and the world through the interchange of a rural route.

Ironically, mail-order houses such as Sears and Roebuck were soon so popular with rural families that some of the businesses in Colchester began to suffer. Without intending to, Arch contributed to the detrimental impact of mass culture on the still-remote little mining town.

Henry's first full-time job was at the Colchester Brick and Tile Company, better known as King's brickyard, located just across the hollow from Vinegar Hill. When he started in 1902, it was running at full capacity, turning out 140,000 bricks a week, as well as huge quantities of the drainage tile that farmers used to keep their fields dry.

Clay was mined in the hollow east of the brickyard. It was blasted loose with dynamite and then shoveled into small open railroad cars, which were hauled up the hill by a steam-powered winch. In the main building the clay was ground up, mixed with water, shaped into slabs, and cut into bricks, which were then put into railroad cars and hauled by teams to the drying sheds. After a few days the semidry bricks were stacked in a round kiln and "burned"—heated to 1,000 degrees. When they were cool enough to handle, they were stacked in wagons and hauled to the railroad.

In those days some thirty hands worked at the brickyard. Several of them were boys, who placed bricks in the dryers, moved them to the kilns, loaded them onto wagons, and finally stacked them in railroad boxcars.

Like the others, sixteen-year-old Henry Wagle worked ten hours a day, sometimes lifting and carrying bricks until his arms were tired and his back was sore. Because he could handle horses well, however, he was primarily a teamster, driving the wagons to and from the railroad.

Henry's outgoing nature made him popular with the other workers, all of whom called him by his old nickname, "Killie." And he apparently liked the owner, Moses King, a small neatly dressed man with a Vandyke beard, who often swore like a sailor in his cockney dialect.

In the winter, when the brickyard was shut down, Henry did not have regular work, but he often helped his Uncle John, who hauled wagonloads of clay to the local pottery, which dried and fired the ware indoors. That eventually led to a better job as a potter's helper. To do that, Henry took long rolls of clay from a pug mill, or mixer, and cut them into sizes that potters could use on their wheels to shape a jar or a crock. The pay was not much better than at the brickyard, but at least he worked indoors and was learning a skill.

When he wasn't working, Henry hung out with other teenage boys, swimming in the Ballast—a pond southeast of town created by railroad excavation—fishing at the mill dam on Crooked Creek, hunting for squirrels and raccoons in the woods, and riding his father's horses. He got along well with a group of teenagers that included "Chick" Hocker, "Clayty" Nichols, and "Flunk" Webster, but they knew he was a hot-tempered kid who was ready to fight when things didn't go his way.

Henry idolized his brother Joe, a strapping, stocky young man who worked as a clay miner and played on Colchester's first football team. Despite the three-year difference in their ages, the two of them spent much time together. Joe was a joker, a big laugher, who was popular around town and easy to get along with. The oldest son of an oldest son, he was liked and admired by his father, whom he resembled. For Henry, admiration did not come so readily.

By 1903, when he was seventeen, Henry was a good-looking youth with sandy-blond hair, big blue eyes, and a charming smile—although when he wasn't smiling, the corners of his mouth always turned down, giving him a kind of melancholy expression. Like most boys his age, he was anxious to be grown up and was already chasing girls. Since they were strongly attracted to him, he eventually caught a few.

The most important of them was Ruth Jones, a pretty, dark-haired girl who lived a half-mile north of the Wagle place, where the Vinegar Hill road crossed Crooked Creek. On the far side of the creek was a rugged, heavily wooded area known as Argyle Hollow, where the small Jones house sat on a hillside just above the floodplain. In the nineteenth century there was no bridge, so that spot was known as Jones Ford, but when Rural Free Delivery began, local folks built a narrow wooden bridge, which worked well enough except during high water. Still, no place near Colchester seemed more remote.

Ruth's father was a coal miner. Born and raised in Wales, George Jones received no schooling and never learned to read or write. He started mining as a boy in the 1850s. When times got worse, he immigrated to America, in 1871, settling first in Pittsburgh, where he married another Welsh immigrant, Naomi Davis, and started a family. In the early 1880s they moved to Colchester. The Joneses were poor, but the land was cheap at Argyle Hollow, so they settled there, close to some of the drift mines. From the edge of their property they could see the dark layer of coal running along the south bank of the creek.

Born there in 1887, Ruth was a year younger than Henry Wagle, and she probably got to know him in school. After the Wagles moved to

Vinegar Hill, she often walked past their house going to and from Argyle Hollow. By the time Henry was sixteen and she was fifteen, they must have known each other well. Of course, their parents knew each other too.

Henry had just started to pay visits to the Jones place, to see Ruth, when a tragedy struck that changed her life. On October 15, 1903, the *Independent* carried an all-too-familiar kind of story:

KILLED IN A COAL MINE

Last Tuesday another death was added to the long list of fatalities which have attended the mining of coal at Colchester. George Jones, a miner, aged 55 years, met his death in a coal bank on the land of William Robinson, three miles northeast of Colchester.

Mr. Jones and his son Clyde, the latter a lad age 16 years, were at work on the opening of a new bank. The entry they were driving ran into old works [an abandoned tunnel] about forty yards from the mouth of the bank. While they were at work a huge stone fell from the roof upon the elder man, crushing him to the bottom. In falling, it missed the boy by a few inches, but he heard his father groan as the great weight fell upon him. The boy could do nothing to relieve his father.

The stone, which was afterwards measured, proved to be four and a half feet wide, eight feet long, and two feet thick.

After the accident the Jones family sank back into poverty. Young Clyde became the breadwinner, and an older, married son also helped out from time to time, but they didn't make up for the loss of their father.

The difficult situation of Ruth Jones probably made her more appealing to Henry, for his own family's experience had sensitized him to the plight of the poor. He felt there was something heroic about people who struggled to make it despite the crushing weight of hard luck.

The details of their courtship are beyond recovery, but Henry and Ruth spent increasing amounts of time together in 1904. To her, the handsome, outgoing, sympathetic young potter must have seemed like a way to escape from unpromising if not desperate circumstances. Whatever the case, by the end of the year, long before her eighteenth birthday, Ruth was pregnant.

Unfortunately Henry was not ready for marriage. When the pregnancy occurred, he was still breaking free from the control of his demanding father and outspoken mother, and he hung out with unmarried friends who were also looking for a good time rather than family responsibilities. Although Ruth naturally was anxious to marry, he resisted, and months went by. Perhaps he wouldn't have gone through with the marriage if there hadn't been enormous pressure from his own family and the Joneses. His mother was especially adamant about accepting the responsibility for Ruth's pregnancy, so Henry finally made plans to marry. That was in the spring of 1905.

Because Henry was only nineteen, Arch had to give written permission before the county clerk in Macomb would issue a marriage license. Then Henry and Ruth were married in Colchester by a justice of the peace, on June 30.

No doubt both families were relieved when the ceremony was over, but Henry's ambivalence toward marriage was unresolved. It did not help matters that their baby was born only a few weeks later, on July 24. It was a boy. Henry named him Archer—and called him "Archie"—as a tribute to his father.

Neither the marriage nor the birth was mentioned in the *Colchester Independent.*

Although Henry's personal life rapidly changed, his job as a potter's helper wasn't changing fast enough, and probably the more he thought of it, the whole situation in Colchester seemed unpromising. He had a deep longing to be more than he was, and he knew that real opportunity lay elsewhere, in larger towns.

Several young men who had left Colchester since the decline of coal mining were apparently prosperous. The new editor of the *Independent,* thirty-year-old Frank Groves, had recently praised them:

> Colchester can point with pride to the young men who have gone to larger cities and into other fields to make their ways in the world. Nearly every one of them has done well. . . . They have succeeded as merchants, in the professions, and in numerous other ventures. They came from a class of sturdy citizens, honest and industrious. Largely due to early training they are capable of making success wherever they chance to cast their lots. Most of

Colchester's boys have done and are doing very well. The great majority of them are successful and highly esteemed.

Whether or not he ever read that article, Henry shared the town's admiration for those young men, and he yearned to count himself among those who had made it. Like others before him, he realized that to stay in Colchester was to conform and have limited opportunity for advancement; to leave was to be independent and have a decent chance to become "successful and highly esteemed." No wonder he resolved to leave, despite his deep attachment to the town.

Another factor in Henry's decision to leave was his much-admired brother Joe. Relying on old friends who still worked for the railroad, Arch had gotten his oldest son a job as a switchman for the C. B. & Q. in Galesburg. Then twenty-two years old, Joe was on his own, living in a more promising place—the same exciting small city that had lured Arch away from Colchester in the 1890s—and occasionally he came home to tell the family about his new life. Of course his younger brother yearned to join him.

By the summer's end Henry too was working in Galesburg. Like his father some years earlier, he did not take his family. He must have roomed with Joe, planning to send for Ruth and the baby when he found a place to rent.

The Wagle brothers worked at the switchyard. It was a gigantic complex of roundhouses, warehouses, and sheds—some forty buildings in all—connected by a mass of tracks, where hundreds of railroad cars and locomotives could be disconnected, reconnected, and if necessary, repaired. One of the busiest yards in the country, it handled 4,000 freight cars every day. The switchman's job called for changing locomotives from one track to another, climbing and riding on the moving cars, and coupling one car to another as they bumped together. Accidents were common. Across the country one switchman in ten was killed or injured. The Galesburg newspaper specialized in articles such as "Struck by an Engine," "Hands Smashed," "Both Legs Severed," and "Crushed by the Cars."

Unlike Joe, Henry worked the night shift, which was especially dangerous. The switchyard lighting was poor, and although the switchmen carried lanterns, the engineers often could not see them as they worked around the cars, moving in and out of the shadows.

However, Henry didn't seem to mind the risk. Not quite twenty years old and anxious to prove himself, he apparently projected a casual confidence, perhaps even a certain recklessness, as he walked atop the moving cars and jumped onto the slowly passing locomotives. Despite the danger, he enjoyed the work.

Ruth joined him in Galesburg shortly before Christmas, and the young couple rented a place on South Chambers Street. Unfortunately Ruth reminded Henry of his responsibilities at a time when he was bent on asserting his freedom, and he may have associated her with his forceful mother. Whatever the case, she later told the McDonough County Circuit Court that he caroused in bad company, and when she criticized him, he became violently angry and abused her. Consequently, she left shortly after the first of the year, taking the baby with her back to Colchester.

Henry went after her, trying to convince her to come back. Whether or not he loved her, he wanted to keep the family together. According to court records, he protested that he wanted to be a good husband, that she was partly to blame, and that Archie needed a father. So she returned with him, briefly to Rock Island, where they needed switchmen, and then to Galesburg.

But Henry didn't change. He apparently had a strong need to dominate his young wife as well as a determination to do what he wanted with his free time. When she objected, he responded like a parent out of control, yelling at her, shoving her, pinching her, and slapping her. By the spring of 1906 Ruth and the baby were back in Colchester again. She eventually went to live in Kewanee with her sister and brother-in-law, Mary and James Kay. Later that year she filed for divorce.

Henry remained in Galesburg, living by himself (Joe had married). To a young man from Colchester, away from his family for the first time, Galesburg must have been an exciting place. Still rapidly growing, it had about twenty thousand people—two thousand more than when the Wagles had come there in 1897. Its factories were booming, putting out everything from typewriters to automobiles, and the two great railroads, the "Q" and the Santa Fe, brought a steady stream of visitors. Galesburg was a busy community, where the twentieth century was off to a fast start and where the people weren't bound together as tightly as they were in Colchester.

Like most small cities, Galesburg also had a wild side. There were two dozen saloons, including several on South Prairie Street, and some had gambling dens. Slot machines were as common as pool tables. Although Henry didn't drink, he was already an ardent poker player, and he soon learned where the action was. Throughout his life, no matter what else he did, his frame of mind was that of an inveterate gambler, forever hoping that the next hand of cards, throw of the dice, or run of the horses would pay off.

The Williams racetrack, renovated and renamed the Galesburg Driving Park, provided an opportunity to bet on the races, and some of the horses were spectacular. Several trotting records had been set at that track, and the legendary Dan Patch set the state pacing record there while Henry was in town. His love for the races, and for betting, must have been developing then.

The city also had a red light district stretching along Ferris and Water Streets, where prostitutes like Maude Garver, Nellie Smith, and Maggie Brown ran bawdy houses without much fear of the police. Henry apparently went there too, as his wife later reported to the court. He seemed to need the company of women who made no real demands on him.

He also made trips back to Colchester, less than two hours away by train, to see his parents, his brother Glenn, and his sister Geneva. He was especially close to his mother, and despite his wild streak, he was always anxious to please her. Because he was separated from Ruth, Henry considered himself free to date other women in Colchester. One of them was Anna Dean, the twenty-one-year-old daughter of an illiterate teamster. Her mother was dead, her family was poor, and she had a reputation for being wild. One of the few women in Colchester with a nickname, she was known as "Coonie."

Henry's work as a switchman and his life in Galesburg came to a sudden end shortly after his twenty-first birthday. On January 25, 1907, the *Republican-Register* carried yet another article about a railroad accident.

SWITCHMAN INJURED

T. H. Wagle, a night switchman at the hump yards south of the city, had a painful accident Wednesday morning shortly before eight o'clock. Wagle works nights and was returning to this city. He was riding on the foot-board of the engine when the board suddenly struck something, causing it to turn under. The switchman's foot was caught between the footboard and the rail and was severely twisted.

The ambulance was called, and the injured man was taken to the hospital. His injuries were confined to the left foot, which was badly twisted at and below the ankle, the bones being badly fractured. At the hospital the injured foot was dressed and placed in a cast.

Henry was on crutches for several months. Unable to support himself financially, he went back home to live with his parents. The foot eventually healed, but for the rest of his life he walked with a limp.

In May of that year, before Henry had completely recovered, the suit for divorce came up in the McDonough County Circuit Court, held at the stately red brick courthouse in Macomb. Ruth was represented by William H. Neece, a brilliant old lawyer and former congressman who had been defending clients since before the Civil War. On the witness stand, before Judge John Gray, Ruth described the abuse that she had suffered from her husband, including one time when he had thrown her down and choked her. She also accused Henry of committing adultery with a prostitute named Lillian Russell in Galesburg and with Anna Dean and others in Colchester. He was, she said, "a man of cruel disposition and low and vulgar habits."

Henry denied all the charges and blamed his wife for their separation, hoping to retain custody of Archie. That was his reason for fighting the divorce. But Ruth provided credible witnesses who had seen him with two young women at the village of Industry the previous summer, and their testimony shocked the court. One of them was Samuel Hawk, Jr., of rural Emmet Township, who was pointedly questioned by Neece:

Q. Now I will ask you if you seen this Henry Wagle at Industry any time; if so, tell about when.
A. I saw him there; it was the 4th of July last year.
Q. What was he doing?
A. Well, it looked pretty bad to me what he was doing the time I saw him.
Q. Well, just tell the court.

A. He was down there; he had a girl with him by the name of Coonie Dean, so he told me her name was, when I ran across him. . . .

Q. Where did she live?

A. Well, I suppose her home is in Colchester.

Q. Do you know what her reputation was for virtue in that neighborhood?

A. Yes sir.

Q. What was it?

A. Well, it was pretty bad.

Q. Now, what did Henry Wagle say to you about this girl?

A. Well, he come up to me, and we got to talking, and . . . he says, "There is the girls I brought over."

Q. How many did he have?

A. There was two of them that were there with him, and he says to me, "We can go together, and we can go out and have a pretty good time today," and I says, "No, you will have to excuse me, Henry, because I am a married man." Well, he says, "I will tell you, if you will come and go with me, I will guarantee it won't cost you anything."

Q. Where did he have the girls at that time?

A. Well, he went along the street from Lawyer's livery barn down towards the railroad tracks.

Q. That was out in the woods like?

A. Yes sir.

Q. What else was he doing there?

A. Well, I seen him several different times that day, and it seemed to me he was kind of rushing business. He told me he was there for that purpose.

Q. Was he trying to get customers for those girls?

A. Yes sir.

Q. That is what he wanted you to do?

A. Yes sir.

Q. Go out there for immoral purposes?

A. Yes sir.

Q. Go out and take one of those girls?

A. Yes sir.

When Hawk finally finished, Asa Cheeseman, who had known Henry for two years, gave similar testimony. He too had been in Industry on the Fourth of July, and Henry Wagle had approached him as well about having sex with Coonie Dean and Ruth Dunsworth. Worse yet, the Dunsworth girl was only fourteen years old.

Henry was stunned by the force of Ruth's attack on his character. He surely had not expected so much to come out in court. The bill of complaint for the divorce had referred to abuse and adultery, which he was prepared to deny, but this was pandering. He was portrayed by Ruth's lawyer as someone with a complete disregard for social mores when it came to sexuality and as a dangerously abusive person when he was aroused.

In many ways the divorce case was the most revealing trial of Henry Wagle's life. It showed a man for whom ego satisfaction was everything. Sexual experience was simply a means to that end. And it was clear from the pattern of marital abuse that any opposition he encountered was a threat to his fragile sense of identity and was likely to evoke a violent response.

When Judge Gray dissolved the marriage, he was unequivocal in his condemnation of Henry's behavior: "The defendant has been guilty of extreme and repeated cruelty, and has committed adultery subsequent to his marriage with the complainant . . . and he is a person wholly unfit to have the care, custody, control, or education of their child."

Henry's first venture out of town had been a dismal failure. Within two years he had lost everything: his wife, his son, his job, and his independence. For a young man obsessed with making it, the impact must have been traumatic. But the divorce case had taught him something: in the future he would be more careful about women and less trusting of everyone around him. Betrayal was always a possibility.

In the meantime there was nothing to do but stay in Colchester, start over, and see if his luck would change.

Social Change
and the Young
Bootlegger

Despite the return of good times to America in the first
decade of the century, Colchester declined in population, from 1,635 to 1,445, and it was rapidly changing in
response to local and national forces. While a small number of townspeople fared well, most did not.

One of those who found the going tough was Van Hampton. When
subscriptions again declined in 1905, he sold the *Independent* to thirty-
year-old Frank Groves, a likable, easygoing editor from Camp Point, and
moved to Macomb for good. Unlike Colchester, the county seat, with
over 5,000 people, was slowly growing, and the future there looked very
bright indeed. The town's most recent asset was Western Illinois State
Normal School, located one mile northwest of the square in a gigantic
brick-and-limestone building that had opened its doors in the fall of
1902. Continually expanding, the college would eventually become the
county's largest employer.

In contrast, Colchester's economic hopes continued to wane. After
the temporary prosperity brought by the coal famine, production at the
local drift mines declined again. As editor Groves pointed out in 1908,
"The small vein coal operator is fast passing from the stage of action,"
and "if he operates a mine at all, he depends upon the local market." By
then Colchester had only eighty-eight coal miners.

Despite the frequent rumors and predictions of a boom in clay mining, that remained a small industry. The big Weir pottery mine northwest of town had changed hands in 1905 and was operated by John Baird, who supplied clay for the Western Stoneware Company in Macomb. He was an able manager, and his operation soon involved three mines and a dozen mule cars on the tramway, but that was the only sizable clay company in town, and its economic impact was minimal. In 1908 Groves summed up the situation in a single sentence: "Fire clay is mined here on an extensive scale, but aside from giving employment to a few laborers, it adds nothing to the commercial growth of Colchester."

To make matters worse, a couple of prominent stores went bankrupt, and late in 1906 the town's only bank failed. The owner of that institution, C. V. Chandler of Macomb, had been the wealthiest man in McDonough County, but he had invested heavily in a local railroad, and when it went bankrupt, his banks in both towns were forced to close. Although most of the Bank of Colchester deposits were eventually paid back as Chandler's assets were liquidated, the process took years.

In a January 1907 editorial Groves asserted that the whole episode symbolized an unfortunate change in national values:

> The insane desire for speed has been the keynote of commercial life in the twentieth century. Men, desiring to break a record, recently sent a train too fast, and death, instead of the division end, was their destination. So too, great financiers, traveling too rapidly toward the goal of wealth, or pulling too many coaches, have derailed their engine, gone into the ditch, and carried with them many innocent and trusting passengers. . . .
>
> For too long it has been impressed on succeeding generations that the aim and end of human endeavor is riches alone, reached by a brand of morality just guaranteed to keep a man out of jail. What we need is a reaction against this tendency. . . .
>
> We need a wisdom that shows plainly that the men with the greatest ambitions are ultimately the men with the greatest disappointments. The workmen of sober, industrious ways, who take pride in their work and excel in it, who throw aside all reckless desires for unearned wealth, and who are satisfied with a laboring man's income, are the best and happiest citizens. . . .

He was contrasting the C. V. Chandlers of America with the modest workmen of Colchester—bold pursuers of wealth with sturdy contributors to community life. It was a call for self-restraint in an age of growing irresponsibility, and more pointedly, it was an effort to reconcile the townspeople to their own "disappointments" in a nation that was achieving, as he said elsewhere in that issue, "unprecedented prosperity."

One man who found it very difficult to make a living in Colchester was Henry Wagle. Although the railroad had paid for his medical bills and provided a small compensation for his injury, he did not work for many months and had expenses related to the divorce. In short, he was broke. When he finally got off his crutches, he worked briefly as a substitute mail carrier on the rural routes, filling in for the regulars while they took their summer vacations, and then he worked from time to time as a railroad laborer.

That was when he found Beulah McConnell. She was a beautiful nineteen-year-old farm girl with dazzling blue eyes and auburn hair, and she was altogether the most remarkable person he had ever met.

Born in 1889 on a farm two miles east of Fountain Green, in neighboring Hancock County, Beulah was the oldest of seven children—all girls. Her father, John McConnell, was a brawny, domineering man whose only son had died as an infant. When he failed to beget another one, he raised Beulah as the boy he never had. It was partly a matter of economics: he needed help on the farm, and she was the oldest. By the time she was a teenager, Beulah could harness a team and drive a planter, a harrow, or a wagon like a man, and she could milk the cows and do other farm chores too.

But McConnell also expected her to share his interests. He taught her to be an expert hunter, and she seldom missed a rabbit on the run or a duck on the wing with her twenty-gauge shotgun. In the wintertime she ran her father's trapline. And she loved to fish, swim, hike, and ride horses.

Because her father was demanding, Beulah developed a certain toughness. If she did something wrong, he didn't hesitate to yell at her or even hit her. But he was permissive with her too, as if she were a son.

Beulah's manlike independence probably led to her early downfall. Attracted to a neighboring farmer's son, whose name is now unknown, she became pregnant at fifteen. Her father's reaction can only be imagined. He sent her to live with relatives in nearby Webster, where she gave birth to a daughter named Pauline on Christmas Day 1905.

Beulah later returned, to live at the farm and help her father, but he was never happy there again—perhaps because his gender illusion about her was shattered. In the late summer of 1907, he sold the place at auction and prepared to move to Carthage, the county seat, some eighteen miles west of Colchester.

That's when Beulah met Henry Wagle. In many ways they were made for each other. Both were outgoing individualists who had known the disastrous consequences of a teenage sexual relationship. In different ways they had felt the force of social condemnation. More deeply, Beulah knew how to cope with a domineering man who was much like her father, while Henry was drawn to an assertive, independent woman who was similar to his mother.

They saw each other regularly for some weeks, and after Beulah left for Carthage, they apparently corresponded. Beulah probably knew little about Henry's life with Ruth, except what he chose to tell her, and she certainly knew nothing about his sordid sexual affairs. When she returned to the Fountain Green area to visit relatives for Thanksgiving, they eloped, getting married in Fort Madison, Iowa, on Thanksgiving Day 1907.

What Henry did for work following their marriage is unknown, but it couldn't have been very promising. He probably continued to work as a railroad laborer. The young couple rented a place in Colchester, but three-year-old Pauline frequently stayed with Beulah's parents in Carthage.

That Henry still longed for attention and had no respect for authority is evident from an escapade that made the front page of the *Independent* in September 1908:

CITY MARSHAL HAS A FOOT RACE

Last Saturday evening about the hour of nine, while the city was thronged with people, all enjoying a good time, some youths purchased a watermelon and proceeded to eat it in the usual way. When the feast was at its height, Henry Wagle happened along and set his No. 11's [shoes] on the melon, thus bringing the banquet to an abrupt end. A warm argument ensued, and as a result Henry landed at the city building in the care of City Marshal James Wayland. While James was at the phone making arrangements to have the prisoner fined, Henry espied an open window and proceeded to use it to his advantage, making his escape.

During the affair, Fred Webster interfered with the marshal and was arrested. But seeing an opening, he also took to his heels, with Wayland in close pursuit. The race was highly entertaining to the large crowd that was present. They went pell mell at a furious pace through the business part of the city, followed by cheers, yells, and laughter. Webster finally drew away and escaped, and both Wagle and Webster left town that night for parts unknown.

Henry had acted like a smart aleck, but the melon eaters didn't think he was funny. When the argument started to get out of hand, Marshal Wayland, a former coal miner known as "Fizzer," had apparently arrested him for disorderly conduct, which carried a $5 fine. Whether Henry ever paid it is unknown.

Because he escaped from a coal-miner-turned-marshal, a man much like Arch had been in the 1890s, it is tempting to see this episode as psychologically revealing and to infer that Henry's lifelong resistance to authority, especially the police, was rooted in a childhood desire to escape the control of his father. If that is true, his later bootlegging must have brought him enormous satisfaction.

Fred Webster, whom everyone called "Flunk," had mined coal at Mystic, Iowa, during the past year but was home for the summer. His own narrow escape from the marshal prompted him to return there—it was time for the mines to start up again anyway—and he apparently encouraged his old friend and fellow escapee Henry Wagle to come with him. Jobs were easy to find there, as the *Independent* had reported in a March 1908 article:

MYSTIC, IOWA

Albert Kipling returned earlier this week from Mystic, Iowa, where he has been mining coal, and he reports that the work there is especially good. . . . Mystic is a great coal mining town, as there are fourteen mines there, and three switch engines are employed switching the coal cars. A large number of Colchester people are

at Mystic, some engaged in mining and others in business. Among
the miners are Will Russell, Fred Webster, Tom Hocker, and Roy
Averill.

Aside from those men, two of Henry's cousins and his uncle Frank
were also mining coal in Mystic, which had been receiving Colchester
families for almost twenty years. By the end of September Henry and
Beulah had moved there too.

Although it was located in a wooded valley in south-central Iowa,
Mystic in 1908 resembled Colchester in the 1880s. Several shaft mines
and many drift mines were in full operation, and the town of 1,800 people, several miles from the county seat, was steadily growing. The business district had a few brick buildings and two dozen small frame ones
clustered along a dusty main street, and railroad tracks ran nearby. Small
homes and shanties dotted the nearby hillsides, and good housing was
in short supply.

Although Henry could have worked as a coal miner, he chose not to
do that. He had grown up hearing stories about death in the mines, and
he had known George Jones well when he was crushed to death, so perhaps for those reasons he avoided the mines. Instead he made use of his
experience in Galesburg and worked as a switchman, helping to move
loaded coal cars from the mines to the main track, where they could be
hauled away. He knew that a switchman's work could be dangerous too,
but it was not as frightening as working in the dark coal mines.

Henry and Beulah remained in Mystic until the spring of 1909, when
most of the mines closed for the summer and coal shipping was all but
discontinued. Then they returned to Colchester, where Henry again
worked as a railroad laborer.

The old hometown was then in the middle of a strange and fearful
experience. Colchester had been fortunate to avoid major fires throughout the nineteenth century, but it had suddenly become the most fire-
prone community in the state.

The first major blaze, on September 3, 1906, destroyed four frame
buildings on Depot Street, including the once-splendid Union Hotel,
which had been the center of community life. Five months later, on
February 3, 1907, a fire farther west on Depot Street burned three more
buildings, including Gib Miller's Cottage by the Sea, which in the old

days had been Jim Hickey's place. Another link to the past, another gathering place that reflected the old pattern of life in Colchester, was gone. Then, on August 6, the Christian Church burned to the ground. Constructed in 1867, it had been a majestic white-frame structure, located on North Street, and its massive, soaring belfry had made it the tallest building in town. For forty years it had stood like a guardian along the main road, and without it Colchester looked like a different place.

Then came another, bigger fire. On the night of October 20, 1907, five more buildings on Depot Street were destroyed, and several others were damaged. By the time the firehouse bell had roused the community and the horse-drawn pumper wagon had been hauled out, the tremendous blaze could be seen fifteen miles away. The townspeople worked like demons in the eerie glow that lighted the downtown streets to keep from losing the entire north side of the business district.

By that time everybody knew that Colchester had a firebug. All the destructive blazes had started after midnight in old frame buildings on the North Side, and during the same period many small fires had broken out, but they had been stopped before doing much damage.

Despite an investigation and massive public concern, the fires continued. In November the firebug tried to ignite a North Side restaurant using an oil-filled bottle with a burning wick, but it was discovered under the building. The following month he set fire to a North Side feed store, but the blaze was put out before it engulfed the building. Someone was trying to burn down the town.

By 1908 several nearby newspapers were carrying articles on the Colchester firebug, and among the worried townspeople suspicion began to center on a young man named Walter Farmer, who was an undertaker. He had been seen on the sidewalk shortly before the feed store fire, and his father, Ed Farmer, owned extensive property on the South Side, which had not been visited by the firebug. Moreover, the Farmer and Sons general store was in deep financial trouble, and it had been closed for two months in 1907 until desperate creditors had arranged for it to continue.

Farmer protested his innocence, and the following April a huge fire did break out on the South Side, destroying some fifteen wooden shops, homes, and sheds. Farmer and Sons lost a storage room and livery barn, but their store was saved. Some townspeople thought that Walter Farmer or his father had started that blaze to divert suspicion, but other suggestions were made too, and no one had any evidence.

The only thing that everyone felt sure of was that the firebug would strike again. It was a time of fear, anger, and suspicion that undermined the old high-trust culture of the town.

On January 31, 1910, the huge Farmer and Sons general store was reduced to rubble in a roaring nighttime blaze that may have been an act of retaliation. After all, Walter Farmer had his undertaking business there. That fire also destroyed the town's opera house, located above the store, which Ed Farmer also owned and operated, as well as the nearby post office.

On the following morning weary townspeople congregated on the east end of Market Street, gazing with blank faces at the smoking ruins and the stacks of salvaged merchandise piled in the street, no doubt wondering whether that enormous conflagration would be the last.

But the mysterious fires continued well into the next decade, consuming the electric light plant, the grain elevator, a department store, a food store, a millinery shop, a cigar store, two restaurants, two barber shops, and other buildings.

Unable to do as well financially as he had hoped, Frank Groves sold the *Independent* in September 1910 and returned to Camp Point. The new editor was John H. Bayless, a tall, stocky, blond-haired man who was thirty-six years old. He had studied business and law in Macomb before moving to nearby Blandinsville, where he sold real estate and then edited the *Star-Gazette* for six years. In Colchester he modernized the *Independent* office by installing a Linotype machine, which his wife and later his sons learned to operate. In many ways Bayless was like Van Hampton—a Republican, a business booster, a temperance crusader, a baseball fan, and a man who soon loved the town.

The first issue that engaged the new editor's full attention was the firebug investigation. In an August 10, 1911, article, following yet another fire, he criticized local authorities and tried to rally the townspeople:

> What about the recent fires in Colchester? Has there been anything done? Is there anything being done?
> This seems to us a neglect of duty, pure and simple, and a people who will lay down at a time like this, when our property and

> homes are constantly in danger of being burned, does not deserve
> sympathy.
>
> The fiend who has been starting these fires is still at large. . . . It
> is up to the citizens of Colchester to do something to stop this
> awful carnage, that is sapping the life and enthusiasm of our fair
> city, and bring punishment to whoever is guilty.
>
> If the authorities do not act in this matter, we are in favor of a
> mass meeting of the citizens for the purpose of considering ways
> and means. He who sits down and allows an enemy to destroy him
> without making an effort is a coward.

Frustrated and angry, Bayless was calling on the townspeople to save
their community by vigilante measures if necessary. Still, no one knew
quite what to do.

As threats and intimidation mounted, Walter Farmer was eventually
forced to leave town. The fires continued after he was gone, however,
until many of Colchester's old frame buildings were destroyed and some
insurance companies dropped their local policies. Through it all there
was much hard talk and finger pointing, especially in the direction of
Ed Farmer, and in 1913 the state fire marshal launched a "sweeping investigation" that lasted for many months, but the Colchester firebug was
never caught.

Despite the problems caused by the frequent fires, the town slowly
edged back toward prosperity. Shortly before he sold the *Independent,*
Frank Groves reported the economic basis for renewal of hope in the
local future:

> With farm prices at a high mark, with our local industries run-
> ning at full blast, prospects in Colchester seem better than for
> years. All local stores are enjoying a good trade. The receipts and
> shipments at the depot are heavy. . . .
>
> Colchester has suffered from many unspeakable reverses dur-
> ing the past years, but we are now preparing to . . . assume our
> proper level of commercial importance.

At that time the most dynamic industrial leaders were George and
Walter Baird, who had taken over their father's clay-mining operation
northwest of town. They increased the number of mines from three to

five and used a steam engine, as well as mules, to pull their clay cars on the tramway. Soon they were shipping out seven or eight railroad cars of clay every day, much of it bound for the potteries in Macomb and Monmouth.

The other sizable clay-mining operation, owned by Charles Myers, was also located northwest of town, and it too was expanding. In 1910 Myers built his own tramway, which ran almost a mile from his massive clay pit to his tipple by the railroad tracks. He used horses and mules to pull the cars.

Moses King died in 1909, but his twin sons, Bennie and Joe, continued to operate the brickyard, which was then producing more drainage tile than bricks. They were also selling "King's Everlasting Silo," constructed of a few thousand hollow clay blocks. By 1910 the King brothers were shipping out ten or twelve railroad cars of clay products every week.

Another pair of brothers were also making their mark. Henry and Ed Terrill dissolved their partnership in 1910—apparently because their wives hated each other and caused friction between them—and Henry built a new general store, with plate glass windows and an upstairs residence, on the corner of Fulton and Market Streets. It was known as Terrill and Sons. Meanwhile his younger brother retained the old family store across the railroad grounds, remodeled it the following year, and eventually established a partnership with his son-in-law, Herbert Hulson. Despite the intense competition between the Terrill brothers, who both sold clothes and groceries, they did well in the years before World War I, when prosperity seemed to be coming back.

In those early years of the century prosperity had a new symbol: the automobile. Destined to change American culture, it also symbolized progress and individualism. The first one in Colchester was a single-seat Maxwell runabout with hard-rubber tires, a right-hand steering column, external brake and gearshift levers, barrel-shaped headlights, and tall, ornate gas lamps. From the front it looked like a huge mechanical insect.

The car was bought from a hardware and buggy dealer, J. E. Carson and Sons, in August 1905, and strangely enough, the buyer was a woman, Mrs. Eliza Tandy, the well-to-do widow of a local railroad agent and telegraph operator. At first she did not drive it, but the oldest of the six Carson boys drove her around in it, to the endless fascination of the townspeople. Then she boldly proceeded to handle it herself—the very image of female independence. The entire episode was an early sign of profound social changes that were coming.

Henry Ford started mass producing the Model T in 1908, and by late the following year Carson had become the local Ford dealer. The arrival of the first Model T was big news, reported in the *Independent:* "J. E. Carson has received a new Ford car, to be used by him as a demonstrator. It is of the touring car type, with top, glass front [the windshield], speedometer, magneto, and gas lamps. The auto is light and compact—weight 1200 pounds. The twenty-horsepower engine is about the size of a water bucket. It is wonderful."

Several other residents soon bought cars, and almost immediately speeding became a problem. The city council set the first speed limit at ten miles per hour, but drivers of the amazing new machines often exceeded it.

One of the speeders was Riley ("Rile") Irish, a tall, husky young man with a mustache who bought a Mitchell runabout in 1908 and raced it around town, making noise, raising dust, scaring the horses, and exciting the envy of other young men. He was finally arrested for speeding, primarily because, while going five miles over the limit, "he ran over T. B. Davidson's dog, flattening him out like a pancake." The episode led to a much-publicized court case that dramatized the town's divided view of automobiles. Some thought they were a danger to the community; others wished they had one. Irish eventually beat the charge.

The speed limit was reduced to six miles per hour, and signs proclaiming it were posted at either end of town, but the speeding continued. So did the car buying, at an ever-increasing pace.

In the socially conservative world of the small town, automobiles symbolized a certain freedom from restraint, a determination to do as you pleased, and consequently no one in Colchester was more fascinated with them than Henry Wagle, but it would be several years before he could afford to buy one. Meanwhile he learned to drive from friends who owned cars, including Rile Irish, who soon became a car dealer.

Henry never returned to Mystic. Instead he stayed in town, working at the brickyard for much of the year and sometimes peddling pottery by wagon to people in the countryside, when the roads were passable and the brickyard was not operating. He and Beulah bought a one-story frame house on North Street, east of the new Christian Church. It was nothing more than an old miner's cottage with a small barn in back, across a shallow ravine, where they kept their horse, buggy, and wagon.

It was a difficult, frustrating time, when they were chronically short of money, and Henry's temper often got the best of him. One time, when the horse pulling his wagon refused to go, he got out, grabbed a short two-by-four, and beat the animal until it screamed in pain and submitted to his control. That's the way he was sometimes.

But he was also fun to be around and popular with the townspeople. In 1909, at the first Fraternal Picnic, which had replaced the annual Miners' Picnic, he and a friend reversed the shafts on his buggy so that the horse could be hitched behind and, in effect, push it. Then they dressed up as country hicks, with Henry wearing an outlandish fake beard. Their humorous buggy-before-the-horse float was the hit of the parade.

Beulah participated in the community picnics too. She commonly won prizes in the ladies' hitching contest and ladies' single-horse driving contest. Not many women could handle a horse as well as she could, and she sometimes took their buggy as far as Fountain Green or Webster, in the next county, to see relatives. Unlike most women of her time, she also eventually learned to drive an automobile.

Beulah and Henry sometimes quarreled, but she was tougher than Ruth, and when he became abusive, she stood her ground pretty well, although she was sometimes bruised. Despite his violent temper, he apparently loved her, and she must have realized that. One time, when he was working at the brickyard, he inscribed their names on two freshly cut bricks, and after they were dried and burned, he took them home as a token of his affection.

In an earlier era Henry might have settled into a thoroughly conventional life, but times were changing, and he changed with them, moving further and further away from the traditional values of the town. He wanted to fit in, of course, and he did, but more than that, he wanted to rise, to make it, to be somebody, even if that meant defying community standards or doing something no one else dared to do. That was the spirit of the new century, and even the *Colchester Independent* sometimes reflected it, as in this 1912 editorial: "Thousands of men and women around us live their indifferent lives and pass away, without doing anything really daring or worthwhile, failing to get the best out of life. . . . Shall we be content to drift along without striving to rise above the level of those who do not care? We are the sculptor, our life is the clay. What shall we make of ourselves?"

Creative writers and social commentators were popularizing the notion that people came in two kinds, "indifferent" conformists and self-created individuals. If community and conformity were linked, so were self-realization and nonconformity. Rising seemed to imply rebellion, and in early twentieth-century Colchester, the best opportunity for a poor man to shape a unique life was rebellious indeed. It was bootlegging.

The ongoing battle between pro-saloon and anti-saloon forces was tipped decisively in favor of the temperance cause by Billy Sunday. The Chicago evangelist was fast becoming a religious superstar when he traveled to Macomb in the spring of 1905 to hold a month-long revival. By providing dozens of meetings in a specially built tabernacle, delighting the crowds with his humorous sermons, and denouncing saloonkeepers and drinkers alike, he dominated the cultural scene in McDonough County during April and May. More than 1,300 people "hit the sawdust trail" to "get right with God," and temperance forces throughout the county were energized.

The churches in Colchester tried to hire Sunday to hold a revival in their town the following year, but he turned them down. Consequently all four churches held separate revivals early in 1906, hoping to keep the religious, anti-saloon momentum going until the city election in April.

Among the preachers was one of the few female evangelists in the country, Sadie McCoy Crank, an ordained minister in the Christian (Disciples of Christ) Church. A Hancock County native who was then living in southwest Missouri, she was a slim, plain, graying, determined-looking woman of forty-three, who had organized churches and attracted converts in dozens of communities. A gifted speaker, she had enormous appeal wherever she went, especially at a time when temperance was the top female issue.

When the election finally arrived, the town went dry by thirty-two votes. No one could have known it then, but that ballot brought an end to legal liquor sales in Colchester until the repeal of Prohibition.

Of course, liquor violations were common that year. Several men were arrested, including a certain Clarence Way, who opened a "gallon house" just outside the city limits. Although his business was legal, the authorities watched him closely and soon got him for selling to minors, "maintaining a nuisance," and whatever else they could think of.

Others were arrested for selling liquor in town, including three young men who brought a keg of beer from Quincy and did a lively business selling it by the glass until they were discovered. Their court case introduced a new word to readers of the *Independent:* "bootlegging."

The election of 1907 brought another victory for the "no license" people in Colchester, but a much more important vote soon took place in the Illinois legislature. The Anti-Saloon League, committed to "the final, absolute annihilation of the saloon in every nation of the world," had taken control of the prohibition movement, and although it was allied with the Protestant churches, it emphasized tough, practical politics. On May 7 the league finally induced Illinois legislators to pass a local-option bill, first proposed in 1903, that provided for a prohibition referendum in each township every two years.

The big test of the new legislation came in the April 1908 election, which was preceded by temperance rallies and revivals all over the state. In Colchester Sadie McCoy Crank held a series of well-attended meetings at the Methodist Church. When the big day came, 1,052 Illinois townships, including Colchester, voted to go dry, putting some 1,500 saloons out of business. That vote extended anti-saloon territory well beyond the city limits of Colchester, and in fact, the only McDonough County township that voted for saloons was Bushnell, more than twenty miles away, which had licensed them off and on for several years.

The Anti-Saloon League printed a map on the cover of *The Illinois Issue,* its monthly magazine, that showed in black and white which townships were still wet and which were dry. A statewide moral war was in full swing. The dark blotches on the map showed where the evil influence of the saloon was not yet abolished by the forces of righteousness.

THE ILLINOIS ISSUE

The Church in Action Against the Saloon

Vol. III.   Chicago, Ill., May 1, 1908.   No. 18

Map of Illinois

Showing the Result

of the

First Year

of the

War

between the

Liquor Traffic

and the

Anti-Saloon League

The White indicates the actual

Anti-Saloon Territory created

by Popular Vote in one year

☐ Dry   ■ Wet

The bootlegger's early career is shrouded in mystery, but he apparently sold beer in anti-saloon territory before 1910. The wagon he used for peddling pottery would have been an ideal way to transport it to his customers, and the countryside with which he was most familiar—his father's rural route northwest of town—butted against the nearest wet territory, in Hancock County. Getting the liquor would have been no problem.

Whatever his beginning was, it must have been modest. It was probably confined to serving people he knew well, whenever the opportunity arose, but since liquor was still available in some townships, prices were still low and so were the bootlegger's profits.

By that time in his life, his friends had started calling him Kelly, the name that eventually marked his new identity.

His first serious brush with the law came in the spring of 1910, and it apparently had nothing to do with bootlegging. The *Macomb Journal* carried the story:

WAGLE ACQUITTED

The much-talked-of holdup case against Henry Wagle, charged with holding up Harrison Cohen, a junk dealer of Burlington, Iowa, at Colchester on the night of May 16, was heard today.

According to Cohen, on this night he was between the mill and the ball park when someone shoved a revolver at him and told him to throw up his hands. He resisted and grabbed the fellow by the throat, and called for help. He also grabbed the robber by the face and scratched him severely. The fellow hit him over the head with the revolver and also got Cohen's thumb in his mouth and chewed it. The man finally broke loose and ran. He jumped on a horse and rode away, while Cohen went up town and informed the police.

The state claims that the story is correct as told by Cohen and that the defendant had marks on his throat and face to correspond with the marks as inflicted by Cohen on his assailant. They also claim that the description of the horse corresponds with the one rode by Wagle.

The defense said that he is not guilty in any way, that he knows nothing of the case. They also claimed that Cohen described a man with a big sandy mustache as his assailant at first, and that description in no way tallies with Wagle. . . .

The justice, after hearing the evidence, released the defendant.

Kelly was lucky that time. The victim's identification was just shaky enough to leave room for doubt, especially after Kelly shaved off his mustache. And Harrison Cohen was an outsider, a Jew from the notorious river town of Burlington, whereas Kelly was a local man, the son of a respected Colchester marshal of the 1890s. So he escaped conviction.

The attempted robbery reveals how poor and desperate Kelly was at that time. The 1910 census, taken shortly afterward, lists his occupation as "railroad laborer" and indicates that he had been out of work for much of the past year. Moreover, he was living with his parents. Whether his temporary separation from Beulah came before the failed holdup or as a result of it is unknown.

One other thing might be gleaned from this episode: young Kelly may have had a romantic view of lawbreakers. Attempting a holdup and riding off on a horse sounds like part of a dime novel about the Old West. Kelly was in fact an expert rider who shared his father's fascination with horses and who loved to hear his grandfather, Henry Walley, tell about frontier days in Illinois and Montana. So the daring holdup— by "a bold highwayman" who "escaped on a sorrel horse," as the *Independent* put it—may reveal much about the bootlegger's mindset as he launched his criminal career.

By 1912 Kelly was making occasional buggy trips to Bushnell, population 3,800, which was still the only saloon town in the county. He undoubtedly sold much beer in those days, for the newest way to beat the liquor law was to set up a "beer camp" near town, in a field or grove, where people could drink and socialize on the weekend. The camp was always gone by Monday morning, so there was nothing for the police to investigate.

Kelly was not very concerned about the police anyway. At that time arrests for liquor-law violations seldom led to convictions. In fact, early in 1910 City Attorney George Falder resigned in disgust for just that reason. Also, in April 1910 Colchester elected a new mayor, builder and businessman John O. Moon, who was tolerant of illegal liquor sales, and he appointed a new marshal who couldn't have been more sympathetic to Kelly. It was Uncle John Walley.

The old boozer and saloon fighter had settled down some as he had reached middle age, but he was still a big rough guy who could handle any man in town, and he was still a heavy drinker. With his handlebar mustache, dark suit, and derby hat, he looked a bit like Wyatt Earp or Bat Masterson, and with eight children to support (the Walleys had lost one to a childhood disease), he was determined to do a good job as marshal. In his first year he made more than forty arrests, including a few for liquor violations. Nonetheless, Kelly knew that as long as he was reasonably discreet, he could sell liquor now and then without fear of the police.

Under those circumstances, it is not surprising that Kelly developed a contempt for the liquor law. He saw that it was a matter not of morality—for there were good people on both sides—but of power. When the majority won in a liquor vote, they could have things their way—officially, at least—until the next election, and then the law might be overturned. It was a game of sorts, with half the public winning and the other half losing at any given time. And his uncle John, the boozer-turned-enforcer, perfectly symbolized the meaningless nature of it all.

While Kelly was becoming involved in bootlegging, his father was facing hard times. In 1912 Arch's eyesight began to fail, so he quit his job as a rural mail carrier and sold his place at Vinegar Hill. He and Alice moved to Galesburg, where they bought a big two-story boarding house at 177 N. Kellogg Street. Alice ran it with the help of Joe's wife, Luella. Geneva was still in school, but Glenn was eighteen, and through Joe's connections he got a job as yard clerk for the C. B. & Q.

While the Wagles were in Galesburg, Alice's father died. Henry Walley, who was called "Hen" by his friends, had been a tough old codger who had continued to work now and again doing odd jobs, although he was seventy-seven. But in July 1913 he was thrown from his carriage during a runaway, and his internal injuries led to pneumonia, which killed him. All the Wagles came down from Galesburg for his funeral, which was held at the home of his grandson and namesake, Henry Wagle, who had always admired the plainspoken old immigrant and homesteader.

Two weeks later, when Alice returned to Colchester to settle her father's affairs, the newspaper commented on her assumption of that traditionally male responsibility:

LOOKING AFTER BUSINESS

Mrs. Alice Wagle, who was the daughter of Henry Walley, who died a couple of weeks ago, was in the city one day last week, settling up the funeral expenses and attending to the business incidental to her father's death. Mrs. Wagle settled those accounts herself.

It was unusual to find a woman "looking after business," but Arch was virtually blind, and Alice had always been an assertive, independent woman. Undoubtedly she was just as capable of running the family business in Galesburg as well.

Indeed, there was little for Arch to do in Galesburg, for his limited eyesight prevented him from getting a job. He disliked the inactivity, however, and he missed both his old friends and Colchester itself. He soon wanted to return home, but Alice had meaningful work at the

boarding house and felt she could support the family better in Galesburg. So, in the summer of 1914 Arch came back to Colchester alone.

He bought a livery and feed barn just east of the park, fixed it up, and
retitled it the Park Livery Barn. At that time it was the only remaining
livery business in Colchester, and he hoped it would allow him a decent
income, at least enough to support himself. He lived on the premises,
in a tiny building that had just two rooms.

Arch was clinging to the past. Like many older men, he had a nostalgic love for horsedrawn transportation, and he never did learn to drive
a car. A 1909 article in the *Independent* surely reflected his sentiments:

IS THE AUTOMOBILE DRIVING OUT THE HORSE?

The liveryman of today, reduced though his numbers may be,
as shown by statistics, is satisfied with the volume of his business
and confident that he will suffer but little from the inroads of the
automobile. There will always be a satisfaction in holding the lines
over a good horse which no amount of rapid traveling in a whiz-
zing machine will satisfy. And there is a feeling of companionship
which a good horse gives, that will be forever lacking in an automobile.

Perhaps a rural mail carrier turned liveryman could not be expected to
feel otherwise, but by the summer of 1914 there were about one thousand cars in McDonough County, and that number was steadily rising.

The automobile was, in fact, helping to bring new economic hope to
Colchester. The most remarkable business of that decade was J. E. Carson and Sons, the Ford dealer, which operated in Macomb as well as
Colchester. In 1912 the Carsons sold well over one hundred cars, and
as the price of a Model T steadily dropped, that number continued to
climb. By 1917 they were selling more than five hundred cars a year and
were the biggest Ford dealership in western Illinois. Meanwhile, three
local businessmen—Revy Hunt, Rile Irish, and Roll Wear—launched the
Colchester Automobile Company, which sold Maxwell, Velie, and Metz
models. For a time they did well too.

Cars and slowly improving roads made it easier for nearby people to
shop and entertain themselves in other communities, so local merchants
vied to attract them. A Colchester group, headed by A. M. Walty, whose

hardware store was still the largest in the county, developed a monthly Booster Day featuring free prizes, band music, and of course, bargains. The first one, in February 1914, was a huge success, and editor Bayless expressed the revival of optimism that it fostered: "Colchester is not dead, even if some of her merchants have been sleeping, and a little publicity like a booster day once a month is going to awaken people to the fact that this is the best trading point in western Illinois."

Everyone certainly hoped so.

Another new business that made a difference was the town's first movie theater. Motion pictures—mostly documentaries like *Theodore Roosevelt in Africa* and early narrative efforts like *The Great Train Robbery*—had been shown at the opera house from time to time, starting in 1907. They were an exciting curiosity that drew increasing public interest, but after the opera house burned in 1910, that kind of entertainment was gone for a few years. It wasn't until 1913 that T. H. ("Tommy") Smith, the grandson of pioneer businessman A. J. Smith, remodeled a store on Market Street to create the 250-seat Princess Theatre.

Seldom were the townspeople so enthusiastic about a new business. Bayless predicted that the theater would "keep our people at home, where they will spend their money with our home merchants, as well as bring the country people to our city to trade," and to a large extent he was right. It helped Colchester strengthen its function as a farm-center community.

Bayless was so anxious to see the town make an economic comeback that he connected the ideal of community itself with the development of local trade as he spearheaded a "buy at home" campaign. Sometimes, as in December 1913, he sounded like a minister preaching the gospel of Colchester:

TRADE IN COLCHESTER

When you spend your Colchester-earned dollar in Colchester, you have a good chance of getting it back again. . . .

Cultivate the family spirit. Colchester is really a big family. Think, talk, act for Colchester. You ought to think that the town you live in is the best town on earth, because you live in it. Keep Colchester in your heart.

Let these words sink in deep. It is money in your pocket, prac-
ticing what is preached herein. The more you do to build up business in Colchester, the more business you will be able to do in
Colchester.

Begin every day right! Let your first resolution be, "I will spend
in Colchester the money I make in Colchester."

Although his immediate purpose was economic development, Bayless
was also reasserting the transcendent value of the town. As he said elsewhere in the same issue, buying at home was a way of saying, "I have
faith in Colchester."

Of course, the problem with promoting economic self-interest as the
highest virtue is that it does not automatically create a sense of community. In fact, it produces a culture devoted to making money and characterized by self-concern. By the summer of 1914 Bayless seemed to
realize that:

LOCALITY IS NOT COMMUNITY

A community is different from a locality. . . . In a locality it is
every fellow for himself and the devil take the hindmost. In a community it is every fellow for all the rest and all the rest for every
fellow. In a community there can not be any "tin can alley" or "dog
town." Things have got to come out right for the more unfortunate
folks.

Bayless was responding to a problem that everyone in Colchester
recognized: the slow deterioration of community. By his own definition,
the town was becoming a mere locality. Unfortunately that was the drift
of twentieth-century America.

As the economic picture brightened, baseball made a comeback.
Occasional games had been played at the turn of the century, but it
wasn't until 1904 that a regular schedule of games was developed. In
some years, however, lack of money was such a problem that the local
team played only a partial season. The pottery grounds, southeast of the
business district, became the new playing field in 1907, and a small
grandstand was built there, but attendance and financial support were
modest for several years.

The turning point came in 1910 when two of the finest ball players in the town's history emerged as leaders of the local team. One was a right-handed spitball pitcher named Ross Dark, and the other was a hard-hitting, left-handed catcher named Clarence ("Cat") Kipling. Together they led the Cyclones, as the team was then called, to nineteen victories out of twenty-three games. That was the best record in McDonough County.

As usual, nothing was more important than beating Macomb's team, the Potters, for the county seat remained Colchester's chief economic rival, and the two baseball teams symbolized that competition. Whenever Colchester won, the *Independent* gloated over the victory, as in July 1911:

MACOMB OUT-CLASSED!
SLAUGHTER OF THE INNOCENTS!
Potters Are Made to Look Like Schoolboys.

The Macomb Potters were overwhelmingly defeated last Sunday on the Colchester ground by a score of 20 to 6. It is no telling how many more runs would have been made, but the Colchester team got tired of running bases and allowed themselves to be put out.

The next year was even better. Colchester lost only one game—to Quincy, by a single run—and during that wonderful season the Cyclones also beat Macomb six times and defeated Galesburg as well. The following year was much the same, but they beat Quincy too.

Even if the townspeople were still struggling to regain their grip on the American promise, baseball made them feel like winners—at least on Sunday afternoons. And for Kelly Wagle, who loved to bet on the games, the second decade of the century brought some very rewarding days at the ball field.

Despite the highly successful revival of baseball, life in Colchester was a far cry from what it had been during the nineteenth century. The sense of community purpose and the feeling of interdependence were largely gone. The townspeople no longer felt connected by a common future. Instead they shared a significant past. The newspaper increasingly celebrated the town's older residents, those who had come there in the early days and had seen "the rise and fall of the great coal industry in Colchester."

The most significant spiritual leader of that era was Abram Newland, the old coal miner, war hero, store owner, coal and clay mine operator, and minister whose life seemed to recapitulate the history of the community. Then in his seventies, sporting bushy gray sidewhiskers and steel-rimmed spectacles, he was living on a farm west of town, near Tennessee, but he continued to preach at churches in Colchester and the surrounding countryside. He was a model of commitment to the common good. Beloved by the old families, he officiated at more funerals than any other minister in the county as the pioneers steadily passed away, and he wrote a short history of Methodism in the Colchester area. He understood the importance of local tradition, which he symbolized.

Newland was also the acknowledged leader of the Civil War veterans, the Grand Army of the Republic, and he frequently spoke at the annual Memorial Day services, held at the cemetery. In 1914, for example, he exhorted his listeners to cherish American ideals and to "honor the memory of those brave men who perished on the field of battle and respect the living grey-haired veterans whose marching line grows thinner every year." He was the voice of a fading generation.

The annual picnics were revived in 1909, as a function of the town's fraternal organizations, but they were no longer a ritual of community, evoking mutual concern and celebrating the struggle of local men. They were simply a summer entertainment, complete with an automobile parade, a balloon ascension, carnival games, and contests of all kinds. Some people picnicked in the city park, but there was no community meal, no inspirational speech, and not much renewal of the bonds that made Colchester a meaningful place.

Thanksgiving was changing too. In 1912 Bayless upbraided the townspeople for failing to maintain a local tradition, the community-wide Thanksgiving service: "It is deplorable that no arrangements were made this year for any kind of Thanksgiving service by any of the churches. It has been the custom in Colchester to have some kind of united religious meeting, but for some cause—neglect, we suppose—no arrangements have been made this year."

During the holidays church and family activities remained important, but the old custom of calling on neighbors and friends early in the new year was gradually discontinued. People stayed home, and their sense of integration with the community was no longer reaffirmed by socializing in small groups as the year began.

Of course, if they wanted to wish someone a happy new year, they could use the telephone, for by 1910 the townspeople had about 150 phones and nearby rural families had another 450. They were all part of a local system called the Farmers Telephone Company, which was busy developing connections to other nearby exchanges. Still, as the townspeople were linked by telephone, they tended to see less of each other.

There were other signs of a changing social consciousness too. Young people were not as constrained by the traditional moral code. In 1914 Bayless complained about what was going on in the evenings:

> There is a bunch of young fellows who have formed the habit of getting in their buggies along about dusk and driving all over town, speaking to every young female that they see, trying to get them to go buggy riding with them. . . . We have been witnesses to a number of these performances during the past few weeks, and it is being carried to such an extent that it is not safe for any respectable girl to be on the streets alone, without laying herself open to insult. . . . And we are sorry that we have some girls who encourage this kind of thing and are indirectly responsible for it.

Bayless was concerned not only about the behavior itself but about the loss of moral accountability to the community that made it possible.

With the end of large-scale coal mining, there were fewer jobs in town for boys, and both sexes were increasingly apt to stay in school. As adolescence became a longer process, the streets of the business district and the always-open depot became weekend meeting places for some of the town's younger generation. Peers became more influential than parents, and teenagers became a distinctive group whose values differed from those held by the rest of society.

In the absence of saloons, men and boys started hanging out at the pool halls, where they could smoke cigarettes, drink beer, play poker, and feed the slot machines. Only the cigarettes were legal.

As the anti-liquor movement crusaded against vice, women became even more central to the cause. They had long felt that suffrage was the key to social reform, and one state leader, Elizabeth K. Booth, chair of the Legislative Committee of the Illinois Equal Suffrage Association, said so in her well-received speech at the 1913 Colchester Fraternal Picnic. That year women won the right to vote in non-constitutional Illinois elections, and they soon began to have an enormous impact. Some towns voted in November 1913, and afterward the *Independent* commented on the contribution of women to the anti-saloon campaign:

RESULT OF WOMEN'S VOTES

The result of the women's vote in the recent elections in driving the saloons from several wet strongholds has given the anti-saloon forces in other towns great encouragement, and they are already planning for a strong fight at the municipal elections next April. At that time several hundred Illinois cities and villages will hold elections. In most of these, however, there will be no serious contest, as they are already "dry" as a result of the men's votes. In a few others that are now "wet," such as Galesburg and Bushnell, the fight will be strongly waged and is pretty sure to result in driving out the saloons. The prospect now is that within a few months the whisky trade in this part of Illinois will be limited to the drug stores and to importation from distant localities.

The article was right: at the spring 1914 election, 114 more Illinois townships went dry, including Galesburg, which had twenty saloons, and Bushnell, which had eight.

Ironically, the growing scarcity of liquor in some areas of the state increased the profits of the remaining saloon owners and liquor dealers, fostered widespread disregard for local laws, and wedded bootleggers to the force that would shape their future: the automobile.

By early 1914 Kelly owned his first car. The make is unknown, but whatever it was, it took him into a new phase of his life. He surely realized that he could use it to become a full-time bootlegger, and he undoubtedly expanded his liquor-selling operation.

From the very first Kelly was dedicated to speed, always driving above the limit in town and going as fast as road conditions would permit in the countryside. He commonly ignored stop signs, and if he was behind a slow car when the oncoming lane had traffic, he passed on the right, racing along the shoulder of the road. He drove with a determined recklessness, as if he were asserting his freedom to do as he pleased, like a child resisting parental authority.

As early as April 1915, he sped off the road going to nearby Tennessee and ended up with a bruised face, a dislocated shoulder, and two cracked ribs. And that was not his last accident.

It is not surprising that he loved the early automobile races, which were held at the Macomb fairgrounds every Fourth of July, starting in 1911. Like so many others, he was excited by the daring exploits of the drivers, who roared around the dirt track at speeds of more than forty miles an hour. As the *Macomb Journal* said in 1912, "It is the man who takes a chance who wins in the automobile races, and it is that display of nerve on the part of the drivers which arouses such interest."

For some of the townspeople in Colchester, Kelly's life soon held a similar attraction.

Unfortunately Uncle John Walley got sick in the spring of 1913 and died in the hospital in Macomb on June 16. He was only fifty-two, but his pancreas had become diseased, a condition that was probably aggravated by years of alcohol abuse. He was buried at Mt. Auburn, and because his widow was poor, Kelly paid for the headstone.

Meanwhile the mayor appointed a new marshal, former coal miner Charles Polonus. A tall, slim, balding man with a bushy mustache, Polonus was a drinker too, but he was committed to enforcing the law. Kelly was no longer immune from arrest.

There was increasing pressure to do something about the beer camps that appeared on the weekends, especially on Sunday afternoons. As Bayless said in the summer of 1914, "The Sunday observance in this city is getting to be pretty fierce, but instead of a day of rest it has become a day of hilarity and dissipation," and he concluded that "it is time for the officers of this city to get a little action on."

In the fall of 1914 the new marshal finally arrested Kelly. According to the *Macomb Journal,* he was charged with twenty-five counts of "selling liquor in anti-saloon territory." Polonus had apparently been told that Kelly was supplying liquor for a beer camp northwest of town and for private groups that met in rented rooms, so he watched those places in September and October, then made the arrest.

Kelly was put in the county jail but was soon free on bond. The details of the case are unknown, but it was difficult to prove that someone had sold liquor rather than given it to friends, which was not illegal. In the spring of 1915 the charges were dropped. The bootlegger was lucky again.

The Wagle case increased the determination of temperance crusaders to clean up the town. Evangelist Sadie McCoy Crank, who by then was loved by the churchgoing portion of the townspeople, came again for the fourth time to hold a revival, and she inspired her listeners, most of whom were female, to get out the vote at the forthcoming election. In April 1915 Mayor John O. Moon and most of his supporters were voted out, and a new, anti-liquor mayor and city council were voted in. The same ballot made it illegal to operate a pool hall in Colchester.

In the following August the city council passed a tough new liquor law that closed all the loopholes. Selling, giving, or transporting anything with alcohol in it was illegal in Colchester, as was gathering at any place to drink, under any circumstances.

The crusaders were finally in control.

World War I and the Bootlegger's Rise

Despite the long struggle to regain its faded promise, Colchester fostered an immense loyalty. The townspeople loved their town. They were sure it was a fine place to live, a community of people you could count on. Nevertheless, as World War I arrived and some residents did not conform, the second decade of the century brought rising tension and social discord.

It also brought the rise of the bootlegger. Devoted to the town but defiant of authority, he symbolized an emerging split in the local mind.

The Great War had an enormous impact, but not at first. When the fighting broke out in August 1914, the townspeople assumed that America would remain neutral. Still, they were horrified by the battle reports from Europe and fascinated by the new technology of war, including submarines and aerial bombing. Early in 1915 the Princess Theatre brought it all to Colchester in a four-reel documentary film promoted as a thrilling and gruesome spectacle:

WAR! WAR! WAR!
The first and only American Motion Pictures of
The Great European War

Soldiers in action, homes being burned, machine guns in operation, buildings blown up, dead and wounded soldiers being car-

ried from the trenches, etc. Reels direct from the blood-stained bat-
tlefields of Europe. Thursday, February 9.

In the spring of 1915, when the Germans used submarines to block-
ade the British Isles, there was deep concern in Colchester, where most
of the townspeople were British immigrants or the children of those
immigrants. And when a German submarine sank the British passenger
liner *Lusitania,* killing over one thousand people, there was outrage.

As the war dragged on indecisively, month after month, with millions
dead or wounded and countless others starving, sympathy for the British, the French, the Belgians, and the other Allies was expressed through
food and materials conservation and relief efforts. So, there was widespread emotional involvement in the war by April 1917, when President
Wilson urged Americans to embark on a great crusade and Congress
responded by declaring war on Germany.

One of the early supporters of the war was Colchester's mayor, Isaac
Newton Boyd, a bank cashier who was elected that spring. A red-faced,
hook-nosed, middle-aged man, Boyd reflected the patriotic idealism of
the period and encouraged young men to join the Allied cause. Although his own son, Wayne, declined to volunteer, a number of Colchester men enlisted and left for training camps that spring. Others were
drafted during July and August, and the conscription process continued into 1918.

The operation of the draft, along with reports of the massive casual-
ties in France, frightened many young men and their families—so much
so that Bayless, who was also an ardent supporter of the war, tried to
assuage local fears with a series of editorials in the summer of 1917.
However, at least one of them, which appeared in mid-August, probably had the opposite impact:

> There are a number of people in every community who are
> working on the fears of men who are being drafted, and are trying
> to scare them about their chances of returning from the war. This
> should be stopped, as it works on the feelings of the young men
> who have to go, so that when they enter the training camps they
> feel as though they are as good as dead.
>
> These men who worry our prospective soldiers should be dealt
> with severely. Records show that the losses in France are not so

great in proportion to the numbers engaged as those at Gettysburg, and yet look at the thousands who survived Gettysburg. . . .

There have been terrible losses, and will be, but not one out of ten will be killed, and probably not one out of four wounded.

The involvement of local men spurred war support activities in the community. Some townspeople bought Liberty Bonds and urged their neighbors to do the same. Many joined the local Red Cross chapter, which soon had more than 300 members, including Beulah Wagle. She and other women made thousands of bandages and face masks for army medical supplies. The *Independent* encouraged young men to enlist, and the Princess Theatre showed pro-war propaganda films like *In the Wake of the Huns* and *The Kaiser: The Beast of Berlin.*

Although the war brought many people together in a common cause, it also fostered resentment. In June 1917 Bayless acknowledged that "many are not yet convinced that we should have butted into this trouble," but he also criticized people who did not actively support the war. "The 'slacker' is not alone disloyal to his country and to his flag, but he is disloyal to his neighbors and friends. They are doing their part, and when he fails to do his, it heaps a greater burden upon them. What are you doing to help? If you are a 'slacker,' folks are thinking things about you. Get busy at something." The editorial was a blatant attempt to make patriotic activism the measure of community acceptance, and it reflected the views of many townspeople. In the spring of 1918 some families had their homes smeared with yellow paint because others felt they did not support the war.

Anxiety about the conflict in Europe was damaging the spirit of community in Colchester.

The war years also brought irregular economic conditions. In 1914 bad weather resulted in poor crops for the second year in a row. Although yields were up the following year, cattle in the county were ravaged by foot-and-mouth disease, which greatly reduced livestock shipping. The war soon strengthened the economy, as American exports to Europe reached record levels, but government regulation kept coal prices low, making it difficult for miners to get ahead. After America joined the war, people bought less, and some small businesses went into a slump. At the same time, the cost of living was shooting upward at an unprecedented rate. All this made it harder for Colchester to make an economic comeback.

The most helpful development was a new company to manufacture flue linings and other clay products. Financed by A. W. Gates and other investors from Monmouth, the Gates Fire Clay Company was constructed south of town, and it opened in 1917. Soon it employed some three dozen men and boys, most of whom worked for low wages—mining, mixing, and cutting clay, moving ware into the kilns, and shipping it out.

Because the new factory needed coal, a new shaft mine was opened southwest of town. It was operated by the Baird brothers, who had expanded their mining operation to include coal as well as clay.

During the war Colchester was slowly changing from a nineteenth-century town to a twentieth-century one. Perhaps nothing symbolized the old way of life, with its slow pace and strong sense of community, as clearly as the old white-painted hitching rail that stretched along Depot and Market Streets. It was still used by country folks on Saturday nights, when they came in their buggies and wagons. But cars were common too, and their cost was still declining. As more of them appeared on the streets, the pace of life in Colchester began to quicken, and townspeople who might once have spoken to each other simply passed by with a wave.

In 1915 the town's first gas pump was installed in front of the Walty Hardware Store, which had once sold more buggies than any other dealer in the county.

As things began to change, there was an upsurge of nostalgia for "the old days" when the townspeople had enjoyed a strong sense of community and life in Colchester had been a promising venture. One expression of that interest in the past came in the form of letters to the newspaper recalling the town's early history.

The first and most important of them was a long letter by pioneer John Pearson, published in two parts under the title "Colchester of Yesterday" in January 1916. Pearson, then seventy-four, had come west with his parents in 1853, and he had witnessed the opening of the early drift mines, the formation of the first coal company, the coming of the railroad, and the founding of the community. Those were the events that had ordered the world of the townspeople, giving Colchester a purpose and determining how life would evolve there. They functioned in the local mind like a myth of origin, sanctioning the way things were.

To Pearson and other long-time residents, the community was a heroic enterprise, and despite the recent economic setbacks, its history was an American success story. As he put it, "From a small business conducted in a little frame building, I have seen the mercantile district grow in Colchester until we have as fine business houses here . . . as any city of our size in the state." In a time of change and uncertainty, his recollection was an expression of faith in, and allegiance to, the community.

Significantly, when characterizing the nineteenth-century coal miners, Pearson mentioned their social concern: "The coal industry continued to thrive for years, and many are the miners who have come and gone in the meantime; some were rough and uncouth, perhaps, but nearly all were good at heart and always ready to help the needy and care for the sick." Like many others in town, Pearson revered the local past because it reflected a tradition of economic development and meaningful community values.

Another old resident, Paulina Vest, who had come with her parents in 1858, recalled when "the new town of Colchester was booming, and . . . the mines were running full blast and attracting many people to this place." Her October 1920 letter to the *Independent* portrays the Chester House, run by her father, as "the social center of the community," where the townspeople partied and danced and "the rich and the poor, the high and the low," were always welcome. Like many others who feared that local residents were drawing farther apart, she idealized the old close-knit coal town.

Another expression of that concern was the Pleasant Valley Club, founded in the summer of 1917 by a group of Colchester businessmen. Its stated purpose was "to stock the creek with fish" at the site of the old mill, which had been torn down in 1909, and to turn that area into "a park or pleasure resort" where people could boat, fish, swim, and picnic. But it was just as obviously an effort to reassert community by providing "a common meeting place for all" on a spot of ground that symbolized the town's heritage and the common experience in Colchester. As the club's organizational statement showed, remembrance created a kind of spiritual community that transcended the recent changes:

The club has been named the Pleasant Valley Club on account of its being on the old Pleasant Valley Mill site, and what name could be more appropriate than this? What a world of pleasant memories the name calls up to all of the old residents in this locality. There probably is not a man, woman, or child who lived here years ago who has not fished, swam, or fallen into Crooked Creek at the old Pleasant Valley Mill. The associations of childhood, of old neighbors and friends, many of them having passed out of this life, are recalled at the name. Pleasant memories cluster around the old mill, and many of the Colchester folks who have wandered away and are scattered unto all parts of the globe are sending back requests for membership in the Pleasant Valley Club.

Clearly membership was a kind of symbolic participation in the old community, so it is not surprising that the club, which started with seventeen member-families, had some two hundred by the end of the decade.

One long-time resident who struggled to maintain a place in the changing community was Arch Wagle. The war years were the most difficult period of his life, except for his final illness. By 1915 he was substantially blind, so he sold his livery business early that year. However, he remained in his shack by the park, where he sold snacks and soda pop. Known as The Blue Goose, the little lunch stand was painted light blue and had a long side window with a hinged wooden cover that could be lowered to make an outside counter. He also bought a popcorn wagon—a small red-painted enclosure on wheels—that he operated uptown in the late afternoon and evening.

The townspeople understood his situation and tried to buy from him now and again, just to be neighborly. Nevertheless, because of his poor eyesight Arch could barely function by himself, and spiteful boys took advantage of his blindness to steal candy from him at The Blue Goose.

Arch also missed his family in Galesburg, but he had too much pride to be dependent on Alice, and he was glad that she could make a home for Glenn and Geneva at the boarding house. Friends helped him write weekly letters to her and then read to him her replies.

Late in the summer of 1915 Arch had a run of bad luck. The September 16 issue of the *Independent* carried two articles about his troubles:

HOUSE CATCHES ON FIRE

Last Thursday evening about eight o'clock the fire alarm was sounded and the citizens rushed out to see what the trouble was, and found that the little building occupied by Arch Wagle at the southeast corner of the park had caught on fire, presumably from a gasoline stove.

The fire department made a nice run and arrived at the fire in short order, but the fire had been put out by a bucket brigade before they arrived.

The origin of the fire is unknown, as there was no one there when the fire was discovered.

SOME BAD STORMS

Last Wednesday afternoon a bad windstorm swept over this city, blowing things around and scaring people into their cyclone cellars, and it was followed by a hard rain. Friday afternoon another hard wind and rainstorm passed over this vicinity, blowing down trees and outhouses, and doing considerable damage.

During this terrible storm the wind blew the roof off the People's State Bank. . . .

Arch Wagle was in his popcorn and peanut wagon across from the Terrill and Brothers store near the well, and the wind blew the wagon over. Arch, being blind, was buffeted around by the wind and was at the mercy of the storm until he was finally rescued by Dick Parnall.

Everyone in town felt sorry for Arch, who had been making a heroic effort to be self-supporting. As Bayless put it, "Arch is seemingly getting all that is coming to him. Burnt out one day and blown away the next, it looks like providence is handing it out pretty hard to a blind man."

When Alice heard about his troubles, she came to see him and urged him to return to the boarding house in Galesburg, but he refused. Arch had been independent since he was a teenager, and he knew that moving from Colchester would mean nothing but dependence and despair.

Shortly afterward Kelly moved to Chicago. His reasons for leaving town are unclear, but he had his own troubles in 1915. Early in the year he was tried on the charge of receiving stolen property. Four automobile wheels and tires had been taken from a railroad car by two young men and later hidden in his barn. The crime was part of an upsurge of theft, focused especially on automobile parts, that plagued the community during the war years. In this case, when the prosecutor failed to prove that Kelly knew the wheels and tires were stolen, he was acquitted.

In September of that same year Kelly was involved in a fight at the roller rink that led to charges against him for assault. It was a seriocomic affair that started with itch powder, according to a front-page article in *The Macomb Eagle:*

A COLCHESTER CASE

A trial was held Saturday before Justice A. W. Falkenthal to establish the facts in the case of the State vs. Henry Wagle of Colchester. The latter, on complaint of James M. Guy of Colchester, was charged with assault and battery on the person of Dewey Guy, son of the complainant.

The trouble occurred at a dance held at the Colchester rink two weeks ago, as a result of someone's having placed itch powder on a number of the attendants at the dance.

Ed Guy charged Henry Wagle with being guilty of the trick, and Dewey Guy also directly accused Wagle. An altercation occurred about which opinions differed widely on the part of the witnesses.

Glen Guy, Dewey Guy, M. T. Wayland, Homer Cain, Vergil Delbridge, Harry Hedrick, Beryl Dorethy, and Mrs. Ed Bayliss were called as witnesses for the complainant. All of those who were in a position to see what was going on corroborated Dewey Guy, who said he was struck by Wagle three or four times.

On the other hand, Bert Vorhees, John Cary, Arthur Goldsberry, Aldo Dorethy, Mrs. Effie King, Cecil Strickland, Mrs. Marie Wayland, and Rollo Reynolds either did not see the trouble or insisted that no blows whatever were struck. . . .

Henry Wagle denied that he was guilty of disseminating the itch powder or that he struck Guy. He explained that in walking toward Guy he was merely trying to explain to Guy and reason with him in regard to the itch powder accusation. . . .

The jury found the defendant not guilty.

Kelly had of course assaulted Guy. No one would have taken him to court or could have provided witnesses for something that had never occurred. But he was lucky once again. And as trivial as it was, the itch powder assault case revealed some things about the twenty-nine-year-old part-time bootlegger: his hunger for attention, his readiness to fight, his dependence on friends, his willingness to lie in court.

By the time this case was reported in the early fall, some people in town clearly didn't like Kelly, but that was surely not his main reason for leaving Colchester. It was, rather, what Chicago had to offer. The big city by the lake was a wide open place of unlimited opportunity, and for that reason it had been drawing ambitious, self-reliant men and women from small towns since before the turn of the century.

Because of his railroad background, Kelly got a job at the Clearing Freight Yards, a new railroad center located southwest of Chicago at the edge of the city. He apparently rented a nearby apartment. Kelly surely did not want to stay in railroad work, but the job gave him a foothold in the city and a chance to find other possibilities.

At that time Chicago was already notoriously corrupt and crime-ridden, and it appeared to lack any real sense of community. In many ways it was the opposite of Colchester—or at least, that's how the townspeople always regarded it. As the *Independent* put it in 1912, Chicago was "a hotbed of political, social, and moral anarchy."

Also, as every temperance crusader and saloon supporter knew, Chicago remained defiantly wet while most areas of Illinois and other midwestern states were going dry. In 1917 more than two-thirds of the saloons in Illinois and most of the state's beer and whisky distributors were located in Cook County, in or near the city. For bootleggers throughout the Midwest, wherever prohibition forces were having an impact, Chicago was the best source of their stock in trade.

Soon it was rumored in Colchester that Kelly Wagle was hauling liquor from Chicago to various downstate communities, and even to distant cities such as Des Moines and Omaha in states that had recently passed an anti-liquor law. In the parlance of the times, he was a "rumrunner."

Of course, there was a certain romantic appeal in that kind of work. At a time when most people seldom traveled, Kelly was always going somewhere, and because of his secret cargo, every journey was an adventure.

Beulah was not anxious to leave Colchester. By 1916 she had a number of friends there, as well as relatives in the next county, and she didn't know anyone in Chicago. She remained behind until February and then reluctantly left on the train to join her husband.

As one might expect, she didn't like the city and was soon begging Kelly to go home. It didn't take long for him to give in. In April they returned to Colchester, moving back into their unsold white-frame house on North Street, just east of the Christian Church.

Kelly may have also decided that he could do just as well in Colchester as in Chicago. Once he knew where to get liquor from a distributor in the city who didn't care whether buyers had a license to resell it, all he had to do was expand his clientele in western Illinois. That's what he started to do.

To appear respectable, he developed a business that might explain to the authorities how he earned a living and why he drove around so much. In April the *Independent* started running an ad for "Kellie's Auto Livery." He had decided to provide taxi service—in a town of 1,400 people.

In a sense, Kelly's Chicago experience was the key to his rebirth as a bootlegger, which took place during World War I. Like a questing hero, he had gone to the great city, gained what he needed to succeed, and then returned to his own community, where his mysterious connection with Chicago gave him a certain stature. While remaining one of the townspeople, he was also associated with modern urban society. And indeed, for the rest of his life he was a man who moved back and forth between two different worlds, the city and the small town.

As the Colchester authorities moved to enforce the anti-liquor law, men who opposed it felt increasingly alienated from the community. That was especially true of younger men, who never quite bonded with the older townspeople as their fathers had in the nineteenth century, and who felt intense anxiety because America had joined the Great War and they were susceptible to the draft. Among them drinking became an act of resistance to an older generation that seemed to be pressing for conformity, and Kelly Wagle, who made resistance to authority a way of life, became increasingly popular.

In July 1917 a certain Roy Goldsberry was convicted of selling liquor and fined $100, a sizable sum at that time. It was the first real test of Colchester's 1915 liquor law, and it was hailed by the crusaders as the start of a much-needed crackdown.

In an impassioned speech to the city council a few days later, Mayor

Isaac Boyd made it clear that bootleggers were betraying the community and the American cause in a time of national crisis. "In spite of the fact that we are in war and every man is asked to do his best . . . we have a bunch of people laying around Colchester who are no good to the city, no good to their families, and no good to themselves," he said, adding that "there ought to be a way of compelling these people to work or be sent to the front." He called for cleaning up the community, and according to Bayless, "The Council, to a man, assured him that they were behind him on the proposition, and told him to use all the money in the treasury to stop the bootlegging."

As the mayor's speech also suggests, the social commitment and work ethic of the older generation were not shared by some of the younger men in town. Coal mining no longer offered a secure, respected place in the community, and other jobs, too, seemed to hold little promise, so they felt alienated from the life of the town. Unable to recall the years of pioneer hope or booming growth, they were living a different cultural story. For them, drinking was an expression of diminished expectations.

As the war continued, the townspeople had other concerns. Dead and wounded soldiers became a reality in 1918. The first man from Colchester to die was Lieutenant Raymond Wakefield, a flyer who was killed on March 11. His funeral a few weeks later was attended by hundreds of people. Before the war ended, seven more young men from Colchester died from wounds or disease.

There was also strict conservation of food and fuel, including meatless Fridays and gasless Sundays. Wasting anything or burning wood, rags, or paper was regarded as a betrayal of the boys "over there." Although large quantities of coal were diverted for the war effort, leaving it in short supply, Colchester did not benefit significantly, because prices were tightly regulated and the remaining mines were small-scale operations. Besides, in 1917 the C. B. & Q. extended a line into the southern Illinois coal fields, which supplied an increasing share of the regional market.

The most difficult experience of the war years for the community as a whole was the great Spanish flu epidemic of 1918. No one knows precisely where it began, but by the spring of that year the virulent flu strain flourished in the military camps of Europe and the United States, killing thousands of American soldiers and sailors. As it spread around the globe, millions of other Americans contracted the disease. Raging fevers and pounding headaches often led to more severe symptoms, especially hemorrhaging in the lungs. In the worst cases victims turned pale and clammy, like wet ashes, and slowly drowned in their own bodily fluids. And oddly enough, most of those who died were young adults.

In Colchester there were about five hundred cases of the flu by mid-October, when the *Independent* reported on the local outbreak:

THE INFLUENZA

In Colchester and vicinity there are hundreds of cases, the doctors being so busy that they are nearly worn out looking after the sick, and there is apparently no check on the disease. The State Board of Health does not hold out much encouragement. . . .

In Colchester all public gatherings have been called off. This includes the closing of picture shows, theatres, or other places of amusement, Sunday school and church services, public schools, etc. A request has been issued for all children to stay on their own premises, and for all men to do the same as much as possible.

Every home was filled with anxiety and fear. Before it was all over, more than a dozen local residents were dead, including the high school principal and the only son and youngest daughter of Mayor Isaac Boyd. Nationwide more than 600,000 people died between the fall of 1918 and the following spring.

Except for Glenn, who was in the army, and Joe, who remained in Galesburg, the Wagle family was back in Colchester when the epidemic started. Alice and Geneva had returned in the spring of 1918 so that they could take care of Arch, whose health was failing. By that time he was a frail, balding man with a bushy mustache, and he walked slowly with a cane. Also, Geneva had married a man named Walter Booth, who worked for the railroad in Galesburg, but for reasons now unknown she was already separated from him and was seeking a divorce. That too may have encouraged the return to Colchester, where Geneva eventually re-assumed her maiden name. In any case, the Wagles moved back into their old house on Coal Street, and Alice worked as a cook in a restaurant near the depot.

The family in Colchester managed to avoid the flu, but Joe and Luella contracted it, along with everyone else at the Wagle boarding house in

Galesburg, so Alice had to return there in October to run the place while her son and daughter-in-law recovered.

It was during the great flu epidemic that Kelly started building a reputation for neighborly concern. Because the Kings lived on Coal Street across the hollow from Vinegar Hill and ran the brickyard where Kelly had worked as a teenager and young man, he had known the family for years. He was especially close to Bennie and Joe King, the twin sons of Moses, who had been operating the brickyard since their father's death. In November of that fateful year, Bennie contracted the flu, and while he was laid up, Kelly stepped in to help the family—running errands, working at the brickyard, and looking in on his sick friend. Unfortunately the flu led to pneumonia, and Bennie died in December. During that same period, Joe King's thirteen-year-old son, LaVerne, shot himself in the foot while hunting along Crooked Creek. After he crawled back home, bleeding severely, it was Kelly who put him into a car and raced to the hospital in Macomb, where the wound was treated.

Thus it was that the Kings became the first of many people in Colchester who felt personally indebted to Kelly Wagle and regarded him as a model of old-fashioned neighborliness. To them, nothing else that he did seemed to matter.

Although the epidemic persisted in Colchester for many weeks, it started to decline in November, and by the time the war ended on the eleventh, many local residents were ready to celebrate. That evening the townspeople poured into the business district, and others came from the countryside, until the streets and sidewalks were jammed, and they all rejoiced together, as the *Independent* later reported.

CELEBRATED IN COLCHESTER

Did we celebrate in Colchester Monday? Well, we would rather guess we did, and where all the people came from that were here we cannot figure out, for the town was full to overflowing. . . .

It was arranged to have the bells ring, the whistles blow, and all kinds of noise start at eight o'clock, and have a concentrated effort for fifteen minutes—and we did have.

At eight fifteen a parade started from the city building and marched all over town. It was a big parade and consisted of floats of various kinds, people on foot, on horseback, in autos, and ev-

ery old way. Several of the floats were well gotten up and represented the Kaiser being done away with in many ways. . . .

After the parade came the singing of popular songs by the audience, led by a male quartette. Then followed the big bonfire out
on the railroad right of way.

It was a big time alright, and everyone went home feeling better.

The community-wide celebration was an attempt to exorcise the anxieties that had built up inside people during the war, and it was apparently successful.

But the postwar period brought new versions of old problems. As
inflation skyrocketed and the wartime strike ban was lifted, labor organizations took collective action. During 1919 more than four million
workers participated in strikes, some of which resulted in violence. In
Colchester the low wages at the Gates Fire Clay Company and the King
brickyard led to the formation of a local union, with the help of organizers from the American Federation of Labor. When the plant owners
refused to recognize the union, the men went on strike.

After that dispute ended in the fall, many local miners joined in a
nationwide strike, shutting down most of the town's drift mines. For the
first time in Colchester's history, the townspeople were confronted with
a shortage of coal, as Bayless pointed out in November:

> The great struggle between capital and labor is on, and over
> 400,000 coal miners in the United States are now on strike. In the
> great coal fields of Illinois, Indiana, Pennsylvania, and other states
> there is not a pound of coal being mined. Thousands of people will
> suffer for want of heat if the situation is not cleared up in a few
> days. . . . Colchester will not be affected quite so badly as many
> localities where coal has to be shipped in, but even here there is
> not enough coal mined to supply the local demand, and already
> there are many coal houses empty. Should a severe winter come
> on soon, there will be a great shortage here.

For lack of coal the Gates Fire Clay Company and the King brickyard
were shut down again, throwing more men out of work, and some stores
reduced their business hours. The shortage affected railroads too, and
soon four of the trains that had been running to Colchester suspended

operations. Fortunately the national strike was called off in mid-December, so massive suffering was avoided, but 1919 was still a difficult year for many of the townspeople.

Of course, those who kept their coal banks operating despite the strike did very well for a short time, as anxious people bid against one another for the scarce loads. Before it was all over, the town was full of resentment—against the strikers, against those who refused to strike, and against operators and haulers who sold to other towns despite the local shortage.

In Colchester, coal mining no longer fostered a sense of community, and high trust was increasingly hard to maintain.

Appropriately, perhaps, the year of the great coal shortage and the strike also marked the end of the Miners' Friendly Society, which disbanded on July 9. The group had fewer than a hundred members then, rendering the death benefit of little value, and they were mostly older men, many of whom no longer worked in the mines, so the great sense of mutual support in the face of common danger had slowly faded.

The fall of 1919 also witnessed a bitter clash over expansion of the high school. For several years some townspeople had wanted to create a high school district that would extend into the countryside and, with that larger tax base, build a new four-year school. Others were afraid of the expense involved. A vote on the issue in 1913 resulted in sound defeat of the proposition. By 1919, however, women were voting in local elections, and they generally favored the plan. As a result, a vote that October, in which almost every eligible citizen cast a ballot, gave a stunning victory to the proponents. A followup vote then approved the purchase of a site and plans for construction.

But the opponents refused to give in. They challenged the high school decision in court on the grounds that women didn't really have the right to vote. Defeated in the circuit court, they appealed to the Illinois Supreme Court, which at first decided in their favor. Then the Illinois legislature passed the "validating act," affirming that all such votes by women were, and had been, legal, so the Supreme Court reversed itself.

The larger high school district was established, but opposition to it continued well into the 1920s as other votes were taken, and animosity returned like a chronic disease. A new building was not constructed for half a century.

While all that was going on, the liquor problem worsened, despite the fact that national Prohibition was finally enacted. The Eighteenth Amendment, prohibiting the manufacture, sale, and transportation of liquor, was passed by Congress in 1917 and ratified by two-thirds of the states, including Illinois, by January 1919. It wasn't slated to become part of the Constitution until the following January, but a wartime emergency act prohibited the selling of liquor as of July 1, 1919, making that the magic date when the great change in American life would begin.

Temperance crusaders such as Bayless of the *Colchester Independent* displayed an enormous naïveté about what prohibition would mean for the country:

THE LIQUOR SITUATION

After next July no liquor can be sold or transported or imported, and the nation will be bone dry. . . . This will end all temperance fights, temperance literature, temperance legislation, temperance sermons, and drunkenness. It will be a great boost toward the millennium. Poor old booze!

Anxious to help enforce the new liquor law, Bayless ran for police magistrate, and he was elected.

In contrast, the soldiers from Colchester started returning early in 1919, and some were even more defiant of local values, including temperance, than the young men who had stayed home. After two years and more of doing whatever they pleased while off duty, they no longer felt accountable to family and community, so they caroused with old friends and patronized the bootleggers.

Among the several dozen young veterans in Colchester was Bert ("Cody") Boyd, who became a notorious boozer and ne'er-do-well, much to the chagrin of his uncle, Mayor Isaac Boyd. Another one was Monte Duncan, a diminutive auto mechanic who was eventually jailed for persistent drunken driving. Still another was Fred Wayland, a coal miner who soon turned to bootlegging himself. All three were in occasional trouble with the police.

Perhaps the most well-known veteran was Abner ("Scabby") Shields, a handsome, athletic, twenty-four-year-old who had been a flight instructor during the war and who afterward did barnstorming exhibitions. Bayless reflected his activities in a September 1919 article:

DRIVING AEROPLANE

Lieutenant Abner Shields of this city has been pretty busy during the past ten days, driving the Roy Pearce aeroplane at Macomb, teaching Mr. Pearce to drive it, carrying passengers, and doing exhibition flying.

Several afternoons at Macomb they have made flights, and Lieutenant Shields has put on some of the most spectacular flying that has been done in this section this year.

He has also carried a number of people who wished to ride, and they have done a good business at $1 per minute.

They have made exhibition flights at Swan Creek and other places . . . and expect to do a considerable business this fall.

Shields was a talented flyer who thrilled the crowds with his dives and barrel rolls. According to an article about him that appeared shortly after the war, his "aerial gymnastics caused many in the crowds to gasp occasionally and wonder if such things could really be possible." A much-admired daredevil, he once bragged that he would fly through a barn if they opened the doors on both ends. Unfortunately the former lieutenant was also an alcoholic, whose flying under the influence gave a new dimension to the concept of reckless youth, so his partnership with Pearce—who later founded the county's first airport—eventually came to an end.

As one might expect, Shields was a friend of Kelly Wagle, who undoubtedly supplied him with liquor as the dark cloud of Prohibition slowly settled over the nation.

Of course, it was difficult to clamp down on local heroes, but Bayless, without referring specifically to the soldiers, called for strict enforcement of the liquor law: "The 'lid' is being pried off very rapidly in Colchester, and if the officials do not get busy very soon, it's going to be a question of the Vigilance Committee. There is a complaint that liquor is being sold indiscriminantly and that even men meet the train here and solicit the business of thirsty-looking individuals. . . . There has been plenty of drunkenness and disorderly behavior."

The rising tension over bootlegging also manifested itself in other ways. A 1918 poem in *The Independent,* for example, was clearly a warning to those who made a business of violating the liquor laws:

THE BOOTLEGGER

His career is short, his way is hard,
And men are on his track.
He is gobbled up at unawares,
For the law is most exact.
They hunt him high, they hunt him low,
They keep hot on his trail.
They catch him up and get his dough
And sock him into jail.

Matters reached a high pitch in February 1919 when someone posted a disturbing notice on a downtown fence: "Will the people in a town of 1500 sit with folded hands and watch a moonshine still in operation right before their eyes?" Rumors began to fly about who it might refer to, and some people even asserted that when the wind was right, they could smell the still in operation. As the newspaper later reported, the anti-liquor crusaders "were for organizing a posse and scouring every nook and corner of the town until the pernicious violator of the law was found and prosecuted."

But it turned out that Tommy Smith, the owner of the Princess Theatre, had posted the sign as a novel way to promote an upcoming film, Fatty Arbuckle's slapstick comedy *The Moonshiners.* The idea worked, but the public outcry showed that liquor violations in Colchester were no laughing matter.

The postwar period was a good time for Kelly Wagle. Because of his Chicago connections and trips to northern Kentucky, he had the best stock of liquor in McDonough County, and because he was willing to go anywhere to sell it, he had new customers in nearby towns like Macomb, LaHarpe, Blandinsville, Webster, Fountain Green, Carthage, Tennessee, and Plymouth. Liquor had become more expensive too. When sold legally, before July 1, it carried a new high excise tax ($4.80 per gallon for whisky), and of course, when it was sold illegally, in dry communities, it was costly because it was scarce. The bootlegger was starting to make good money.

He was also starting to race horses. Kelly had gone to the racetrack in Galesburg when he was there working for the railroad, and after his accident he had traveled to races in Illinois, Iowa, and Missouri with his uncle, John Walley, who owned two racehorses late in his life. Aside from the horse that pulled his pottery wagon and buggy, Kelly had owned a couple of ponies as far back as 1913. He didn't race them; he simply liked horses. In the summer of 1914 one of his ponies got into the newspaper when it jumped a fence and escaped, getting as far as Dallas City, thirty miles away, before it was eventually caught.

After buying his first car in 1914, Kelly had no use for the buggy that had once belonged to his father, or for the horse that had pulled it, but he kept them anyway for a few years. Finally, in August 1918, he put a brief ad in the *Independent:* "I have a horse, harness, and buggy for sale. Henry Wagle." Done when his bootlegging career was on the rise, that transaction symbolized his break with the world of his father.

Kelly also had a Shetland pony that he allowed little children to ride and that pulled a two-wheeled cart they could sit in. He was always interested in children and always kind to them. But in the summer of 1919 he put another ad in the newspaper: "For sale. Shetland pony, 6 years old, sound and gentle for children.—Henry Wagle." After that the only horses he kept were for racing. For a time they were stabled in his own barn, and a man named Earl ("Chiny") Rhodes groomed and exercised them. Later he kept them at the county fairgrounds in Macomb, where there was a half-mile track they could run on.

The first horse that made money for Kelly, and the one that really drew him into racing, was a brown-faced white pony named Sparkle, purchased in 1918 and often kept at the farm of his old friend Chick Hocker, southeast of town. By August of the following year it was winning races at nearby county fairs and getting some newspaper attention:

WAGLE PONY WINS RACES

"Sparkle," the white pony belonging to Henry Wagle of this city, was over at LaHarpe last week at the fair and cleaned up in the races nicely, and demonstrated that it was some runner.

On Friday there was a special purse of $40 put up for a race between it and the Davis pony of Blandinsville. The betting, it is said, especially on the part of the Blandinsville bunch, was pretty spirited, but the Wagle pony took the lead from the start, and the Davis pony never had a look in at any time.

On Saturday, in a race with all girl riders, with Nellie McConnell riding Sparkle, it again won out against three other ponies in
a spirited and well-ridden race.

By that time, largely because of his car and horses, Kelly's personal
property tax assessment was $102, putting him in the upper quarter of
Colchester taxpayers. In contrast, Arch Wagle's assessment for 1919 was
only $12.

As Kelly became increasingly successful, he became more well respected. People admired a man who could make good money, drive a
new car, and own a few horses while others in town were struggling. And
if he broke the law by selling liquor where it was illegal, well, a lot of
people did that. He knew how to get ahead—that was for sure. And to
increasing numbers of people, that was what really counted. In Colchester, as in much of postwar America, virtue was no longer the price of
acceptance.

Also, as his bootlegging operation grew and he saw that people admired him, Kelly's self-image began to change. He was not just a young
man on the make; he thought of himself as a smart operator who could
always outwit the law and a daring individualist who did whatever he
wanted—and was highly regarded for doing it. He was transforming his
life, advancing in the direction of his dreams like a Horatio Alger hero,
and his new identity was confirmed every time he made a sale to some
grateful customer. After the defeats and disappointments of the previous decade, Kelly seemed to have control of his life, and he must have
been thrilled by the opportunities that anti-liquor legislation provided.

Unfortunately for her, Beulah did not support Kelly's new identity.
During the war years she repeatedly asked him to stop bootlegging, and
according to a later newspaper account, she even had her father talk to
him about it. But all the pressure simply turned him away from her. Long
before the end of the decade, she must have realized that breaking the
law had become a way of life for Kelly, and he wasn't going to change.

The Omaha Mystery Girl

Postwar America had a growing fascination with sex and violence that was fed by films and newspapers. It seemed as if things long repressed had suddenly surged to the surface, and even rural and small-town people were affected.

Perhaps the most popular movie of that era in Colchester was *Woman and the Law,* shown in the winter and spring of 1919. The story of a desperate woman who murdered her husband, it was "based on the sensational Jack DeSaulles case, the most interesting domestic tragedy ever known in New York," as the publicity stated in the pages of the *Independent.* The Princess Theatre was packed to the doors.

Later that year McDonough County had its own sensational murder case, which was followed with enormous interest by readers of the *Independent* and other county newspapers. A physician named George Alverson, who practiced in the village of Sciota, and a woman named Alice Clugston, who lived in Bushnell, were arrested in August and charged with poisoning her husband. The most damning evidence was a series of love letters written by the doctor to Mrs. Clugston. Many of the letters were published in the newspapers during the trial, and everyone in the county read them, talked about the case, and rendered a verdict. Early in 1920 the lovers were convicted and sent to the state penitentiary at Joliet.

The people of Colchester, like others in the county, viewed the Alverson-Clugston case as an example of the shocking evil that modern selfish values could foster, but at least justice was done and the moral order in McDonough County was reaffirmed. Ironically, late in 1919 a Colchester couple was involved in a far more sensational murder case—one of the most disturbing and mysterious crimes of the era—but the townspeople knew nothing about it.

Throughout his marriage to Beulah, Kelly continued to take an interest in other women. They were important psychological support for a man who craved admiration. His frequent trips out of town often included female companionship—and probably sexual relationships.

One of his women was a redhead named May Thornburg, who lived in a nearby town and who apparently spent time with him off and on for several years. Nothing else is known about her.

By late in the decade Kelly and Beulah often quarreled over his women and his bootlegging. On more than one occasion he beat her, so she often thought about leaving him, but she was afraid of what he might do. According to a later interview with her father, Beulah discussed the situation with her sister and once remarked, "He told me that if I ever double-crossed him, he would follow me, no matter where I went, and find me and kill me."

She was locked into an abusive relationship and felt that any attempt to get out of it would end in death. Partly for that reason, she sent Pauline, who was then a teenager, to live permanently with her parents.

By 1919 the most important woman in Kelly's life was Blanche Loop, of Carthage. She was an attractive young widow, twenty-four years old, with blond hair, blue eyes, and a lovely smile. Like Ruth Jones and Beulah McConnell, she was also poor and desperate.

Blanche came from an old Carthage family. Her great-grandfather, Squire Davis, had been sheriff of Hancock County in the 1850s and then circuit clerk until his death in 1866. His son, Andrew Jackson Davis, also served as circuit clerk, during the 1870s, but he didn't do well at that job and spent most of his life working as a laborer. He was well respected but had a meager income. In 1881 his only daughter, Dora, married a cabinetmaker named James Swain and moved to nearby Hamilton. The

Swains eventually had five children, the oldest of whom was Blanche, born in 1895.

Swain became an alcoholic and eventually worked as little as possible. Consequently, the family faced enormous hardship. Early in the new century the Swains were separated, and Dora returned to her father's home in Carthage, leaving her two sons but bringing her three daughters. That was where Blanche spent most of her childhood. It was a stable but impoverished environment. She wore nothing but secondhand clothes, and her only toy was a pale-faced, blue-eyed doll made from a doll's head she had found and a body sewed by her grandmother. By the time she was a teenager, Blanche felt that local people looked down on her family because they were poor.

On March 3, 1913, shortly before her eighteenth birthday, Blanche married a young meat cutter named Lloyd Loop, who worked in a butcher shop on the square. The following year they had a daughter whom they named Elinora. Although the Loops had little money, Lloyd was a good worker and a well-liked young man. Things looked promising.

Unfortunately he contracted influenza during the epidemic of 1918, and it led to pneumonia, which killed him shortly before Christmas. Blanche was devastated by the loss, and she had to move back into her grandfather's home. But within a few weeks she asked her mother to mind Elinora and went to work as a telephone operator.

Blanche had been a widow for about a year when she met Kelly Wagle. She was walking rapidly to work one morning when he saw her from his car, pulled up near the curb, and asked her where she was going in such a hurry. She said, "To work, and I'm late." He offered her a ride, and she took it. That led to a series of dates with the handsome, charming, generous man from Colchester.

Kelly told Blanche that he was married but didn't get along with his wife. She didn't care. He also told her that he sold liquor where it wasn't legal. She didn't care about that either. She was tired of being poor and anxious to have a good time.

That was something he always understood.

It is doubtful that Kelly planned to leave Beulah. He had no grounds for divorce, and his experience with Ruth had taught him that awful things might be revealed in a divorce court. Beulah could describe beatings and threats, adultery and bootlegging. The divorce could easily lead to criminal prosecution. Besides, he had Beulah under his control and Blanche to run around with. That was probably the way he wanted it.

Nevertheless, things finally flew apart. In late October 1919 Kelly and his brother Joe drove to St. Louis with Blanche and another woman. (Joe's marriage to Luella was deteriorating and would soon end in divorce.) They got rooms at a hotel and planned to stay through the weekend, but Beulah found out where they were, drove there, and confronted Kelly. He flew into a rage and beat her.

She returned home, determined to leave him, and she apparently planned things out with an old boyfriend named Earl Harper, who had been raised in Carthage and was living in Omaha. He was a thirty-year-old department store employee with a wife and a daughter, and that fall he had returned to Carthage briefly to move his mother out of town. He and Beulah evidently planned to go to California, where he had lived for several years.

Because the Eighteenth Amendment had been passed by Congress and ratified by the states, and the wartime emergency prohibition act was already in force, although not very effective, Kelly had amassed a large stockpile of liquor. He knew the price would rise as soon as liquor supplies dried up, and he wanted to make a killing. While he was away from town, however, Beulah sold his cache to a bootlegger from Galesburg for $1,400—enough money to buy a modest home in 1919—and then she took Kelly's new red Buick and his handgun and fled to St. Louis. She stayed there for several days, evidently meeting with Harper and planning to go west. It is possible that he was simply an old friend who was trying to help Beulah get away, but it is more likely that they had plans to be together. In fact, her mother-in-law, Alice Wagle, later told the police "that she had seen Beulah on the day of her disappearance, and the girl had told her that she could not stand it at home any more and was going to run away with the Omaha man [Harper]."

Before she left St. Louis early in November, Beulah cashed a $1,000 bank draft and mailed two postcards. One was to Kelly's sister, Geneva, with whom she had hunted and fished. Her message remains unknown. The other one was sent to Mrs. Carrie Rhodes, the mother of Chiny Rhodes, who took care of Kelly's horses. It simply read, "I'm going west, and headed to h____." At the very least she was ambivalent about what she was doing. Beulah also telephoned her sister back in Carthage and said, "I'm going to Omaha, and on to California. I'll write you when I get there and send Pauline some money."

That was the last time the family ever heard from her.

In 1919 Omaha was a world away from Colchester. A fast-growing city of almost 190,000 people, many of whom were foreign born, it had been under the control of crime boss Tom Dennison since the turn of the century. He ran a protection racket that corrupted the police force and allowed gambling dens, brothels, and speakeasies to flourish. Beyond that, theft of all kinds was on the rise, and local newspapers referred to "The Worst Crime Wave in Omaha History." The city was sometimes called "Little Chicago."

Although Nebraska had passed a state constitutional amendment authorizing prohibition in 1916, there was no provision for enforcing it, and in Omaha prohibition was very unpopular in the business community and among most ethnic groups. Anyone who paid protection money could haul in unlimited quantities of liquor and find a ready market.

During the war Kelly Wagle had started selling liquor in Omaha, apparently making runs from suppliers in Chicago, and he continued to do that after the wartime prohibition act went into effect. By the fall of 1919 he was familiar with the notorious, wide-open western city, and shortly after discovering that Beulah had double-crossed him, he found out she was headed there.

On Thursday, November 20, the *Omaha Evening Bee* carried a late-breaking headline story that would soon captivate the entire city:

OMAHA WOMAN FOUND MURDERED NEAR BLAIR
Victim Slain and Body Thrown
From Swiftly Moving Car

The body of an unidentified woman was found along the road four and one-half miles north of Blair, Neb., toward Tekamah, according to a report telephoned to Omaha police by the sheriff at Blair late this afternoon. . . .

The woman, who was murdered, was believed to be a resident of Omaha.

According to the sheriff, it appears that the woman was murdered and then thrown from a swiftly moving automobile. The
body was found at the foot of the embankment along the road.

On the front page of the next issue the *Bee* carried a sketch map of
the area fourteen miles north of Omaha where the body was found.

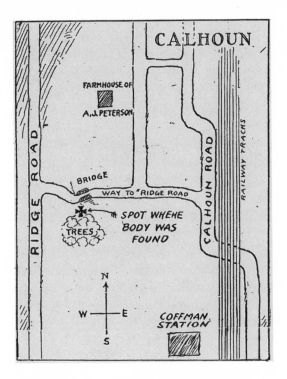

A farmer named Peterson discovered the body near an old wooden
bridge on a little-used country road that wound through the hills. According to the sheriff at Blair, "The victim was a woman about 25 years
old, with auburn hair and medium build, wearing a blue crepe de chine
waist, blue skirt, and brown hosiery." Someone had held a gun behind
her left ear and fired a bullet into her brain.

The body had been thrown head-first to the bottom of the embankment, where it lay face down among the fallen leaves and brush for two
or three days before Peterson spotted it. With daytime temperatures in
the forties and fifties, it was starting to decompose. Also, while it lay
there some animal had chewed on the right side of the face. Still, au-

thorities were struck by the beauty of the young victim, who was soon known throughout the state as the "Omaha Mystery Girl."

The body was taken to Calhoun, the seat of rural Washington County, where an inquest was held on November 21 at a place called, ironically, Johnson's Amusement Hall. After more than an hour of questions and testimony, nothing was determined except what everyone already knew: the young woman had been murdered.

State's Attorney Grace Ballard was a feisty, outspoken, middle-aged woman who knew everyone in the county. The only female state's attorney in Nebraska, she was determined to crack the case, so she dressed the corpse in a cream-colored shroud, put it in a cheap black coffin, and took it to a local funeral parlor. Then she invited the people of Washington County to come and see it. During the next twenty-four hours hundreds of people filed past the coffin, staring and whispering, shedding tears and shaking their heads, but no one recognized the victim.

Identification was difficult because the killer had removed items of clothing that might have helped—shoes, hat, and coat—as well as the woman's wedding ring. Since the body had apparently been thrown from a car down a twenty-foot embankment, there were no footprints.

On Saturday, November 22, the headline of the *Omaha Evening Bee* reflected the frustration of local authorities: "POLICE FAIL TO THROW ANY LIGHT ON BRUTAL MURDER OF WOMAN." By that time the other two daily newspapers, the *World-Herald* and the *Daily News,* were also carrying headline stories about the case, and the public's attention was riveted to the Mystery Girl investigation.

The *Bee,* known for its sensationalism, was so anxious for the victim to be identified that it ran a lurid photograph of her bruised and partly mutilated face, and above it was a plea for help from the public: "Can Anyone Identify This Woman Who Was Murdered?"

Of course, no one in western Illinois saw the photograph, and although major newspapers like the *Chicago Tribune* and *St. Louis Post-Dispatch* carried articles on the baffling murder case, the Colchester, Macomb, and Carthage newspapers did not. And no one in those communities yet suspected that Beulah Wagle was dead.

Authorities in Omaha felt that the young woman must have been murdered in the city and then taken to the remote countryside. For that reason, and because the investigation in Washington County was going nowhere, the body was released to Omaha officials. It was taken to the city by undertaker John A. Gentleman, who put the original clothes back on it and opened his mortuary on Farnam Street to the public.

On Saturday morning the *Omaha Bee* ran another headline about the case: "MURDERED GIRL ON VIEW HERE." By that time the entire city was following the investigation, and during the next few days perhaps ten thousand people streamed through the mortuary to get a look at the Mystery Girl. Many left in tears.

Several tentative identifications were made, and local newspapers jumped on the most promising ones. The headline of the November 24 *Omaha Bee* reflected the swirl of competing information: "BODY IS IDENTIFIED AS THREE DIFFERENT WOMEN." But those and other identifications were soon checked out by the police and discounted.

On Wednesday, November 26, officials in Omaha conducted a second inquest, but little was added to what was already known. The Douglas County coroner testified that the dead woman had eaten a meal shortly before she was killed and that "some of the bruises and contusions on her head and body had been inflicted before death." Someone had beaten her and then killed her. It appeared to the police that the Mystery Girl murder was a crime of passion.

Late that afternoon the six-man coroner's jury delivered a verdict that was simply a tissue of unknowns: "Said unknown person came to her death from a 38-caliber bullet fired by unknown parties at a place to this jury unknown."

Frustrated and depressed, the Douglas County authorities went home for Thanksgiving.

By Friday, November 28, the weather turned cold, just like the murder investigation that had started more than a week before. With the approval of local officials, the undertaker sealed the decomposing body in a more expensive, silk-lined coffin and took it to the city cemetery. The newspapers made even that event into a front-page story, full of touching details, as shown by the *Omaha Daily News* account:

MURDERED GIRL'S BODY GOES TO CEMETERY VAULT SANS MOURNERS

Quietly and without ceremony the body of the "Mystery Girl," viewed by thousands at the John A. Gentleman morgue since last Sunday, was taken to West Lawn Cemetery at 4 p.m. today.

There it will be placed in a receiving vault for ten days, and if not identified within that time, it will be given final burial in a plot donated by H. C. Shook, superintendent of the cemetery, who refused to permit the murdered girl to occupy a potter's field grave.

Funeral services will be held in the West Lawn Chapel at the time of the final burial.

The girl's body now reposes in a silver-gray crepe coffin, the personal donation of undertaker Gentleman, who provided it to replace the $16.50 box in which the Washington County officials had encased the corpse. . . .

A marcelline silk pillow holds the head of the girl. Spartan silver handles are on both sides of the coffin. The interior of the death box is lined with lavender cushions. A cream-plaited robe, which the undertaker's wife donated, enfolds the corpse. . . .

A neatly-inscribed silver plate tops the casket's cover. It reads: "At Rest." Another plate within the coffin reads, "The Unknown Girl."

The *Bee* headline for that day, "POLICE SAY MYSTERY MAY BE SOLVED," turned out to be just another dead end, and the Mystery Girl story finally faded from the front page.

A few weeks later, on a bleak, windy December 21, Gentleman held a graveside service at West Lawn Cemetery. Five reporters and one policeman who had worked steadily on the Mystery Girl case acted as pallbearers. As a score of people watched, the fancy casket, covered with fading flowers that had been sent during the past few weeks, was finally lowered into the frozen ground. The beautiful young woman whose dead body had stumped dozens of investigators and troubled the entire city for over a month was finally laid to rest.

Later that day the *Omaha Bee* carried one more story, reviewing the case and referring to the burial as "the final chapter in the most baffling murder mystery in the history of the Middle West." Baffling it was, but the final chapter was a long way off.

An anonymous donor soon provided a granite headstone, which symbolized the frustration of local authorities:

> **MYSTERY GIRL**
> Found Nov. 20, 1919
> Buried Dec. 21, 1919

That might have ended the case, but it didn't. The public could not forget the beautiful murdered girl whose body lay unidentified and unclaimed in the city cemetery at Omaha. Back in Washington County the ghost of the Mystery Girl began to haunt the old dirt road near the wagon bridge where her body had been found. By the day after Christmas it was front-page news in the *Omaha World-Herald:*

SEEING GHOST OF MYSTERY GIRL

Has the ghost of the "Mystery Girl" found murdered fourteen miles north of Omaha returned to haunt the lonely spot where her assassin pitched her body to the bottom of a deep gulch? Superstitious residents of the countryside tell of seeing a strange apparition hovering over the ravine. At times, they say, the airy form darts over the hilltop that leads down into the gully, but in a flash it is back among the trees that overhang the roadside. . . . Timid persons living in the vicinity are said to have misgivings about traveling the Coffman Road after nightfall.

While people in eastern Nebraska were troubled by a mysterious dead body, four hundred miles away others were troubled by a mysterious disappearance. When no one had heard from Beulah Wagle by Christmas, her family in Carthage became worried, and they called around to see whether anyone else knew anything. No one did.

By January the townspeople in Colchester began to wonder what had happened to Beulah. An enormous uncertainty settled on the community. Some thought that a woman who ran off was very likely to find trouble, but others, recalling that Kelly had beaten and threatened her, began to speculate that he had also killed her.

John McConnell contacted the police that winter, but since Beulah had left for St. Louis, there was little that local authorities could do. Kelly was questioned, of course, but all he said was, "She took my car and liquor, and she beat it." He never encouraged the police to investigate, and he never showed much concern about where she had gone or whether she would ever be coming back.

By that time Blanche was already living with Kelly. She had left her six-year-old daughter with her mother and grandparents in Carthage and had moved into the Wagle house on North Street. In a weak effort to avoid scandalizing the community, Kelly referred to Blanche as his "housekeeper," but the beautiful blue-eyed blond, who often went out of town with him, was obviously more than that.

Before the winter was over, Kelly received some anonymous notes from outraged townspeople saying that the sinful cohabitation would have to cease, but Kelly wasn't about to send Blanche away, nor would he consider leaving town. National Prohibition had started on January 16, and increasing numbers of people were violating the law. He was building a large clientele.

For her part, Blanche liked Colchester. She had always felt that people in Carthage looked down on her family, but in Colchester she was as good as anyone. Of course, she was also pressing Kelly to marry her, and since she knew about the beating of Beulah, the selling of Kelly's liquor, and his quest to find her, Kelly undoubtedly realized that marriage was a good idea.

Shortly before Beulah's disappearance, Joe's wife, Luella, had left him. They were living in Louisiana, Missouri, at the time, so early in 1920 Joe filed for a divorce there on the grounds of abandonment. He published a formal notice in the newspaper at Bowling Green, the county seat, and when Luella didn't show up for court, the divorce was granted.

Kelly went to visit Joe and talked with him about the divorce process. When he returned to Colchester, he told people that he had filed for a divorce in Missouri. Later he said the divorce had been granted. In reality, he never filed for a divorce from Beulah, in Missouri or anywhere else. He knew that he was already free to remarry.

Unfortunately John McConnell felt that Earl Harper was probably responsible for his daughter's disappearance. After searching for several months, he finally located Harper in St. Louis, in August 1920, and he talked the police into picking him up. They questioned him thoroughly, but Harper denied knowing anything about Beulah's disappearance, and since there was no dead body in Colchester or St. Louis, and no crime to investigate, there were no grounds for holding him.

Harper was surely lying. He had apparently planned to run off with Beulah, and she had probably traveled with him to Omaha. She had no other reason for going there. But Harper must have changed his mind, for he remained married to his wife and continued to work in a department store. He was not a lawbreaker anyway, and he certainly would not have brought Beulah to his hometown to kill her when St. Louis, where neither of them lived, would have been a much safer location.

However, it would not have been difficult for Kelly to locate his red Buick in Omaha, or to locate Harper, whose name could have been obtained from several sources in Colchester, including Kelly's mother and his sister, Geneva, to whom Beulah had disclosed her plans. Either the car or the man would have led him to Beulah.

After the Mystery Girl's body was discovered near Omaha, Harper must have realized that he was mixed up in a murder case. Shortly afterward he moved to St. Louis, where McConnell eventually found him and the police interrogated him.

Meanwhile the authorities in Nebraska knew nothing of Earl Harper's involvement in the case or of John McConnell's search for his missing daughter. Despite the fact that Beulah said she was going to Omaha, her father never traveled there.

That summer the police in both Washington County, where the body was found, and Douglas County, where Omaha was located, put up rewards of a few hundred dollars for information pertaining to the Mystery Girl, but no one seemed to know anything.

McConnell did question Kelly, but despite the beatings Beulah had received and Kelly's threat to kill her if she ever double-crossed him, the distraught father didn't think Kelly was a wife killer. As McConnell said much later, "I can't figure that he had a motive."

That shows how little he actually knew about his former son-in-law. He didn't realize that Kelly feared divorce proceedings because Beulah knew too much and might talk in court. He also didn't realize that nothing in the world angered Kelly so much as betrayal. And more important, he didn't realize that Kelly had been in the process of reinventing himself, creating a new identity as a big-time bootlegger, when Beulah sold the stockpile of liquor that was going to finance his transformation. She even ran off with his new car, which was his means of making a living as a bootlegger and the very symbol of his new identity. He would have tracked her all the way to California, much less Omaha, to retrieve his money, his car, and his chance to make it big.

There were also clear signs that Kelly had money that year. He bought a new car, of course, shortly after Beulah left, and he traveled extensively, but more important, in August 1920 he started building a new house. It was a project that attracted enormous attention from the townspeople.

The excavating began right after his old house burned to the ground in a mysterious, unexplained fire, which the *Independent* described on August 19:

HOUSE BURNED

The house owned and occupied by Henry Wagle of this city was burned to the ground Wednesday night or early Thursday morning, together with much of its contents.

Mr. Wagle was at home at the time and he, together with his housekeeper, had a narrow escape from death, the entire north end of the building being a mass of flames, and the flames and fire sweeping through the entire house when they escaped.

In an interview with Mr. Wagle just as we went to press, he stated that they had cooked supper on an oil stove, as usual in the evening, and had turned the stove off. They had then taken an auto ride, returning shortly before ten o'clock. They had retired immediately, probably by ten o'clock, and were fast asleep.

Mr. Wagle was awakened a few moments before 12 o'clock by the crackling of the fire, and jumped out of bed to find the house a mass of flames. . . .

Mr. Wagle has no idea how the fire originated, and there are several theories, but the real cause of the fire seems to be unknown.

The house was insured, so Kelly was suspected of setting the mysterious blaze, but no one could prove anything. In any case, he knew exactly what he wanted to build, and work began on the new place immediately.

Kelly supervised the construction himself, often working alongside the eight or more men who were on the job every day. The new place was a pretty, one-story bungalow with a hip roof and a front porch—the kind of modern home that would be increasingly common in the 1920s.

But Kelly added something strange, something that set the whole town talking. When the workmen were pouring the basement, he had them make a vault, a separate room with cement walls, just below where the living room would be. For that purpose he bought a thirty-inch-tall safe, took the back off of it, and had the workmen set it into the concrete wall. That became the door to his vault, although it was so low that Kelly had to crawl through it on his hands and knees. Inside the vault he installed electric lights and wooden shelves. It was a perfect place to keep something in a world where no one—not even a wife—could be completely trusted.

Once the basement was done, Kelly hired a big crew of carpenters to finish the house in a short time. By late December, only four months after the fire, the *Independent* reported that "Henry Wagle has completed his new home in the first ward and has moved into same. It is a pretty bungalow and will make a pleasant home."

Bayless did not mention that the occupants of the house had just gotten married. He knew that Kelly's personal life was controversial, that the townspeople wondered and gossiped about what had happened to Beulah, and he apparently decided to leave the whole matter alone.

Kelly and Blanche had gone out of town, all the way to Woodstock, northwest of Chicago, to get married. He had apparently been running liquor in the suburbs that summer and fall when he wasn't back in Colchester supervising the construction of his house. They were married on December 18.

Both of them used false addresses on the marriage license. Kelly indicated that he lived in Louisiana, Missouri, and Blanche said that she resided in Peoria. Their apparent reason for not connecting themselves with Colchester was that Illinois law prohibited divorcees from remarrying within a year after the divorce, and people in Colchester knew—or thought they knew—that Kelly had gotten a divorce from Beulah only six months earlier. This way, no official in Woodstock could possibly connect them with the town where Kelly's life was the spice of local conversation.

The only witness from Colchester at their marriage was a young friend of Kelly's named Bill McGrann, a former coal miner who was temporarily working in Chicago. Later, under Kelly's influence back in Colchester, he would also become a small-time bootlegger.

With the burning of his old house and the building of his new one, complete with a vault to store his money and his liquor, Kelly must have felt that he was making a fresh start. He had left the past behind him and was launching a new life. He was going to make lots of money. He even painted the new house green.

But the townspeople who watched it all happen developed an unshakable anxiety, as if they were exposed to hidden danger. Too much was unexplained. Where did Kelly go on his frequent trips out of town? Why did his old house, where he was cohabiting with an attractive young blond, suddenly burn to the ground? What was the vault in his basement for? And most troubling of all, what had happened to Beulah?

The townspeople were used to coping with sudden death, but this was different. Something dreadful had happened to Beulah, but what? There was no closure to the dark mystery of her disappearance. That Kelly went on with his life as if she had never existed only made the whole matter seem more unnatural.

It is not surprising that the coming of the new decade was marked by visits of the Woman in Black. She was often seen around the north side of town at night, walking the streets, cutting across yards, lurking in the shadows, even peering into windows—always showing up when least expected, like a suddenly remembered nightmare. Although Bayless, like Van Hampton before him, was always skeptical about ghosts, early in 1921 he finally reported what was happening:

WOMAN IN BLACK IN COLCHESTER

She is here! She has been seen by various people, peering in at windows, etc., and she disappears so quickly that she can't be recognized.

One night last week a lady on Coal Street saw her all dressed in black, and when the lady went to the phone to call a neighbor, who rushed across the street to capture her, biff—she was gone.

Two young girls on their way to church saw her out in the middle of the street, angling across the road near the Charles Zimmerman house, and they ran home in fright. . . .

If anyone sees this awful "Woman in Black," the *Independent* hopes they will go right up to her and get acquainted, for we would very much like to know her.

In the meantime, a good many of our timid ones are staying off the streets and pulling the curtains pretty close of nights.

Other evidence of the town's anxiety came in the form of rumors that were intended to explain Beulah's disappearance. They were all connected with Kelly. He had killed her and left her body in St. Louis. He had killed her and buried her body in his backyard. He had killed her and then burned her body in his house fire. He had killed her and hidden her body in a secret vault in his basement.

All of them were partly right.

Of course, in time the townspeople stopped thinking about Beulah. After all, no one knew anything for sure, and the McConnells were not from Colchester, so there was no one in town who might have kept her on everyone's mind. Besides, Kelly was not accused of anything, many of the townspeople liked him, and he came from such a good Colchester family.

The automobile comes to Colchester, ca. 1912. *From left to right:* an International Motor Buggy, a small Maxwell, two Model T Fords, an International, an Apperson Jack Rabbit. Car dealer J. E. Carson is standing between the two cars on the right. (Photograph courtesy of Larry Carson.)

The ruins of the Farmer and Sons general store on Market Street, February 1, 1910. Some credited that blaze to the Colchester firebug; others regarded it as retaliation against Ed Farmer and his son Walter, who were suspected of setting the fires.

Smoldering ruins from the last firebug blaze, which consumed eight buildings on Depot and Coal Streets, April 3, 1913.

Beulah and Kelly Wagle, soon after their marriage in 1907.
(Photograph courtesy of the *Omaha World-Herald*.)

Morgue photograph of Beulah Wagle in November 1919, when she was the Omaha Mystery Girl. The *Omaha Bee* printed this lurid picture under the caption "Can Anybody Identify This Woman Who Was Murdered?" (Photograph courtesy of the *Omaha World-Herald*.)

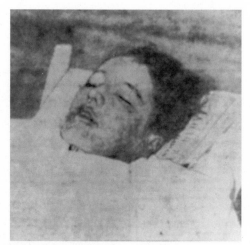

The gravestone of the Mystery Girl. (Photograph courtesy of the *Omaha World-Herald*.)

Alice Wagle (sitting), with her daughter Geneva and son Glenn, in 1918. (Photograph courtesy of Marilyn Richey.)

Blanche Wagle, the bootlegger's third wife, in the 1920s. (Photograph courtesy of Elinora Zeisler.)

Kelly Wagle in the early 1920s.

The printing office of the *Colchester Independent,* ca. 1920.
Editor J. H. Bayless is on the right.

Market Street in the mid-1920s, showing Kelly Wagle's taxi service.

Hattie Polk, the only female mayor
in Illinois in the early 1920s, as she
appeared in the *Chicago Tribune* on
November 23, 1923.

McDonough County state's
attorney Wallace Walker, ca. 1930.

McDonough County sheriff
Paul Eakle, ca. 1930.

The old McDonough County Jail, where Kelly Wagle spent six months in 1927.

Macomb Street in the 1920s, showing the spot where Kelly Wagle was murdered in 1929.

This photograph, which appeared in several newspapers in 1929, shows the bootlegger a few months before he was murdered.

The Colchester Methodist Church as it looked at the time of Kelly Wagle's funeral.

The Bootlegger
and the
Early 1920s

In Colchester the Twenties began with a terrible irony. J. H. Bayless described the problem in a front-page article that appeared in August 1920:

COAL IS SCARCE

The coal situation in Colchester . . . looks pretty dark. In years gone by the name "Colchester" suggested coal, and vast quantities of coal have been shipped away from this city. But this is a thing of the past.

At this time a very small percentage of the coal used here is mined from local mines. There are some banks still running, but they are only a drop in the bucket, and it has now become necessary to ship in coal.

But it is hard to get coal shipped in at this time, and the price is soaring, until it has reached the highest price in the history of the coal industry.

Of course, that situation also dampened local hopes for industrial development, especially in pottery and brick making, which depended on ready access to coal. For the previous two years, the King brickyard had been shipping in coal to fire its kilns.

Nevertheless, Colchester enjoyed a certain prosperity, simply because nearby farmers did very well. In fact, they had done well since the late years of the war. Mechanization had allowed them to increase production, and with a food shortage in Europe, they generally sold their crops at high prices and boosted their earnings to record levels.

The result was soon evident in the Colchester business district, as Bayless pointed out in May 1920:

A CROWD IN TOWN

A stranger dropping into Colchester last Saturday evening would have thought that there was a celebration of some kind in town, for there was about the biggest crowd in town that we have seen here in many a day.

We had occasion to take an automobile ride around town, and it looked to us as if there were a thousand cars parked on the streets of the city. They were stuck around in every conceivable place, and the stores were crowded to full capacity. At many of them the force of clerks were not sufficient to take care of the customers.

The country folks were investing in automobiles, especially Model Ts, and buying a host of other manufactured products, so Colchester seemed well on its way to prosperity as a farm-center community.

Meanwhile Prohibition led to contempt for the law on an unprecedented scale. Despite the raw, unsanitary quality of most moonshine and the danger of poisons in reprocessed industrial alcohol, people drank as much as ever. It was the fashionable thing to do. Drinking even became an assertion of individualism, a protest against the repressive moralism of the anti-liquor crusade.

But it also created massive social problems, including government and police corruption, political hypocrisy, and the spread of organized crime. As grateful drinkers patronized bootleggers, often viewing them as respectable men with the courage to flout the authorities, the line between right and wrong slowly faded, and the American social order started to fall apart.

However, people soon realized that the increase in crime and corruption was rooted in the public's response to Prohibition. As early as March 1922 the *Independent* carried an article that bluntly stated the awful truth:

THE BOOTLEGGER

Bootlegging has developed into a huge industry, involving millions of dollars of capital. No big city in the country can be truthfully described as dry. Scandal has characterized the situation with regard to law enforcement in a score of cities. Law violators and their aids in the local, state, and national enforcement ranks have grown rich in the liquor trade. . . .

Conscience strikes a blind spot when it comes to prohibition. So long as this feeling exists among a large element of our so-called average citizens, so long will bootleggers flourish, and will officials conspire with them to make illegitimate wealth out of the liquor traffic. . . .

One can see very little hope for improvement in these conditions, which are bringing the laws into contempt and demoralizing society generally.

There is not the slightest doubt that criminal disregard for the law has doubled since the advent of prohibition.

The problem was worst in the cities, and in the public mind, at least, the worst of the cities was Chicago. By 1921 more than five thousand speakeasies operated there, and gangster Johnny Torrio was grossing millions of dollars from illegal liquor and associated forms of vice, such as gambling and prostitution. The mayor, William Hale ("Big Bill") Thompson, and many police and court officials had links to organized crime. And unfortunately that was just the beginning. With the help of his nephew, Al Capone, Torrio soon spread his operation into the suburbs, setting up brothels and roadhouses, bribing officials, corrupting elections, and killing those who got in his way.

Like so many other places, McDonough County was also entering a period of unprecedented lawlessness and corruption. Soon after Prohibition began, many people started making and selling beer, and some sold hard liquor. The profits were substantial: a bottle of home brew would sell for twenty-five cents—about an hour's pay for most workers— and a quart of whisky or gin would bring five to ten dollars. Homes, restaurants, bowling alleys, and even gas stations became places where the public could buy "booze," as the newspapers liked to call it.

Local police sometimes winked at illegal liquor operations because they knew the people involved or were secret drinkers themselves, but the most blatant violators were usually arrested. Early in 1922, for example, the county sheriff nabbed three moonshiners who operated a still in an old building just four blocks from the courthouse in Macomb. Many people knew it was there because the cooking of fermented corn mash created a stink, like rotting garbage, that pervaded the neighborhood. Of course, it was much harder to catch those who merely sold liquor, especially if they were at all discreet.

One of the most troublesome McDonough County bootleggers in the early 1920s was a short, slim, sandy-haired man named Verne Lawson, whose career illustrates the problem of enforcing Prohibition. In 1919 he moved to Colchester from nearby Industry and bought a restaurant. After he failed to make a go of it, he started running a poker den, for which he was arrested in April 1920. Brought up before a local magistrate, he received some financial help from one of his gambling cronies, according to the town's justice of the peace docket: "Verne Lawson said he was guilty of the above charge . . . and was fined $50. Henry Wagle paid it by check." The latter also probably got him started in bootlegging, for soon afterward Lawson began selling liquor from his home on North Coal Street. His bootlegging was especially noisome to local authorities because, as the *Independent* later reported, "He was selling to young boys, habitual drunkards, and anyone else who had the money."

Lawson was arrested twice in 1921 and four times in 1922, but liquor-law violations were hard to prove, especially since customers were reluctant to testify, so prosecution often failed. When Lawson was finally convicted, he paid a small fine, only $60, and went right back to bootlegging. Finally, early in 1924, he was convicted of selling liquor to minors and was sentenced to one to two years in the penitentiary at Joliet.

When Lawson got out after eleven months, he was soon arrested again, for selling liquor and violating his parole, and he was sent back. Paroled again after another year, he returned to bootlegging once more, but he was soon involved in a theft case that landed him in prison for a longer time.

Verne Lawson was not a smart operator, but Kelly Wagle was. He got some of his liquor in Kentucky, but much of it came from a supplier at Thirty-fifth and Halsted Streets on Chicago's near South Side. He would park his car next to a warehouse, leaving his keys and some money in it, and go have lunch. When he got back, the trunk would be filled with tin cans of alcohol. He never saw the men who put it into his car and they never saw him. After running the liquor downstate, Kelly sold mostly to people he knew, in Colchester and other towns. It was a safe operation as long as he was cautious.

Although he sometimes sold liquor from his house, Kelly often took it to his customers, so that people were not constantly coming to his back door. Paid in advance, he commonly concealed a quart bottle or a gallon can of liquor at an agreed-upon place—near a tree, a mailbox, or a fence post—where the buyer could later find it. And he often hid his liquor supply somewhere off his own property, in a barn or shed, for example. That made it especially hard for the police to prove anything.

Kelly also did well because, like a Hemingway hero, he had a personal code. He himself never drank. If anyone asked him why, he would say, "Liquor is for selling" or "I don't like the taste of it." He also never sold to youngsters—that is, to school-age boys—or to habitual drunkards. And he never encouraged anyone to drink. Some people respected him because he did seem to conduct his business with a certain integrity.

And Kelly was simply well liked, for he knew how to relate to local residents. He spoke to most of the people in town whenever he saw them, and to the men he made jovial remarks that implied they were old friends. Sometimes they were.

That made it hard for the townspeople to believe some of the dark rumors they heard about Kelly—that he used a blacksnake whip on a man from a nearby town, that he beat a rival bootlegger half to death in the next county, and that he tied up another man who had stolen some of his liquor and dragged him behind his car all the way to Blandinsville.

Perhaps nothing symbolized Kelly so clearly as his new house, with its open front porch facing the street and its secret vault that no one ever entered but him. By the summer of 1922 there was a rose trellis at one end of the porch, and the house was surrounded by a broad green lawn set off here and there with newly planted flowers and shrubs.

The house seemed to put distance between itself and other buildings, and that impression resulted partly from the disappearance of a small white place that had been close by on the west. It had been rented by two single men who were in the building trades, but soon after Kelly and

Blanche moved in next door, the little house mysteriously caught fire one night and was so damaged that no one could live in it. Shortly afterward Kelly bought the building and tore it down. Then his lawn ran all the way over to the Christian Church, and things were pretty quiet in that part of town, except on Sunday mornings.

Kelly's cars also revealed something about him. He liked big closed models, which were known in the Twenties as "touring cars." They had powerful engines and lots of space in the back seat and the trunk. They were ideal for a bootlegger.

After 1920 Kelly never owned just one car. In 1921, for example, he owned a black Ford, a white Cadillac, and a blue Marmon. All three were touring cars, and the last two cost over $2,000 apiece. In the minds of local people, Kelly's cars symbolized his rise to success, his mysterious occupation, and his transcendence of the town.

Sometimes he owned as many as five cars at once. Given his business, Kelly did not want to be easily identified by the car that he drove, so he often switched cars for a second or third trip to a particular place. He traded them frequently too.

The practice of changing cars gave rise to a number of stories about Kelly. The one most likely to be true asserts that when he wanted to obtain another car in a hurry, he went to a dealership owned by the Davis brothers in nearby Blandinsville. He would simply pull in, pick out a new car, pay cash for it, and drive off. Kelly may have done that a time or two, when he wanted to dispose of a car that the police might be looking for, but then again, it may be folklore.

Other stories are more colorful and improbable, such as this one, which has several versions:

> One day when Kelly was coming back from Chicago with a load of liquor he stopped to eat at a hotel in Bushnell. While he was there, someone called the police and said that Kelly Wagle was in town and probably had booze in his car, so the police came to watch the hotel. But Kelly suspected a trap, so he phoned his wife in Colchester, and she drove right over in a Dodge touring car that was identical to the one he had parked out in back. She switched the cars. Later, when Kelly came out to drive away, the police nabbed him and then searched the car, but it was empty. He had outwitted the police once again.

Kelly's driving also became part of his emerging legend, which frequently pitted him against the police. People claimed that when he was carrying a load of booze he drove so fast that the police could never catch him; that when he was being pursued, he wouldn't hesitate to drive through a fence and into a cornfield; and that if he was almost caught, he would spin his car around while going full speed and head back in the other direction, racing past his pursuers. Whatever he did, he always escaped.

Clearly, some of the townspeople wanted to believe that Kelly couldn't be caught. In a period of mounting regulation of people's lives by edicts like speed limits and liquor laws, he was becoming a kind of hero, always daring to resist the demands of authority.

Late in 1920 he had an accident with his Cadillac, and a report in the *Macomb By-Stander,* reprinted from a Galesburg newspaper, reflected his habitual fast driving and his contempt for the law:

SAY COLCHESTER MAN BAD DRIVER
Henry Wagle Wanted in Knox County on Warrant

Galesburg, Dec. 31—A warrant has been issued for the arrest of T. H. Wagle of Colchester, Ill., by Brimfield men, who charge him with reckless driving. Thursday morning Mr. Wagle passed thru Brimfield in a new Cadillac car. There was another man and two women in the car with him, according to all reports. It is said that the Cadillac was traveling at a fast rate of speed as it passed through the main streets of the village.

Just before getting out of town, the Cadillac was driven head on into a Ford touring car, which was almost demolished by the collision. The occupant of the Ford received a bad cut on the head and had several teeth knocked out. It is feared that the man is injured internally. Residents of Brimfield who saw the cars collide stated today that Mr. Wagle did not stop to find out whether the man was seriously injured or not, but continued toward this city at a neck-breaking speed. The car was traced by Brimfield people as far as Knoxville.

The car was finally located at a garage in Galesburg. Kelly was arrested and charged with "assault and destruction of property." In court some weeks later he blamed the accident on the other driver and got those who were with him to say the same. He beat the charges.

At the time of his accident, Kelly was already facing assault charges of another kind. He and his brother Joe had always been close, but as Kelly's bootlegging continued, their relationship became strained. Perhaps it was because Kelly increasingly expected those around him to do whatever he wanted, and Joe, as the older brother, was unlikely to give in to that demand. Whatever the case, they eventually had an open quarrel. In November 1920 they started slugging each other at a restaurant, and Kelly beat Joe over the head with the butt of a revolver. Both men were arrested and paid small fines for disorderly conduct, but Joe also brought assault charges against his hot-tempered brother. Two months later, when that case came up in court, Kelly pleaded guilty and paid a $100 fine.

It was a disturbing episode for Arch and Alice, who eventually promoted a reconciliation, but Joe and Kelly were never again as close as they had been.

By that time Arch's health was rapidly deteriorating, and before the end of 1921 he was bedridden. Besides being blind, he had a serious liver problem. Nevertheless, he remained popular with older residents of the town, who occasionally stopped by to look in on him.

On April 5, 1922, the former coal miner, railroad man, marshal, and mail carrier finally died at the old Wagle house on Coal Street. Ironically for someone who didn't drink and had often arrested those who did, he died from cirrhosis of the liver, a disease common among alcoholics. His funeral was held at the Methodist Church, where Alice was still a member, and he was buried at Mt. Auburn.

It is difficult to know what Arch's death meant to Kelly. On the one hand, he admired his father as a man who had come from a poor family and had struggled hard to make a living. On the other, Arch reflected the moral values of the town, which the bootlegger persistently rejected. Kelly probably also viewed his father as a good man who did not deserve the bad luck that had slowly defeated him.

Arch had lived only sixty-two years, fourteen less than his hard-drinking father.

In the early 1920s, as he became a successful bootlegger, Kelly developed an enormous reputation for good deeds. If someone had a car in the ditch, he would pull it out. If people needed a ride to another town, he would offer to take them. When a poor man hurt his leg and couldn't walk, Kelly bought him a pair of crutches. When a friend was hospitalized in Chicago, Kelly drove the man's family to visit him. When a rural family that he knew was in dire need, he repeatedly brought them food. When a coal miner died and Kelly served on the inquest jury, he gave money to the bereaved family.

His generosity and kindness were often extended to children. He frequently gave some boy or girl a quarter to buy treats or invited a group of kids over for ice cream on his front porch. When the county fair was held in Macomb, he sometimes took a car full of youngsters—and gave them money to spend too.

Kelly still loved to play marbles, so he often bought enough to fill his pockets and then challenged the local boys who played in the streets. He always played to win—and sometimes got upset and kicked the marbles out of the circle if he lost. But if he did win, he would always give the boys his marbles anyway.

Kelly loved sports and sometimes expressed his community spirit by backing a local team. When Colchester High School, which had only 150 students, organized its first football team in 1921, there was no money in the school budget for uniforms. Local merchants were expected to chip in but failed to contribute, so Kelly outfitted all the boys himself. He also let them practice on land that he owned north of his house, and he often stopped by to watch them and lend encouragement. They needed it: most of them had never seen football played before.

The opening game of that season, against LaHarpe, was a close one. In the second half a fight broke out among the spectators, and Kelly was in the middle of it, throwing punches at several opponents. Before it was over, he had a few bruises, a bump on the head, and a dislocated finger. Worse yet, Colchester lost, nineteen to twelve, and he had placed some bets on the local boys.

He did better, however, as time went by. The team ended that year with a winning season—seven victories in ten games. In the following year they were undefeated, averaging forty-nine points a game, and they developed a regionwide reputation.

Neither the school nor the town ever forgot Kelly's generosity. To some, he became a kind of community father, deserving respect because of his interest in the youth of Colchester.

Another act of community support became a McDonough County legend. It also occurred in 1921, but the sport was baseball.

Macomb and Colchester had been rivals for almost forty years, and in 1921 both teams were very good. Sponsored by a new patriotic organization, Macomb's team was called the American Legion. Colchester's team was the Redmen, sponsored by a fraternal group, the Improved Order of Red Men, which maintained a ball field northeast of town.

When they played each other in Macomb on the Fourth of July weekend, the Legion and the Redmen split a two-game series in front of hundreds of spectators from each town. Colchester won a second game later in the month, and Macomb won a second game in August. By then both teams had won most of their other games, and they were rivals for the county championship. Finally there was only one game left in the season—against each other. Heavy bets were laid, and both teams looked forward to the "great battle," slated for September 11 at the county fairgrounds in Macomb.

Throughout the season Macomb had made a practice of "strengthening" its team by hiring outside players with minor league standing or college experience, and although that defeated the idea of local, amateur baseball, there was no rule against it. One of their best added players was Adolph ("Ziggy") Hamblin, a black man from Galesburg who had been the finest all-around athlete in the history of Knox College. He played for Macomb throughout the 1921 season. For the championship game, they also added a little-known major league pitcher, two minor league players from Rock Island, and others from Galesburg and Monmouth.

When the Redmen learned that most of the Macomb team would be outsiders who were paid to play, they announced that they would bring in a college player and a minor leaguer from Chicago whom they had used in previous games against Macomb. But they also had deeper plans: Kelly Wagle, who always bet heavily on the Redmen and was one of the managers of the team, was secretly negotiating with members of the Chicago "Black Sox." The infamous White Sox players, who had been paid by New York gamblers to throw the 1919 World Series, had just been barred from professional baseball, and they were trying to play wherever they could find a game. Kelly, a long-time White Sox fan, had seen the final game of that World Series, and he admired the disgraced heroes, who were never convicted in court.

When the fateful Sunday finally arrived, more than two thousand people thronged the fairgrounds. After both teams had warmed up and the game was about to start, suddenly "three players clad in rather seedy looking uniforms with stars on their shirt fronts came over from an automobile and took their places," as the *Independent* later reported. The astonished crowd slowly recognized who they were: Shoeless Joe Jackson, the greatest hitter in baseball after Ty Cobb; Ed Cicotte, one of the finest pitchers in the game; and Swede Risberg, the most acclaimed shortstop in the American League.

When it was all over, Bayless wrote the greatest baseball story of his newspaper career:

MACOMB IS SHUT OUT!
Colchester Wins Championship of the County
National Celebrities in Game
Locals Put One Over on the County Seat Team:
Cicotte, Risberg, and Jackson in the Line-up

The Colchester Redmen baseball team are the champions of McDonough County. In a game full of thrills, and in which men of worldwide reputation, perhaps the very best there is, participated, the Colchester team defeated their ancient enemy, Macomb, last Sunday afternoon by a score of 5 to 0. . . .

Cicotte simply toyed with the batters, not passing a man and striking them out when necessary. Wilson of Rock Island, the idol of Macomb fans, struck out every time he was at bat.

Joe Jackson loafed on "Boots" Runkle's hit to left field, to see if he wouldn't try to take second on the hit; and "Boots" took the bait alright. Then old Joe tried out his good right arm and Risberg did the rest. [Runkle was out at second.]

Later, Risberg ran back of second base and, running full speed away from the plate, caught a fly that brought the crowd to their feet. . . .

Not a Macomb man reached second base, and only four scattered hits were registered off Cicotte's delivery. . . .

> This little frame-up on Macomb was one of the cleverest pieces
> of work ever pulled off here.

According to one story about the game, Kelly had bet someone that he had a player who could get more hits than the best player for Macomb, who was Wilson. Then he told Cicotte, "I don't want that guy to get a hit," and Cicotte struck him out every time. Meanwhile Jackson, Risberg, and Cicotte all got hits for the Redmen. That story may be Kelly Wagle folklore, but it reflects a certain truth: Kelly had a pile of money bet on that game.

For the townspeople, the great game was a moment of glory—not just because they won the championship but because they defeated the more prosperous county seat and showed that "Colchester was able to handle a deal of that magnitude," as Bayless put it.

Of course, Macomb fans saw it differently. The *Macomb Journal* editor complained that "Colchester played three of the blackest of the 'Black Sox,'" and he objected to the game on moral grounds: "Our team will not again play against those players whom Judge Landis has barred from professional baseball because of their crookedness." Macomb's other newspaper, the *By-Stander,* reviewed the entire 1919 World Series scandal and concluded that by hiring three of the "Black Sox," Colchester people had "permitted their desire to win a ball game to warp their standards of honesty."

Clearly the Macomb fans were sore losers, and they failed to connect their own do-anything-to-win practice of hiring professional players with the surprise use of the "Black Sox." But there was a moral point to be made: the degeneration of American values, symbolized by the great baseball scandal, was not limited to the big cities. The use of the "Black Sox" and other imported players to decide the McDonough County championship surely demonstrated that.

Kelly's gambling was not limited to football and baseball games. As his bootlegging career flourished, he became a frequent poker player, often winning or losing more than a hundred dollars in games with Verne Lawson, Bennie Kipling, Raymond ("Bumps") Moon, Cecil Underhill, Harry ("Turk") Stephens, and others. Eventually he ran a poker game of his own in the basement of a garage located near the ravine behind his house. He nicknamed the place "Monte Carlo." In September 1922 he and six cronies were arrested while playing there, but he simply paid the small fine and went right back to it. So much gambling and liquor selling went on at the Wagle house that Blanche frequently reminded her daughter never to tell anyone what she saw or heard at home.

Meanwhile, in 1921 Kelly built a two-story brick building on Depot Street, next to the People's State Bank. The downstairs became a bakery, and the upstairs, officially rented by the Red Man Lodge, became a dance hall and gambling joint. Kelly often played poker there, and a crap table was set up on Saturday nights. Later, when local officials tightened up on gambling, the upstairs was converted into a pool hall.

Kelly also frequently bet on fights—prizefights, cockfights, even dog fights. He loved the intensity of a fight, and putting money on one of the combatants always heightened his sense of involvement.

Of course, Kelly also continued to bet on his horses, which he raced at fairs and other events in the summer. If he wanted to show off for the local folks, he himself would ride. In August 1921 he won the pony race at the Colchester Fraternal Picnic, held south of town.

Oddly enough, he developed an interest in the annual mule race at the McDonough County Fair. In the early 1920s he owned a mule named Julia and hired someone else to ride it. But even in that tongue-in-cheek kind of competition, Kelly would do anything to win, as suggested by a 1922 *Macomb Journal* report:

DEAD HEAT IN THE MULE RACE
ON FIRST DAY OF THE BIG FAIR

A dead heat in the annual county mule race, and the runoff thereof, were the features of the opening yesterday of the big fair. Elzie Haines of near Colchester, mounted on "J. Patterson," was the final victor. Kelly Wagle's mule, "Julia," was second. . . .

Both the heats kept the crowd in a continuous uproar. "Patterson" and "Julia" headed into the stretch of the first heat, neck and neck, and the excitement in the race was augmented when Kelly Wagle threw his hat at his mule, as the animal raced by him just above the grandstand. A warning from the judge prevented his repeating it in the runoff, which was almost as close a finish.

Later in the decade Kelly rode in the mule race himself, and he often delighted the crowd by doing something outrageous, such as riding across the infield of the track to get ahead of the other entries. He loved to be the center of attention.

By the early 1920s Kelly Wagle was a well-known figure. After all, he was the leading bootlegger in McDonough County at a time when bootlegging was a glamorous occupation, and in that mysterious role he did whatever he pleased, regardless of what anyone else thought. He became the model of twentieth-century individualism in Colchester, and many of the townspeople admired him.

Two young men who did were Fred Wayland and Jay Moon. Born in 1891, Wayland was the oldest of six sons in a coal-mining family. He was a good-looking, muscular man with light brown hair and gray eyes. After serving as a truck driver in World War I, he got married and worked as a carpenter and brick mason for John O. Moon, a prominent builder and community leader.

One of Wayland's closest friends was the builder's son, John W. Moon, who was always called "Jay." Born in 1896, he was still in his mid-twenties when the Prohibition era began. A slim, dark-haired young man who always dressed well and looked handsome, Moon was one of the most sought-after bachelors in town. He worked for his father and lived at the family home on East North Street, the main road coming into town from Macomb.

The two young men first came to public attention early in 1921 when they were arrested for stealing forty-four automobile tires and thirty-six inner tubes—together worth over $1,000—from a train that had stopped on the switch track at the west end of town. Although no one had witnessed the theft, people had seen Wayland and Moon in nearby towns offering tires for sale at very low prices. In mid-January the sheriff located most of the tires in an abandoned house near Mt. Auburn Cemetery and at the home of a young coal miner, Harry ("Punk") Averill, who was a close friend of the other two.

Wayland and Averill were indicted, but the charges against Moon were eventually dropped. Some townspeople thought that his influential father had pulled strings behind the scenes, but no one knew for sure. Before the winter was over, Wayland pleaded guilty to burglary and larceny, and Averill admitted that he had been an accomplice. Both were sentenced to the state penitentiary at Joliet.

Although that case was rapidly cleared up, local authorities knew that

Wayland, Moon, and Averill were part of a gang of "some eight or ten men, and young men . . . who have been making a living without any perceptible labor," as Bayless put it, and who had been suspected of "various offenses which have been allowed to go on for years," including bootlegging.

In fact, at the end of January 1921, while the tire theft case was still in the news, McDonough County authorities discovered a moonshine operation near Averill's home, in the countryside north of town:

LOCATED A STILL

Deputy Sheriff James Wilson came to this city last Tuesday and drove to the Ed Leach Farm, where he had a hunch that he would find a still and accessories. He found the accessories all right, but it is said that a man from this city went out a few days ago and removed the still, secreting it in a new place.

Mr. Wilson found a keg containing about 20 gallons of sour corn mash and a barrel containing some 40 gallons of the same fluid, all ready to be run through the still and turned into tangle foot with a kick like a Missouri mule. One of the casks was hidden under the corn in a crib and the other was near the crib, along the fence by where Harry Averill has been living and where the stolen tires were found. A piece of coil from the still was found in the cellar, we are told, where Averill lived.

Just who the still belonged to is a question, but the theory of most of the officers seems to be that Averill was at least one of the owners, and probably there were others.

It is likely that the Averill-Wayland group was producing moonshine for Kelly Wagle or Verne Lawson, the two most active bootleggers, but the investigation never went any further, so nothing is certain. It is apparent, however, that Kelly knew all those young men, and he had already started to employ Wayland and Moon for running loads of liquor.

Shortly after the tire theft case was resolved, Jay Moon's father ran for mayor on a platform that promised "Law Enforcement and Good Business Administration." In April he was elected.

A thin-faced, dark-haired man who was blind in one eye, John O. Moon was perhaps the leading figure of his generation in Colchester, and he came from a well-known pioneer family. His father, William Moon, emigrated from Cornwall early in 1855, saw the railroad come through, and "dug the first car of coal ever loaded at Colchester," as his obituary proudly put it. He was also a saloon supporter who was arrested more than once for drunkenness. John, born in 1861, was always called "Jack" by his friends—and that eventually included everyone in town. He grew up mining coal but turned to carpentry and by the end of the century was a partner in a lumber yard. Later he had his own millwork shop. He built homes, schools, and churches in Colchester and several nearby towns, and by the early twentieth century he was a very prominent businessman.

He was also an extremely popular, outgoing person who shined in the limited social world of the town. In the late nineteenth century he was a mainstay of the Colchester Literary Society, often giving speeches or debating current issues. He also acted in local plays, which were put on at the opera house by the Colchester Dramatic Club. In later years he was a leader in the Modern Woodmen and Knights of Pythias fraternal groups.

Perhaps no one in the history of Colchester exerted broader civic leadership than John O. Moon. In the 1890s he organized and headed the town's first fire company. In the early twentieth century he served for years as president of the school board and made dramatic improvements in the local educational system. He was a founder and long-time president of the Colchester Club, devoted to business improvement, and was also president of the Building and Loan Association. At the same time, he was a constant leader in city government, serving as alderman for many years and as mayor twice before, from 1910 to 1911 and 1914 to 1915.

Moon was deeply committed to the town—no one ever questioned that—but he was also a drinker who was not anxious to enforce Prohibition. He was a pragmatic businessman, not a moral crusader, and he saw that all the pressure to stamp out drinking simply divided the townspeople.

When he took office in 1921, Colchester no longer had a significant identity as a coal town, although some drift mines still operated, employing a few dozen men. Clay mining had dwindled, too, although the Baird Clay Company was still operating a few mines and Charles Myers was operating one. The Colchester Pottery was closed, and the only producers of clay products were the brickyard and the Gates Fire Clay Company. Colchester was becoming less of an industrial town and more of a farm-center community, dependent for prosperity on the merchants, who looked to Moon for leadership.

While he was in office, the city council addressed the need for a waterworks system, installed many cement sidewalks, improved the streetlights, and pressured the state to bring a "hard road" through town. At the same time, the merchants were organized to promote "a bigger and better Colchester." Moon also launched a campaign to license pool halls. When that failed, two or three of them operated anyway, as semisecret private clubs, and the city government simply pretended not to know about them. They were good for business.

It is difficult to say exactly why Kelly Wagle and Jay Moon became partners, or business associates, but they did. Like many other young men, Moon must have been drawn to Kelly as a kind of social rebel who led an exciting life, made good money, and didn't have to work too hard. Kelly, in turn, must have recognized the value of drawing the mayor's son into his bootlegging operation. Beyond that, both men came from old Colchester families and had well-respected, tolerant fathers, and both were nondrinkers but inveterate gamblers. Moon also had a reputation for saying little about himself or his business and for taking orders without complaint, and that must have suited Kelly very well.

One other factor was surely important: by 1921 Moon was dating Kelly's sister, Geneva. She was twenty-four then and had blossomed into an attractive young woman with light brown hair and sparkling blue eyes. She worked as a switchboard operator in Macomb, so she had her own spending money, and unlike most women of that era, she knew how to drive a car. A stylish dresser, she liked to wear her blouses tight and her skirts short, and she exuded an air of carefree independence that most men found very appealing. She was a good dancer, too, and loved to do the Charleston and the Black Bottom. Like Kelly, she was outgoing, hot-tempered, and ready for anything. Unlike him, she smoked and drank—mostly gin. In the parlance of the Twenties, she was a "flapper."

Blanche and Geneva got along very well, and the two couples frequently went out together, chiefly to restaurants, sporting events, and speakeasies in other towns. They all liked to have a good time.

Kelly and his young associate knew how to avoid trouble with the authorities. First of all, they quietly supplied liquor—high-quality moonshine—to some of the leading men in town, including the president of the People's State Bank and certain members of the city council. Also, they maintained close ties with Colchester policemen, especially Thomas Tones and T. C. Dark.

Tones, whose nickname was "Reuben," had worked at the King brickyard for many years and knew Kelly very well. During World War I he also became the city weigher, working at the stockyards and the grain elevator. After going into police work, while he was in his forties, he began raising and training English bloodhounds, which soon had a statewide reputation. During the 1920s Tones worked for the police in dozens of towns, including Galesburg, Quincy, and Chicago, tracking thieves and killers. Sometimes Kelly volunteered to help him transport the huge tan dogs to the scene of a crime, and later Jay Moon did the same. Tones returned the favor by ignoring their bootlegging. In fact, he was also a heavy drinker who probably got his own liquor from them.

Thomas Campbell Dark, always called "Cam," was the night policeman. Then in his sixties, he had an old-fashioned sense of community, and he tried to get along with everybody. He was also a drinker, and so were his sons, Sam, Ross, and Dwight, so he was not anxious to enforce the liquor law. Besides that, Dark was a poor man, a former teamster and hay dealer who had almost died when a chain snapped and cut him open across the abdomen. He was laid up for many months. He had always struggled to support his eleven children, so he was glad when Kelly Wagle and Jay Moon paid him to tip them off when the heat was on.

By 1922 the corruption that was sweeping the country had a firm foothold in Colchester, where the most widely known businessman was a bootlegger.

The Mayor, the Bootlegger, and the Klan

As crime and corruption spread across the country like an epidemic, law enforcement became the hottest issue of the decade. In Colchester J. H. Bayless wrote one editorial after another that called for public action. In May 1922 he used the notorious Chicago situation as an example of what can happen when lawbreakers take control: "Chicago is passing through a period of crime and degradation, which always happens when good people lay down and turn the government over to unscrupulous men. . . . Murder, robbery, bombing, and all forms of crime are now so common there that one pays very little attention to them, and a conviction is hard to get. This situation will prevail until the God-fearing and law-abiding people get together and assert themselves." In other editorials he talked about the apparent "moral breakdown" that was producing "all kinds of lawlessness," and he declared that "something should be done to curb it."

That kind of sentiment was widespread in America, and it contributed to the rise of the Ku Klux Klan. Revived in the South in 1915, the organization remained small and regional for a few years, but after World War I it spread through most of the country, becoming strongest in the Midwest. By the mid-1920s Illinois alone had some 100,000 Klansmen, who were located primarily in the small towns.

Thriving on fear of social change, they viewed themselves as guardians of the American way of life. And in truth, they were not bloodthirsty bigots but ordinary men who wanted to bring back a more rigid moral code and reestablish the highly unified communities of the past, infused with patriotism and Protestant faith. In short, they felt alienated in the new postwar America, and not realizing the complex reasons for the rise of individualism and rapid social change, they blamed various groups for the national decline: Catholics, Jews, blacks, aliens, bootleggers, and others.

In 1922 Klan recruiters, called "Kleagles," started seeking members in McDonough County. They worked through the newspapers by placing ads that were directed to native-born Americans, often asserting their commitment to "the tenets of the Christian religion," "a closer relationship through Americanism," "protection of our pure womanhood," and other traditional-sounding values. The ads did not mention the Klan but offered one or more Post Office boxes where inquiries could be made. Once local interest was shown, organizers came to launch the new chapter, which then conducted its own membership drive.

In January 1923 the *Macomb Journal* discussed the Klan's recruiting effort, pointing out in a surprisingly well-informed article that "the Klan did not take very well in Macomb, where a great many refused to join," but "in Colchester, it is understood that a large percentage of the men joined." The Klan also did well in Blandinsville, Bushnell, Tennessee, and other small towns.

The recruiting continued through that year, feeding on public concern about immorality and lawlessness. In May Bayless said flatly in the *Independent* that "a good [Ku Klux Klan] organization should be perfected here," for "there is work for it in Colchester." Two months later he published a vivid account of the first local Klan rally:

BIG KLAN MEETING HELD HERE

In response to a printed invitation sent through the mail, a representative of the Independent attended a big meeting of the Ku Klux Klan, held in a field just east and a little north of the Harry Bunt house northwest of this city on last Thursday night.

The invitation was a printed one on a white card:

"Your friends state that you are a 'Native Born American Citizen,' having the best interest of your Community, City, State, and Nation at heart, owing no allegiance to any foreign government, political party, sect, creed, or ruler, and engaged in a legitimate occupation. You are therefore invited to attend a lecture on 'True American Principles and Ideal Americanism.'

Place: One-fourth mile west and one-fourth mile north of Mt. Auburn Cemetery, Colchester, Illinois. Time: 9:15 p.m. Date: August 9th. This invitation will admit you.

Klan, Invisible Empire, Invitation Committee

Knights of the Ku Klux Klan"

At the appointed time, with others who had received similar invitations, we drove as directed, and one had little trouble in finding the place for there was a constant stream of cars going in that direction. . . .

On arriving at the gate entrance to a field, a number of white-robed figures stopped each car, inspected the invitations, and motioned for the autos to proceed. On entering the field, other white-robed figures directed the parking of cars, they being parked in a large circle around the field, which was patrolled by other figures in white.

Everything was in darkness with the exception of the auto lights as they came in and took their places. Also, the Klansmen carried flashlights. Everything was done in silence, and it made a fellow feel a little like he was in a haunted house on a dark night. The silence was impressive, and in our judgment there was near a hundred cars in the circle when a tall, hooded figure stepped over to the center of the circle and lighted a cross. The cross was fed by gas from a small tank of some kind, and it afforded considerable light, by which the Klansman-lecturer read his address.

The speaker commenced by giving a short history of the Ku Klux Klan and the work that they had done. He outlined the principles of the Klansmen as follows:

For 100 percent Americanism.

For the Public Schools.

For the tenets of the Christian religion.

For the separation of church and state. . . .

They are not in favor of mob violence and do not uphold violence of any kind, but are strictly in favor of lending assistance to the regularly constituted officers in the performance of their duty and in the enforcement of the law. They believe in the church, and in the teachings of the Bible and that Christ was crucified and rose again. This is the reason that the Jews do not work in harmony with the Klan. . . .

Cards were distributed at the commencement of the meeting, and all were asked to sign them and, if wanting to join, to place a cross so it could be seen. Then the meeting was adjourned and the crowd silently wended its way homeward.

There were many prominent and foremost residents of the city and vicinity at this meeting. The closest attention was given to the speaker, and a casual observer would get the idea that a very large majority of those present were in sympathy with the organization and the principles they stand for.

Several other Klan rallies were held that year, including one in September that took place on the railroad grounds near the Princess Theatre. It featured a lecture by a hooded Klansman who was a leader in the national organization. Like an old-time preacher, he spoke for more than two hours, lashing out at lawbreaking, corruption, and immorality. The crowd swelled to hundreds of people, and some of them signed cards to apply for membership.

At private meetings in the countryside, always after nightfall, the Klansmen held their initiation ceremonies, at which the new members came forth, lifted their hoods, kissed the American flag, and took the Klan oath by the glare of a burning cross. Sometimes a Klan leader spoke about "100 percent Americanism." By the end of 1923 the Colchester chapter of the Ku Klux Klan had well over one hundred members.

Of course, not all the KKK activities were harmless. Fired by self-righteousness and shrouded in secrecy, the Klansmen dealt in intimidation. Many people in town received anonymous letters telling them to stop doing something that the Klan found objectionable. A few, including Kelly Wagle, had crosses burned on their property late at night as a warning to heed the demands of the Klan. In Colchester, where there were no blacks or Jews and very few Catholics or non-British immigrants, the Klan's biggest concern was the bootlegging that everyone knew was going on. To the Klansmen, Kelly Wagle symbolized the moral breakdown that threatened their community and the American way of life.

Spurred by accounts of Klan violence and intimidation, the state government passed a 1923 anti-Klan bill, making it illegal even to appear in a public place while hooded and robed to conceal one's identity, but since local officials were often in the Klan, the law was seldom enforced. In Colchester support for the Klan was considerable. Those who had been temperance crusaders over the years looked on the Klansmen as legitimate enforcers of the law who would finally eradicate the liquor traffic. As Bayless said in 1923, "The Ku Klux Klan is to our law officers what the fraternal orders are to the church, doing their work that they have long neglected."

Because they espoused Protestant Christianity and offered free membership to ministers, the Klansmen also had the support of the churches. Shortly before Christmas 1923, a group of Klansmen suddenly marched into the Colchester Methodist Church, interrupting a Sunday service to promote their organization, and the startled congregation was very impressed, as the *Independent* later reported:

KU KLUX KLAN ACTIVITIES

The Ku Klux Klan has been quite active in this city during the Christmas season, and several demonstrations have caused a buzz of excitement. . . .

On Sunday night the congregation of the Methodist Episcopal Church here was thrown into great excitement when eleven white-robed figures silently marched inside the door while the pastor, Rev. Hardy, was offering prayer, and when the prayer was finished the Klansmen formed two columns in the aisle and the leader marched down between the lines to the pulpit and handed the pastor an envelope containing $25, with a note instructing him to distribute the contents among the poor of the city as he deemed best. The envelope also contained the poem "God Give Us Men," which the pastor read to the congregation. The Klansmen then marched out as the congregation cheered them.

That kind of response energized the local movement and bolstered the recruiting efforts.

Among those who cheered the Klan that morning was the most influential woman in the church and the town's foremost moral crusader, Harriet O. Polk, whom everyone called "Hattie." By then she was the mayor.

Born in Colchester in 1871, Hattie Polk was deeply rooted in the anti-liquor campaign. Her father, George Welch, was a pioneer farmer who had settled north of Pleasant Valley Mill in 1849, and he was a teetotaler for all of his eighty-seven years. Her mother, Margaret Welch, was a long-time Sunday school teacher and eventually a member of the Women's Christian Temperance Union. In the 1890s Hattie became a member too, and except for the Methodist Church, it was the only organization she ever joined. In 1893 she married Edward Polk, a short, balding, mild-mannered store clerk who was himself an ardent Methodist and a Good Templar. A big-boned, assertive woman, Hattie easily dominated him. She also taught Sunday school for thirty years, and by the early 1920s she was president of the local WCTU chapter.

Like so many temperance crusaders, she felt that drinking alcohol of any kind was a sin that led to moral degradation, and she had an intense hatred of the liquor traffic. Temperance for her was more than an interest or a commitment; it was a way of life and a worldview.

When she decided to run for mayor early in 1923, Hattie Polk was a rigidly erect, iron-jawed woman of fifty-two, with graying hair and steel-rimmed glasses. She looked like an old-fashioned, no-nonsense schoolteacher, and people saw her as a determined enforcer of the law. She made it clear that she was running "to clean up the town," and everybody knew what that meant. Illegal liquor was the only issue in the campaign.

Polk attacked no one, but her candidacy inevitably focused criticism on the administration of Mayor John O. Moon, who was blamed for protecting the bootleggers and who was not a candidate for reelection. In April she trounced her Republican opponent, former mayor John Hunter, and became the most well known and widely admired woman in the town's history.

Because she was also the only female mayor in Illinois, Hattie Polk was something of a celebrity. Women in many towns sent their congratulations, and shortly after the election she was interviewed by the *Macomb Journal*. Sounding like the Christian crusader that she was, she declared, "Moral uplift and righteousness will be the aim of the new administration," and she referred specifically to "the liquor problem."

But putting a stop to the bootlegging was difficult, if not impossible, because Colchester was still a complex web of personal relationships. Most of the men in town had known each other forever—had played baseball and marbles together, had worked with or for each other, or had been "brothers" in a fraternal order. They depended on one another for business support, they swapped stories at the pool hall and the barber shop, and they knew each other on a nickname basis. Consequently, it was hard to find officials who would strive to arrest or prosecute the bootleggers. In fact, many would help an arrested friend beat the charge. As Bayless pointed out in July 1923, "It is against the law to sell liquor, but . . . if a law violator is arrested, then the underground organization gets busy and all the ropes are pulled to get him loose." He declared that "the fellows who are in sympathy with the lawbreakers should be rooted out," but through one relationship or another, that included most of the men in Colchester. By the mid-1920s Kelly Wagle, Jay Moon, Verne Lawson, George Dickerson, Bill McGrann, Ernie Polk, Turk Stephens, Fred Wayland, and Charlie Zimmerman were bootlegging, and all but Lawson were lifelong residents of the town.

To avoid the difficulties in Colchester, Mayor Polk and her reform-minded city council worked closely with the county authorities in Macomb, and they had some success. At that time the state's attorney was Andrew L. ("Les") Hainline, a handsome, well-educated, idealistic, thirty-six-year-old man who was the son of *Macomb Journal* editor W. H. ("Doc") Hainline. Crippled since childhood, the young state's attorney walked with a cane, but he had enormous energy and great commitment to Macomb and McDonough County. Wealthy and influential, Hainline was the foremost civic leader of his generation. He had been elected state's attorney in 1916, at the age of twenty-nine, so he had extensive experience by the time Hattie Polk's crusade to clean up Colchester was rolling. By the end of May, Wagle and Moon had been arrested by the county sheriff and charged with "transporting intoxicating liquor" to customers in Macomb.

On November 23, 1923, Hattie Polk delivered an address in Chicago to the Illinois League of Women Voters, to whom she was a heroine. After accepting the applause of hundreds of women, she commented that being mayor was "just housekeeping on a larger scale." Then she reported on her crusade. "We're cleaning up Colchester," she said, "and we've got several indictments, including one against the worst bootlegger."

On the following day her photograph appeared in the *Chicago Tribune,* and an article with it quoted her as saying that "Colchester has one bad bootlegger." Clearly, to Polk and her supporters Kelly Wagle was Public Enemy Number One.

And by then he was, in fact, the bootlegger's bootlegger. Although many people made their own beer, Kelly supplied most of the hard liquor sold in McDonough County and nearby areas. For many small-time bootleggers, he was the supplier, the wholesaler.

But by the fall of 1923 Kelly was indeed under indictment—and not just for bootlegging. Since late summer he had been the central figure in the most widely publicized Illinois auto theft case of that era. On September 8 the *Macomb By-Stander* provided the most extensive early report:

STOLEN CARS HERE: MAY BE MORE
Henry "Kelly" Wagle to be Taken
to Chicago, Questioned

Indications of the distribution of stolen automobiles in McDonough County through the operation of a clever theft ring with probable headquarters in Chicago, uncovered here two weeks or more ago by George M. Cole, state automobile investigator of Macomb, today resulted in the detention of five cars and the arrest of Henry "Kelly" Wagle of Colchester, who sold at least three of the cars to their present owners.

Wagle was arrested at Colchester today by Deputy Sheriff W. R. Purdum and Deputy S. B. Howard, and was brought to Macomb to await the arrival of members of the Chicago police department, who will take him to Chicago for questioning. . . .

Wagle claims to have bought the cars he disposed of here from a Chicago man who cannot be located at the address given, which was in a prominent part of the downtown section. For that reason, the officers caused his arrest and are referring him to the Chicago police department, where he will be given a stiff questioning in an effort to establish the identity of the persons really guilty of stealing the machines. . . .

Two or three weeks ago the By-Stander carried a story relative to the work of tracing a band of automobile bandits operating throughout central Illinois. In that dispatch it was stated that at least 100 stolen cars had been distributed throughout this section of the state.

Kelly was, in fact, part of a huge auto theft ring centered in Peoria. They often stole cars in Chicago, filed off the engine numbers and changed the license plates, and then sold the cars to agents like Kelly, who transported them to other counties or states and resold them.

Before he was taken to Chicago, Kelly was interviewed by a reporter for the *By-Stander.* He naturally denied knowing that the vehicles were stolen, and in the process he revealed something about his use of cars: "'Killie' told the By-Stander Saturday evening that he has owned a total of thirty automobiles during the last eight or nine years. Of these, seven were Fords and others were Hudsons, Buicks, Dodges, Interstates, Hupmobiles, Cadillacs, Marmons, Durans, and Packards. He said he would run them awhile and then trade them in for new cars. He was a hard driver and frequently burned out bearings and had other mishaps. Wagle says he can account for all three cars—where he bought them and where he sold them."

Later that month Kelly was indicted for auto theft and receiving stolen property, and so was Jay Moon, who resold two of the fourteen cars recovered in the investigation.

Hainline worked hard to line up evidence that would convict Kelly Wagle and Jay Moon of participating in the auto theft ring, although the case was ultimately tried in Chicago. Kelly was afraid of being convicted and tried every approach to avoid it, including offering to reimburse anyone who had bought a car from him that turned out to be stolen, but neither the young state's attorney nor the Chicago authorities wanted to bargain.

On November 22 things took a dramatic new turn: someone bombed Hainline's house. The county seat was literally stunned by the blast, which shook the north part of town like an earthquake. On the next day the *Macomb Journal* carried the headline story:

RESIDENCE OF STATE'S ATTORNEY HAINLINE BOMBED
Bomb under Steps Ruins Portion of Large Residence

The residence of State's Attorney A. L. Hainline, 635 North McArthur Street, was partially wrecked by a bomb about 10 o'clock last night, and the escape of Mr. Hainline and his wife and parents, Mr. and Mrs. W. H. Hainline, was simply miraculous.

The force of the explosion was felt all over the city, and the report was heard as far away as Bushnell. Windows were broken in houses two blocks away, and with the fire alarm following, there was much excitement. Fortunately, the residence did not catch fire from the explosion, and the damage is confined to that force alone. It will be large, however, being estimated at $2,000 to $5,000.

The cause is attributed to some person or persons whom the state's attorney is prosecuting or has prosecuted. Who, it is not yet known, but the officers are working on some clews that may lead to the guilty parties. Indignation runs high at the outrage.

Hainline was slightly injured by flying glass, and local police felt that the bombing may have been an attempted murder. Whatever the case, it was front-page news throughout western Illinois, and in Macomb the citizens raised a $2,500 reward for information leading to the bomber's arrest.

Naturally Kelly was the prime suspect. Hainline had him arrested, but the bootlegger said that he was at home in Colchester at the time of the explosion, and no one could prove otherwise. Nevertheless, the young prosecutor was sure that Kelly was responsible, believing that he had employed "hired thugs" from Peoria to plant the bomb.

The investigation continued for weeks, with the help of an experienced detective from Quincy, but Hainline was unable to compile enough evidence to charge Kelly with the crime. By the first of the year he was deeply frustrated.

In early February, however, the crusading state's attorney got the chance to convict Kelly in a bootlegging case. He and Moon were charged with delivering two gallon cans of liquor to Lambert Hillyer, who lived on East Washington Street in Macomb. Hillyer was one of the many small-time bootleggers for whom Wagle and Moon were the suppliers.

Because the bombing was still on everyone's mind, and because Kelly Wagle was a notorious figure, the courthouse was packed. People came to see whether Hainline could get him.

It was a hard-fought case that symbolized for many people the whole issue of law and order in the Prohibition era. As Hainline said to the jury, "The big question involved in this case is whether our laws shall be enforced, or whether we shall be still more a nation of lawbreakers."

Fortunately, there was not just circumstantial evidence—cans and bottles of liquor from Hillyer's home—but an eyewitness, a policeman who saw Wagle and Moon deliver the booze. And Hainline's powerful summation, a plea for support of the law in an era of moral decline, visibly affected many people in the courtroom.

On February 8, 1924, the jury finally rendered its verdict: guilty. The young state's attorney was overjoyed, and so was Hattie Polk, who viewed the conviction as a turning point in her battle to clean up Colchester.

Two weeks later the convicted bootleggers were fined $300 each and sentenced to seventy-five days in the county jail. Of course, they planned to appeal.

Encouraged by that victory, local authorities kept up the pressure. Because Hattie Polk and others asserted that the Colchester police were corrupt, Hainline brought in state detectives, known as "dry agents," to investigate. On February 14 the *Independent* reported the arrest of a policeman:

A SENSATIONAL ARREST
Constable T. C. Dark
Accused of Having Liquor

One of the most sensational moves that has yet been made in the prosecution of the liquor cases in this city came last night when constable T. C. Dark, who is also the merchant night watchman, was arrested by secret service men who have been working in this city, after they had secreted themselves in a closet in the city building and listened to a conversation between the constable and Jay Moon. . . .

According to rumor it seems as though Dark has been suspicioned and accused of tipping off violators of the law in this city for some time, and also, it was said that he kept and used liquor in the city building.

Dark was eventually convicted of "drinking on duty" and paid a fine. He also lost his job as a policeman.

However, some of the townspeople didn't like the idea of surveillance by the secret service—men hiding in closets and listening in on conversations just to arrest someone for drinking. The Cam Dark case simply increased the hostility between supporters and opponents of Prohibition.

Although the Wagles supposedly moved to Chicago in 1924, they did not sell their home, and in fact, Kelly had no intention of staying away from Colchester. He was simply trying to avoid surveillance of his boot-legging activities while working with Peoria and Chicago lawyers to beat the auto theft charges and the liquor sale conviction.

Because he had built up an enormous trade in central western Illi-nois, Kelly was still making frequent trips in the area and was still hid-ing his liquor in various places. Acting on a tip that he had hidden a load in the barn behind his house, the Colchester police, headed by the new marshal, Herman Kratzer, raided his home in early July. Every newspa-per in the county carried the resulting story of Kelly's struggle to avoid arrest. This version is from the *Macomb By-Stander,* which by then considered itself the authoritative chronicle of his battles with the law:

GET ALCOHOL AT WAGLE RESIDENCE
Kelly Wagle Makes Escape with
Dozens of Cans in Auto

It has often been said that "you can't teach an old dog new tricks," and the fact that they certainly do persist in their old stunts was proven yesterday at the home of Henry "Kelly" Wagle, who bears a wide reputation as a bootlegger.

Officers visited the Wagle residence yesterday, armed with a search warrant, and obtained two cans containing alcohol, but Wagle escaped with dozens of other cans, said to contain alcohol.

The raid was conducted by city officers of Colchester—Herman Kratzer, Luther Kessler, and Tom Moon—who had obtained a search warrant issued through a Justice of the Peace officer in Colchester. They accosted Wagle at the gun club near Colchester and advised him of their possession of the warrant. He demand-ed a duplicate of the paper for himself, and the trio returned to town to have the extra document issued.

Wagle in the meantime is said to have rushed to his barn, where several dozen tin cans of alcohol were stored, and with a chisel, he was demolishing the containers when the officers arrived. They succeeded in getting possession of two cans containing the liquid and rushed with them to the city building, where they are being held as evidence. Again in the meantime, Wagle took advantage of their absence and loaded the spoiled cans and the remaining good ones into his Dodge car and sped away.

The McDonough County sheriff's office was notified of the raid and Wagle's escape, and they set about to guard the south and west roads leading into Macomb from Colchester. Wagle did not appear, however. It is believed that Wagle drove into the country and dumped the liquor.

Kelly was soon arrested and charged with "possessing, storing, and transporting intoxicating liquor in the City of Colchester." Later that month he was tried in the court of Justice of the Peace Lyman Burrows before a jury of six townspeople. By that time Kelly felt that he was being persecuted by the Ku Klux Klan, which included Marshal Herman Kratzer, so he and his lawyer made a special effort to keep Klansmen off the jury. Perhaps that made a difference, for he was declared innocent.

The case was a major disappointment for Mayor Hattie Polk, who had planned the raid with her new marshal, and it revealed the difficulty of convicting Kelly in his hometown, where many people resented police efforts to enforce Prohibition.

Despite the setback, Polk instructed her city attorney, William Harris, to prosecute Kelly for violating the Illinois Prohibition Law (rather than the Colchester law), so that the court would have a second chance to convict him for the same offense. That plan was foiled when Kelly somehow stole the evidence—the two gallons of confiscated liquor—from the city building. That, too, was front-page news in the *Macomb By-Stander*, which carried the June 23 story under a stunning headline: "WAGLE IS FREED: EVIDENCE IS STOLEN!"

For those who admired Kelly, the whole episode was a marvelous story, often retold, that proved he was too smart for the local authorities.

That impression was reinforced early in January 1925, when an appellate court threw out the much-publicized conviction of Wagle and Moon for selling liquor to Lambert Hillyer. As the court put it, "there is no proof that the cans seen carried into the house [by Wagle and Moon] contained liquor."

At about the same time Kelly managed to beat the various charges of larceny and receiving stolen property that had been brought against him in Chicago. The prosecutor there could not prove that Kelly knew the cars were stolen.

Those were frustrating developments for State's Attorney Les Hain-line, but by then he had something far worse to deal with. On the first night of the new year two enormous blasts had resounded throughout the county seat, causing destruction, panic, and fear. Someone had bombed the Macomb City Hall, at the southwest corner of the square, and then, later that night, the home of circuit court judge T. H. Miller, a few blocks away.

On the following day the *Macomb Journal* carried the story under a two-inch headline:

TWO BOMBINGS SPREAD REIGN
OF TERROR HERE LAST NIGHT
City Building and Home of
County Judge Partly Wrecked

Terror struck its fangs deep into the mental make-up of Ma-comb's citizenry last night and turned an otherwise peaceful night into one of great apprehension following two mysterious bomb blasts directed at law enforcement officers here. The detonations, severe in both the effect and report, partially wrecked the city building and the residence of county judge T. H. Miller, and oc-curred scarcely four hours apart. Buildings in near proximity to the blasts were rocked and windows shattered as the handiwork of law defyers was demonstrated, imperiling the lives of scores of per-sons. . . .

At the time of the first blast last night, shortly before 8:00, Chief of Police Elmore Coats, Night Policeman Henry Hammer, and Jud Blevins were seated in the police office at the city hall, first floor, rear. There was a sudden detonation that shook the entire build-ing and plunged a portion of it into darkness. . . . Fourteen per-sons, mostly women and children, were on the second floor of the building, which is used as a flat, and they were frantic when the officers arrived. . . .

The bomb was placed at the foot of the rear stairway, and when it exploded, it wrecked the stairs, the rear door, and a frame struc-ture at the rear of the city building used as a garage and a general storage room. Plaster was torn from the walls and ceilings of the stairway and the second story of the building, and every pane of glass on that floor was shattered. Windows in neighboring homes and stores were blown out by the severe concussion. . . .

Hardly had the perturbed nerves of citizens become partially settled before a second blast was heard—that at the home of county judge T. H. Miller, 313 S. McArthur Street. A charge of explosives had been placed against the foundation at the southwest corner of the house. A portion of the foundation was blown in, the first floor joists were snapped, the front porch ceilings ripped, and every window in the house and several in neighboring residences shattered.

On the following day the Macomb bombings were front-page news in the *Chicago Tribune* morning edition and in many other newspapers. City-type violence was spreading to small-town America. A Ku Klux Klan leader in Galesburg who was quoted by the *Tribune* said that the bombings were retaliation against the Klan, which had been holding a meeting in Macomb that night. He was wrong, but McDonough County was developing a reputation for lawlessness.

Within two days the county board and local civic groups put up a $3,500 reward for information leading to the arrest and conviction of the bomber.

Many were convinced that Kelly was responsible. Of course, he was questioned by the police, but as the *By-Stander* reported, he was "bitter in his denunciation of the bomber" and declared, "Hanging would be too good for a man who would jeopardize the lives of women and children to get vengeance against anyone." That sounded like a sincere reflection of his personal code.

Moreover, when the Macomb police asked Reuben Tones to use his bloodhounds, Kelly assisted him in bringing and handling the huge dogs. They sniffed the air at the shattered home of Judge Miller and led the authorities north past the square to Chandler Park, but unfortunately, the bomber's trail led only as far as the railroad depot.

Within a few days the police shifted their attention to another suspect. A sixty-year-old florist named Sam Danley, who had an extensive greenhouse on the west edge of Macomb, was arrested and charged with the bombings and with writing threatening letters to public officials.

Danley had been in trouble with the law for years, mostly because he had made and sold wine and occasionally whisky as well. In 1912, for example, he was convicted on ten counts of selling liquor and spent three months in jail. After an arrest and conviction for liquor sales in 1917, he broke jail and was later discovered at his home. When he refused to come out and surrender, the police set fire to one of his buildings and fired shots into the windows of his house, narrowly missing his wife. Danley fired back with a shotgun. During the fracas he slightly wounded three policemen. Convicted on assault charges, Danley served a short jail term and then went back to his flowers, but he was always bitter toward the police and toward Judge Miller, who had been the state's attorney when he was prosecuted in 1912. After the 1925 bombings, Sheriff Ira Atkinson, Judge Miller, and Mayor Samuel Russell received anonymous letters advising them to resign, and those were traced to Danley.

He had also been angry at State's Attorney Hainline, who had refused to prosecute the police for setting fire to his building. After Hainline's house was bombed in 1923, the young state's attorney had also received two anonymous letters advising him to resign. The handwriting was similar to those written two years later, so Danley was charged in connection with that case, too. Unable to provide the $10,000 bail bond, he remained in jail until the fall term of the circuit court.

In October 1925 Danley was convicted of sending the threatening letters to Hainline and was sentenced to six months in the county jail. The following year he was convicted of perjury in connection with that trial and was sentenced to one to fourteen years in the state penitentiary at Joliet.

Strangely enough, Danley was never convicted of the bombings. The authorities were probably satisfied that he was in prison on other charges, and they must have felt that it would be difficult to further convict him since he had alibis for his whereabouts when the bombings occurred. Also, and perhaps more important, Les Hainline remained convinced that Kelly Wagle had bombed his house and that Danley had simply seized the opportunity, more than a week afterward, to send the threatening letters ordering him to resign. The later bombings were probably Danley's own idea; Hainline wasn't sure about that, but he always felt certain that Kelly Wagle had brought the big-city crime of bombing to McDonough County.

Worried about the safety of his family, Hainline bought a specially trained German shepherd guard dog that watched his house at night. Although he was not intimidated by the bombings, he was disappointed by the lack of public support for law enforcement and frustrated by a legal system that seemed to favor the lawbreakers. In the spring of 1925 he did not run for reelection.

By that time the Ku Klux Klan was thriving in McDonough County, which supposedly had some two thousand Klansmen. In Colchester it was the largest and most influential secret society, and the city government cooperated to help promote it.

The evening of March 12, 1924, was designated as Ku Klux Klan night, when more than two hundred Colchester Klansmen triumphantly paraded the streets and then simultaneously ignited four huge crosses scattered along the railroad grounds, as if they were laying claim to the whole town. Later they held a ceremony and banquet at the Fraternity Building. That entire week was designated "Birth of a Nation Week," for Klansman Tommy Smith, owner of the Princess Theatre, had arranged to rent D. W. Griffith's masterpiece, *Birth of a Nation,* which depicts post–Civil War Klansmen as heroic defenders of white America. For members of the Colchester Klan, who filled the theater in their white robes and pointed hoods on March 12, the racist film dramatized their fears about cultural degradation and confirmed their identity as crusaders for Americanism and enforcers of Christian morality.

In the following August the Klan presented the annual Colchester Chatauqua—renamed the "Klantauqua"—a program of "music, entertainment, and lectures" that allowed Klansmen to propagandize about the principles and practices of the organization. According to the *Independent,* "It was one of the most successful entertainments ever held in this city and the most extensively attended." The city council and the churches had vigorously supported it.

Although the Klan did not commit overt acts of violence in Colchester, it continued its campaign of intimidation, polarizing an already divided community. Men who refused to join were viewed with suspicion, and if they were merchants or tradesmen, Klansmen pressured the townspeople not to do business with them or socialize with them. Some of the stores on Depot and Market Streets had signs in their windows saying "Trade with Klansmen." All that pressure only increased the anti-Klan sentiment, as did newspaper reports of Klan violence in other communities.

Klan criticism of Kelly Wagle led to personal animosity and, ultimately, to fistfights between Kelly and a couple of the Klansmen, one of whom was a member of the city council. Threats were issued on both sides, and when Kelly moved back from Chicago in the winter of 1925, he started carrying a handgun in his car.

Despite the intimidation, he never stopped bootlegging. And because he resisted the Klan, Kelly was admired by an increasing number of people who feared the organization.

At the same time, Hattie Polk felt so threatened by Kelly and the other bootleggers that she also bought a handgun. With the help of a local Klansman, she practiced firing it at a woodpile in the lumber yard.

Local controversy over the Klan got worse in February 1925 when Mayor Polk joined with hooded Klansmen to hold ceremonies at the two public schools. The *Independent,* always sympathetic to the organization, presented those events in a positive way:

KU KLUX KLAN VISITS SCHOOLS

The public schools were visited Wednesday by a delegation of Klansmen in uniform, and a short service was held at each building, and an American flag was presented to each school, and a Bible was given to each room.

The Klansmen secured the services of the Mayor, Mrs. Hattie Polk, who accompanied the delegation to the two schools and made a short talk on the Bible and the flag.

The service was an impressive one, and she read the 21st chapter of John after her address. . . . Then all stood and repeated the Lord's Prayer in concert, and the meeting adjourned.

The townspeople were used to overt religious proselytizing in the schools, especially during Polk's administration. In 1923 all the grade school and high school students were required to attend a revival at the Methodist Church, and in the following year they were forced to attend one at the Christian Church. Since the Klan was a Christian and patriotic group that had the firm support of local ministers, Polk felt that it was appropriate to join with them in holding the Bible and flag ceremony.

However, townspeople who opposed the Klan were outraged. As if to fight fire with fire, several black-robed figures soon created a huge flaming circle on Depot Street, near the railroad grounds. That was the symbol of an anti-Klan group called the Knights of the Flaming Circle. Although there was probably no formal chapter of the Knights in town, some residents wanted to put the Klan on notice that opposition was mounting. Others complained that Mayor Polk and the Klan had violated the separation of church and state, and some wondered whether the Klan was giving orders to the city government.

The backlash was so considerable that when Polk ran for reelection later that spring, she issued a pamphlet denying "the erroneous rumors . . . that your present Mayor is a member of the Ku Klux Klan" and asserting that she and the Klansmen had placed the Bibles in the schools simply because "the Bible is a textbook." Besides, she added, WCTU leaders in Illinois had also urged her to do that.

The same pamphlet carried an endorsement by all four of the town's ministers, who viewed Hattie Polk as the champion of decency against the forces of corruption and immorality.

WHAT A VOTE FOR MRS. HARRIET POLK MEANS

A vote for Mrs. Polk is a vote . . .
For a better and safer town
For the BOYS and GIRLS
For the SCHOOLS
For the CHURCHES
For arresting the Bootlegger
  as well as the Drunkard
For all that is Decent and Wholesome
For LAW and ORDER
For the BIBLE.

We, the undersigned, believe that the good people of Colchester have no choice in this election, and that means either to vote for Mrs. Polk or stay home. We feel that no one could vote for either of the other candidates with a clear conscience, since we know what some of the forces that are working so hard for them have done to our boys, and brought shame and disgrace upon our town. There are no BOOTLEGGERS working for Mrs. Polk. . . .

Rev. Edw. Hardy, Methodist Episcopal Church
Rev. F. Hibbert, Free Methodist Church
Rev. R. A. Diver, Christian Church
Rev. J. B. Kelley, Baptist Church

The effort to enforce Prohibition had, in fact, isolated reformers and enforcers like Hattie Polk from many others in the community who resented their coercive approach. One week before the election, Herman Kratzer, the marshal appointed by Mayor Polk, announced in the *Independent* that he was through with law enforcement because the townspeople did not support his efforts: "Heretofore in Colchester, the citizens as a whole stood by the Marshal, but with me it has been different. I have had the majority of citizens working against me."

By that time Polk herself had become such a controversial figure that neither party nominated her, but her constituency—mostly women and ardent churchgoers—finally prevailed on her to run as an independent. Then, as the newspaper later put it, "The fireworks commenced." Accusations about bootlegging, drinking, intimidation, corruption, and the Klan were hurled back and forth by Polk supporters and Polk opponents at meetings and rallies as the town's smoldering animosities suddenly flamed and burned. When it was all over, Bayless remarked, "A general campaign of the wrong kind was carried on," and "Some who were friends before are now not on good terms." That was putting it mildly.

When the votes were counted, a feed store owner named William S. Mote, who was a drinker and a critic of the Klan, beat Hattie Polk by a comfortable 119 votes. John O. Moon, who had the closest association with the bootleggers, came in third, but he and Mote together represented a significant anti-Polk, anti-Klan majority.

For the moral crusaders, it was a resounding setback.

On the following evening, at about midnight, "a fire of mysterious origin" broke out on Market Street. The townspeople jumped out of bed at the sound of the fire bell, and hundreds of them watched in the roaring glow that lit the railroad grounds as gasoline cans and ammonia tanks exploded and flames surged into the night sky. Within an hour two of the finest brick buildings in town were totally destroyed, despite the combined efforts of the Colchester and Macomb fire departments. By morning there was nothing left but smoldering rubble.

A woman who lived in the Leach Hotel, near the two stores, later reported that "she heard a noise, which sounded as if someone had thrown a brick through a glass window, and then the whole backyard [of the hotel] was lighted up, almost as bright as day, by a sheet of flames."

The *Independent* said nothing at all about the cause of the blaze, which consumed the J. B. Smoyer (formerly the Henry Terrill) general store and the Carson and Sons hardware store, which shared a common wall, and severely damaged the adjacent showroom of the Carson auto dealership and a small frame house owned by the Carson family. However, the *Macomb Journal* reported that many in Colchester blamed "factionalism and bitter feeling." Indeed, car dealer Leo Carson and his brothers were all drinkers and outspoken opponents of the Klan, and some months earlier Klansmen had burned a cross in front of the dealership. Still, no one had enough evidence to accuse anybody, and the investigation led nowhere.

The townspeople never learned anything for sure about the cause of that postelection fire, which did $100,000 in damage, but they were all glad the election was over. As it turned out, so was the era of the Klan, which by 1925 had strong opposition in most communities. The local chapter soon disbanded, and Hattie Polk, the defeated crusader, left town and never returned.

The Legendary Bootlegger

The 1920s brought good times for many Americans as industrial production soared and new businesses were launched, but the general prosperity did not extend to farmers and miners. Mechanization led to increased agricultural production, but the cost of farming also rose dramatically. Worse yet, farmers kept on producing at high levels throughout the decade while the demand for exports dropped after the war and commodity prices plummeted. Before the decade ended, agricultural income was down by more than one-third, many farmers were mortgaged to the hilt, and foreclosure was on the rise. Likewise, with the advent of electricity and oil as alternative sources of power, the demand for coal sharply declined, so mine operators cut back on production and pay, forcing thousands of Illinois miners to seek other jobs. Neither development was catastrophic for Colchester, but the farmers and miners who shopped there had less money to spend.

One event that brought renewed optimism and temporary prosperity was the coming of the "hard road." Throughout the 1920s the state was engaged in an all-out campaign to "pull Illinois out of the mud" by developing a system of paved highways, and early in 1923 the public works commissioner decided that Route 9, running from Peoria to Carthage, would pass through Colchester. The townspeople could hardly wait. They regarded the hard road as their new link to the American promise. It would end their provincial isolation and unite them with the march of national progress, or so it seemed.

The work on Route 9 moved along rapidly, and early in 1925 it was clear that Colchester would soon be connected by pavement to the rest of America. Scores of workers and their families started arriving in February, and by early March Colchester resembled a military camp. Every available house and room was rented, dozens of tents were put up, and the landscape was littered with trucks, road graders, concrete mixers, and other equipment. A special tramway was built to carry carloads of concrete and other materials to the construction site, and more than forty horses and mules were brought in for hauling and grading.

The town hadn't looked so busy since the 1880s. The townspeople watched while the road builders worked, and others came from miles around just to see the big noisy paver turn carloads of concrete into finished slabs of highway. As long as the great construction project continued, the hotel was booked, the restaurants were jammed, and the stores were busy.

In the middle of that wonderful summer, J. H. Bayless proclaimed that Colchester was finally rising out of its thirty-year slump, reborn as a thriving clay town and commercial center.

COLCHESTER STILL ON THE MAP

Hope springs eternal in the community as well as the human breast, and it is never safe to say that a town is dead, even though the undertaker is in the offing.

Consider the case of Colchester. Here is a town which looked like it had been literally worked out. Its industry was mining thin-vein coal, and for some thirty years its mines were busy. Then the coal gave out, and for some years Colchester has been out of the coal market.

But when things looked blackest, Colchester came back. Folks had been overlooking that it had some of the best clay to be found anywhere, another natural product that could be turned into wealth. They began converting Colchester into a clay products town, and now with an increase in retail activity, it enjoys a substantial boom.

When the road building was completed, the townspeople celebrated. They held a four-day event, the "Hard Road Opening and Fall Trading Festival," that climaxed on September 24, the day when Route 9 was opened from Carthage to Macomb. The celebration featured a "pavement dance" that drew 4,000 people, fueling hopes that Colchester would attract crowds of shoppers from a wide area.

The merchants who sponsored the big celebration also developed a new slogan for the town: "The hard road leads to Colchester."

No business attracted more out-of-town people than the new Princess Theatre, built in 1926. The South Side fire of 1925 had left a stretch of what the newspaper called "horrible ruins" in the business district, but movie show entrepreneur Tommy Smith soon bought the land where Smoyer's (formerly Terrill's) store had stood and announced that he would build a new brick theater, complete with a lighted marquee and modern projection equipment.

When it was completed the following April, the new Princess Theatre was the most elegant building in town. It featured a five-hundred-seat auditorium elaborately decorated in blue and gold, a large stage with a modern gold-fiber screen and a heavy rose-velvet curtain, and a massive Wurlitzer pipe organ that could sound "like a ten-piece orchestra." The gleaming lobby had a separate candy shop and a soda fountain.

The townspeople regarded the new Princess as "the finest small-town theatre in the state," and it probably was. It even received a write-up in *Motion Picture Magazine.* The opening was an event of enormous local importance, like the dedication of a new church.

The shining double doors were magic portals that led to other worlds peopled by the likes of Douglas Fairbanks and Rudolph Valentino, Pola Negri and Mary Pickford. Even without sound the Hollywood stars projected glamorous individualism, and in films like *Passion, Scandal, The Flapper,* and *The Jazz Age,* the spirit of the Twenties came to Market Street.

On Saturdays, when the country folks came to shop and brought the kids, the Princess offered less sensational, ten-cent movies, such as Our Gang comedies and Hoot Gibson westerns. The theater was always packed.

The one promising industrial development of the later 1920s was a new clay mine northeast of town. In 1926 the Northwestern Terra Cotta Company of Chicago sank a 135-foot shaft and started mining a tall vein of pure, hard, gray clay—known as "potter's clay"—with compressed air drills and dynamite. By the following year twelve men and two ponies were producing eighty tons of clay there every day. Brought up by an electric hoist, it was crushed, hauled to the railroad, packed in boxcars, and shipped out—primarily to Chicago, St. Louis, and Ottawa, Illinois, where terra cotta building materials were manufactured. Before the decade was over, Colchester clay was used in scores of major construction projects, including the Wrigley Building, the Merchandise Mart, and the Stevens Hotel (later known as the Chicago Hilton).

The manager of the Terra Cotta mine was D. Clinton Gates, an engineer who had spent most of his life in the gold mines and coal mines of the Rocky Mountain West, but the foreman was a local man whose experience reflected the mining history of Colchester. Thomas ("Tige," pronounced "Tag") Cooper was a stocky, outgoing fifty-one-year-old man who had already spent four decades working underground. When his father died of typhoid fever in 1886, Cooper was only eleven years old, but he dropped out of school to work in the coal mines. His mother soon remarried, but the family remained poor. When the shaft mining declined, Cooper moved to Mystic, Iowa, but he later returned and worked as a drift miner for many years until the Terra Cotta operation got started. By then, no man in town had a better reputation as a miner.

If Tige Cooper symbolized the mining heritage of Colchester, the new mine itself—which had electric lights and power equipment—represented the brighter industrial future that always glowed on the horizon.

While Colchester was struggling to regain its economic momentum, the *Independent* was twice sold. After fifteen years of hard work, J. H. Bayless was disappointed that the circulation had not grown, so he secured an appointment as postmaster and sold the newspaper in the summer of 1925. The new owner was Charles Hayden, a former linotype operator for the *Peoria Journal*. Like Bayless, he realized that the town's future was at stake, and he was soon lecturing his readers on the need for community activism. Too many townspeople showed no commitment to the common good, he said in August 1926, and "no community will go very far if the majority of its citizens think that they have no civic responsibility or obligations." Hayden was a good newspaperman and a promising leader, but he soon developed health problems, so in October 1926 he sold the *Independent* to Harry Todd and L. D.

Gustine, who had worked together for many years on a newspaper in Lewistown.

Gustine focused on business matters, so Todd was the new editor. A tall, outgoing, ambitious man, who wore rumply suits and plain bow ties, Todd mixed well with the businessmen in town, and he immediately launched a "buy at home" campaign and started organizing the merchants to promote their stores. Sounding like Babbitt in the best-selling Sinclair Lewis novel, he celebrated local businessmen as "the backbone of the community" and proclaimed that "community boosting" would make Colchester into "a live, enterprising town."

Unlike Bayless—and Van Hampton decades earlier—Todd was not a moral crusader. Shortly before selling the *Independent*, Bayless had reiterated his view that "Colchester needs a good cleaning up, for moral conditions have been growing steadily worse," but Todd never made a similar comment in his five years as editor. In fact, he was so concerned with how the town was reflected in his newspaper that he seldom focused on crime of any kind. When a hardware store owner named Howard Vance suddenly vanished in the summer of 1928, Todd wrote a four-sentence article expressing the hope that "he will return and clear up the situation," whereas the *Macomb Journal* reported that investigators were finding evidence of embezzlement. Of course, bootlegging and gambling also received no attention from the new editor, who soon bought out his partner and became the sole owner of the *Independent*.

While Harry Todd tried to promote a positive image of Colchester, others urged moral reform. Early in 1926 the four local churches cooperated to bring in evangelist Grady Cantrell, who had held very successful revivals at other small towns in the region and was billed as "a second Billy Sunday."

A slim, middle-aged man with a great shock of wavy brown hair and a broad smile, Cantrell was a dynamic speaker and a good organizer, if not quite the showman that Sunday was. Starting in mid-February, he held revival meetings at the high school auditorium, and hundreds of people came every night to hear him condemn "the jazz life" of the modern day and call sinners back to Christ. A talented humorist, he often made witty replies to questions from the audience. "Will I go to hell if I smoke?" one man asked. "No, but if you're not saved, you'll smoke in hell," Cantrell replied.

Night after night the audience laughed and clapped, prayed and shouted. When it was all over five weeks later, the entertaining evangelist had saved some 250 souls and had produced the biggest revival in the town's history. Local crusaders felt that "the devil was on the run" in Colchester.

Despite that effort, however, most of the townspeople were more ambivalent about immorality and lawlessness than ever before, and in that respect, they were like the American public everywhere else.

Prohibition had brought an enormous increase in crime and corruption, but it was difficult for drinkers to regard bootleggers as enemies of society. Instead, they saw them as bold, accommodating businessmen, serving the public in a repressive era.

Even gangsters received a certain adulation and respect, and the best example was Al Capone. After Johnny Torrio was seriously wounded by gunfire and then jailed for nine months in 1925, he returned to Italy, and Capone took over as Chicago's crime boss. Using machine-gun violence to eliminate rivals and part of his enormous profits to pay off the police, Capone soon controlled most of the city's illegal activities, and he became the most famous Chicagoan.

People downstate and elsewhere in the country learned about him through a multitude of news reports with titles like "Gang War Flares Again in Chicago" and "Capone's Killers Still on the Warpath." Feature articles sometimes glamorized him in the process of deploring his criminality. A prime example is "Al Capone, Lord of Chicago's Underworld," which appeared in the *Macomb Journal* late in 1927, accompanied by a romanticized sketch of Capone as a darkly handsome, powerful-looking figure. The article calls him "a swarthy, scarfaced desperado" with "a reputation for ruthlessness" but also observes that many people regard him as "a square shooter" with a certain integrity. Moreover, he is depicted as a self-made man: "Like most other prominent Americans, Capone worked his way up from the bottom and can attribute his success to hard toil and singleness of purpose."

The era of the gangster hero had arrived.

By 1926 or 1927 Kelly Wagle was acquainted with Capone, whom he admired. His introduction to the notorious gangster may have come through Neva Walley, a daughter of John Walley, who had divorced her first husband and moved to Chicago, where she dated one of Capone's bodyguards. It is also likely that Kelly purchased redistilled industrial alcohol from Capone's gang, which controlled the distribution of it in most of Chicago and the southern and western suburbs.

Although rumors later circulated that Kelly was "a rumrunner for Al Capone," that is doubtful. He liked to work for himself, and he continued to serve an established clientele in western Illinois. He often traveled to Chicago, but the center of his world was Colchester.

Nevertheless, like Capone, Kelly became a kind of hero—at least to some of the townspeople in Colchester. They knew he was a daring rumrunner, so they told stories like this one, which appeared in the *Macomb Journal* the year after he died: "Once when Wagle was hauling a load of booze [into Omaha] a policeman stopped him, and then jumped onto the running board of his car, ordering him to drive to the police station. On the way to the station, Wagle knocked the officer off the running board and escaped." That account came from an Omaha newspaperman, so it was probably true.

Another story puts him in Kentucky, where he was being chased by the police after picking up a load of moonshine. After disappearing over a hill, he ran through a field and right into a haystack, which covered his car while the police went by, letting him escape. That is almost certainly Kelly Wagle folklore, but he did run moonshine from Campbell County, Kentucky, near Covington, in the early 1920s.

Another story that is surely folklore finds him running from the police somewhere between Chicago and Colchester. They were gaining on him, so he threw a case of liquor behind him on the road—quite a feat, considering that he was driving—and the police car smashed into it. Of course, Kelly got away that time too.

Other stories depict him as incredibly clever, especially with respect to hiding his liquor. The most well known one involves the Christian Church near his home. It seems that one morning some people came to the church for a baptism, and when they uncovered the huge font, it was full of gallon cans filled with liquor. Kelly was hiding his booze there. The people went to get the sheriff, but when they came back, the cans were gone. Kelly had moved them to another place.

That story has a certain factual basis. When the furnace of the Christian Church was changed from coal to oil, the coal bin in the church basement went unused. Through a friend in the church, Kelly got access to it and stored a load of liquor there. When word started to circulate among the congregation that Kelly was storing booze in the coal bin, a member of the church board named Alta Hunt told him that his secret was out, so he moved the cans to another location.

The story got changed around because Kelly was becoming a legendary figure whose audacity and cleverness always put him one step ahead of the authorities. Similar stories find him hiding his booze in the freight room at the depot, in coffins at the nearby Williams Mortuary, or even in a secret passage somewhere in city hall. Others tell of a secret tunnel that connected his basement to his barn across the ravine, so that he could move his liquor without being seen. Still others have him shipping it out in railroad boxcars, concealed beneath apple crates, as if he manufactured it in huge quantities, or hauling it by horse and wagon to steamboats at the Mississippi River, as if cars and trucks were too conventional for the great bootlegger.

All these stories reflect a major theme of the Kelly Wagle legend: escape from, or avoidance of, imposed authority. That was, of course, a deeply held, if sometimes repressed, desire in the American mind during the Prohibition era.

In one case an automobile accident was shaped into a heroic story that became one of the most widely known parts of his legend. In May 1925 a Ford coupe slammed into a telephone pole just north of Colchester, and a nine-year-old girl was severely injured. The *Independent* gave a brief account:

A FEARFUL ACCIDENT

Edna Belle Clark was the victim of a very serious accident last Friday evening. . . .

She was thrown forward through the windshield [of Ray Dunsworth's car], and her head and neck were fearfully cut on the left side, and the jugular vein was exposed. A large gash was cut across her right cheek, and she was scratched and cut in a number of other places.

Drs. Harrison and Dillon were called and were at the scene in a few minutes and gave first aid, and then she was taken in Henry Wagle's car to the hospital in Macomb, arriving there in twelve minutes.

The doctors at the hospital went to work immediately, and

stopped the flow of blood and stitched up the cuts, and at this time she is doing very well.

Kelly had played an important role in saving the little girl, and soon he was the solitary hero of a well-circulated story, which later appeared in a short-lived newspaper called the *McDonough County News:* "Two years ago when Edna Belle Clark was slowly dying of strangulation after her windpipe had been pierced by glass in an automobile accident, Wagle grasped the child in his arms and lifted her into his automobile, and was speeding toward Macomb before witnesses realized what he was about. He made the six miles in six minutes, and at the hospital at the county seat an operation was hurriedly performed which saved the child's life." An innocent child was saved by the decisive and daring bootlegger, who used his well-honed driving skill to do what the townspeople otherwise could not have done—or so the story implies.

Another story that circulated but never made the newspapers involved Kelly's niece, Nellie Creasey, who was one of the daughters of Uncle John Walley. She and her family lived across the creek, in a poor rural neighborhood called Ragtown, and one time in the mid-1920s she became distraught and decided to commit suicide. She swallowed an overdose of medicine and wandered off into the woods to die. When the family discovered what had happened, they called Kelly, who immediately borrowed the bloodhounds of Reuben Tones and tracked her to a shed down by the Pleasant Valley Mill dam. Taking the nearly unconscious young woman in his arms, he carried her to his car and sped to the doctor's office, where her life was saved.

The bootlegger had done it again—if this story is true at all.

Another aspect of Kelly's life that became part of his legend was his generosity, and the most well known story of that sort involves the Methodist Church. He never attended services, but his mother, wife, and stepdaughter did, so once a year he gave money to help support that church. Some say that on his birthday he always gave the church $10, or $20, or $50 for every year that he had lived. No doubt the amount got higher as the story circulated. By the time he died, one version claimed that "once a year on his birthday he gave every church in town a wallet full of money"—an ironic twist, considering that the churches were flatly opposed to the liquor traffic and to him.

The benevolent bootlegger was the focus of other stories as well. When in 1926 Colchester developed a "hard road fund" to promote additional paved roads, Kelly made a $100 contribution, just as Thomas Baird, J. E. Carson, Henry Terrill, and other prominent businessmen did. According to a story that later circulated, however, when the town was seeking contributions for paving Hun Street, which adjoined his property, Kelly was asked to contribute, but he simply took the pledge sheet, tore it up, and told the official that he would foot the entire bill because other townspeople along that street were poor. Of course, Kelly was never that well-to-do, or that generous, but the story was widely told anyway.

Other service-to-the-poor stories—that he paid the mortgage of a farmer who was facing foreclosure, that he gave a horse to an impoverished drayman whose own horse had died, that he paid the funeral expenses for poor coal miners, that he provided food for destitute farmers whose crops had failed—are also probably folklore, produced as Kelly Wagle became a symbol of neighborly commitment in the minds of many townspeople. He stood for what Colchester most deeply meant in a changing America. That Kelly was also an expression of that change, an example of self-serving individualism and betrayal of community values, was seldom acknowledged.

Kelly's well-known generosity to children was reflected in his legend too. In addition to routinely giving children money for treats and occasionally inviting all the neighborhood kids over for ice cream, he did help a particular child now and again. Once, when Kelly offered to take his stepdaughter, Elinora (whom he always called "Smitty"), to the state fair, she asked whether a girlfriend could come along. Kelly said yes, so Elinora asked her to go, but the girl hesitated to accept because she was from a poor family and didn't have a nice outfit to wear. When Kelly found out, he simply bought her some new clothes, and they went to the fair.

That kind of generosity eventually led to a story that has several versions but goes something like this: "One day Kelly went to a man who owned a clothing store and told him, 'I don't want to see any ragged kids running around, so you supply them with clothes, and I'll pay for them.' Sometime later he happened to see a poor boy who had no shoes, so he went back to the store owner and gave him hell for not doing what he told him to do, and then he bought the boy a pair of shoes."

Another story has him providing clothes for a whole group of unfortunate schoolchildren in Ragtown: "The kids in Ragtown, north of Colchester, were very poor. One time, when several of them were going to graduate from the Ragtown School, Kelly heard that they didn't have any decent clothes, so he bought new clothes for all of those kids. That was the best graduation they ever had in Ragtown."

Later Kelly Wagle folklore even depicted him as a kind of Colchester Santa Claus, who bought toys for children and left them anonymously on the doorsteps of needy families at Christmastime. Clearly the townspeople were anxious to regard the controversial lawbreaker as someone who acted to help the unfortunate. And that, of course, made his presence in the community easier to accept.

The legend of Kelly Wagle—the daring rumrunner, the clever bootlegger, the timely rescuer, the community supporter, the benefactor of children—flourished in the minds of the townspeople after he died, but it clearly got started while he was still alive, perhaps as a counterforce to the other, darker rumors about him that continued to circulate.

Kelly's heroic stature was also a product of his success. By the later 1920s he was the leading bootlegger in central western Illinois, at a time when bootlegging had become a glamorous occupation. Moreover, by 1925 he was achieving success at something that was equally glamorous: horse racing.

After selling Sparkle to the Terra Cotta mine, which used ponies and mules in the tunnels, he had decided to try his hand at training and racing thoroughbreds, which he sometimes bought in Kentucky. His early mounts, Tottie Toast, Honest Tom, and Abe Lincoln, were often raced at county fairs in Illinois, Iowa, and Missouri, and they occasionally finished in the money. However, none of them was a great runner.

Then, in the summer of 1925 Kelly bought a two-year-old mare named Katherine Dillon, which had been raised on a farm in Louisville. She and Honest Tom won half-mile races at the McDonough County Fair that August, but that was only the beginning for Katherine Dillon, who was trained by H. J. Hockenbury of Bushnell. Later that season she won the Chicago Handicap in Springfield, in front of a record crowd of 80,000 spectators, netting a $300 purse, a blanket of roses, and a tall silver trophy called "The Governor's Cup." Back in Colchester the townspeople started to talk about Kelly's victories at the racetrack.

By September 1926 Katherine Dillon had raced thirty-four times and had an amazing record: first twenty-seven times, second four times, third twice, and fourth only once. Most of the purses were small, but Kelly did accumulate $2,259 in winnings—more than most men earned in a year—not to mention what he made through bets.

His streak of luck with Katherine Dillon suddenly came to an end on September 10 of that year at the Adams County Fair, and the story was soon reported in the *Independent*:

KELLY WAGLE LOSES FINE RACE HORSE

Katherine Dillon, the three-year-old running mare owned by Kelly Wagle of this city, was fatally hurt in the closing race at the Adams County Fair at Quincy last Friday.

In the running of the five-eighths mile novelty race with four starters, Katherine Dillon and Yellow Pine were running first, almost side by side, going into the first turn, with the Wagle horse between Yellow Pine and the inner fence. Yellow Pine, bearing in going into the first turn, caused Katherine Dillon to hit the fence with her left front leg, breaking the leg just above the knee and causing her to fall, dismounting her rider, Dale Hardy of Carthage, who broke his collar bone. . . .

A veterinarian was called at once, and upon examination said there was no chance to save the horse. Humane officer Colus immediately shot her.

Despite that calamity, the success of Katherine Dillon had taken Kelly's life in a new and promising direction: from then on he was firmly committed to racing thoroughbreds.

Meanwhile, his partner Jay Moon wasn't doing so well. Early in 1925 he pleaded guilty to violating the Prohibition law in a case involving twenty-one cans of liquor that the police had found in his car more than a year earlier. He paid a $250 fine, and the circuit court judge warned him that a second offense would land him in the penitentiary. Moon promised to mend his ways.

By that time, however, he was a committed rumrunner who had brought many other loads of liquor into the area under Kelly's direction, so even after his conviction he lived entirely by bootlegging and gambling. Often accompanied by Geneva, with whom he had a long-

standing sexual relationship, Moon commonly went to Campbell Coun-
ty, Kentucky, near Cincinnati, for moonshine and up to Port Huron,
Michigan, for Canadian liquor that was smuggled across the St. Clair
River. He also made runs to Chicago.

In the process Geneva had become a small-town version of a gangster's moll. Like Kelly she loved fast cars and enjoyed the challenge of
matching wits with the police. She was blunt about how she regarded
people, too. "He (or she) can kiss my ass" was a common remark about
someone she disliked. Rumor had it that Geneva even transported liquor in her car at Moon's request, but whatever the case, she was a
rough-talking, hard-drinking, good-time girl who had no more respect
for the law than her brother or her boyfriend did. And like them, she
sometimes carried a gun.

In the summer of 1926 the partnership between Kelly Wagle and Jay
Moon came to a dramatic end, and Geneva, whether innocent or not,
was caught up in their dispute. The details are sketchy, but the main
problem involved a very big load of liquor bought by Kelly; he had it
picked up by Moon and Geneva at Port Huron, and it was subsequent-
ly hijacked. A few years later, after Kelly's death, Geneva briefly told a
reporter what had happened: "Once he [Kelly] tried to kill me—fired
three shots at me and then struck me over the head with his revolver.
He had accused me and my sweetheart, John Moon, of stealing 18 thousand dollars worth of whisky and selling it." After pistol-whipping Geneva, Kelly went looking for Moon, who made himself scarce for a few
days. When Kelly eventually spotted his partner driving north on Coal
Street, near the cemetery, he forced Moon's car off the road, smashed
the driver's side window, and punched him repeatedly in the face, swearing at him all the while.

Whether he threatened to kill Moon at that time is unknown, but for
Kelly the hijacking was a matter of betrayal, the one thing that he could
never tolerate.

In later years the mysterious hijacking inspired a story of domestic
betrayal that was set in the familiar world of Colchester: "One Sunday
Kelly was invited to his mother's home on Coal Street. After having
dinner, he fell asleep on the couch. Meanwhile, Geneva played the pi-
ano loudly in the next room while her sweetheart, Jay Moon, came over
and stole a load of liquor that had been hidden under the house. When

Kelly found out that it was gone, he was furious, and he never trusted Moon or Geneva again." (Another version asserts that he eventually stole it back.)

This story explains the break between Kelly and Moon in local terms, but it reduces the major hijacking to a more limited theft and omits the bootlegger's violent confrontations with his sister and his former partner. The townspeople who repeated this account must have viewed the local bootlegging as a harmless competition between clever rivals. However, Kelly never would have hidden liquor at his mother's house (respect for her dislike of drinking was part of his code), nor would Moon have waited until Kelly was around before stealing it. Some Colchester residents believe that Geneva was the source of this story, and if so, she spun it for her own reasons.

Soon after the violent split between the two bootleggers, State's Attorney William Harris, who had succeeded Les Hainline in that office, received an anonymous tip that Kelly Wagle had a big supply of liquor upstairs in his building on Depot Street. The upper rooms were still used as a gambling place, although Kelly would soon turn them into a pool hall. On November 4, 1926, the police moved in, as the *Macomb Journal* reported the next day in a headline story:

SEIZE 70 GALLONS OF ALCOHOL AT COLCHESTER
Arrest of Kelly Wagle is Ordered

A raiding party, composed of Sheriff Ira Atkinson, Deputy Paul Eakle, Policeman Joe Reid, State's Attorney Bill Harris, and Marshal Kipling of Colchester, last night swooped down on a building in Colchester that adjoins the Colchester State Bank on the west and, armed with search warrants, seized 70 gallons of alcohol.

The alcohol was in one-gallon cans, and at current bootlegging prices it has a retail value of approximately $3,000.

State's Attorney Harris was today preparing to file information in the county court against Henry "Kelly" Wagle of Colchester, on charges of illegal possession and transportation of liquor. A capias is to be issued for his arrest. . . .

The haul was the biggest ever made in McDonough County, and in the belief of officers its seizure strikes directly at the source of much local bootleg alcohol.

Kelly was not in town at the time of the raid, but he was later arrested and then released on $1,000 bond.

When his trial came up a month later, he pleaded guilty in the hope of getting a light sentence, but instead he got the maximum: six months in the county jail. On December 16, 1926, the McDonough County authorities finally had Kelly Wagle where they had wanted to put him for several years.

Neither his arrest nor his conviction was reported in the *Colchester Independent*.

The McDonough County Jail was an old red-brick building that had been constructed in 1876. Located on Jackson Street one block west of the square, it had an office, several small cells, and living quarters for the sheriff's family. Kelly started serving his time there on December 16.

While he was in jail, some of his friends stopped in to see him now and again, including Fred Wayland and Chick Hocker, who occasionally ran errands for him. His mother came every week. Since Arch's death four years earlier, Kelly had looked after her, often buying things for her, and they remained close. Alice never criticized him, and like many others, she related to Kelly as he presented himself to her and ignored everything she heard or read about him.

Blanche came every day. She had to. Kelly refused to eat the jail food and told her to bring his dinner in the late afternoon. It was an imposition for Blanche to travel to Macomb every day, seven days a week, but Kelly had exploded at her many times—he had probably hit her too—and Blanche was afraid of him. She usually did whatever it took to avoid his rage.

Kelly had one other regular visitor. Every Sunday afternoon Edna Belle Clark, well recovered from the injuries that had almost killed her, walked over from her house on Randolph Street and brought him a pint of ice cream.

Despite the visitors, Kelly was terribly bored in jail, so he enjoyed talking with the new sheriff, Paul Eakle, a tall, wiry, dark-haired man who had been raised on a farm near Colchester and had married a local girl. Before his election, he had lived on North Coal Street. The thirty-five-year-old Eakle was the youngest sheriff in the county's history, but he was experienced, having served as a deputy for several years. In 1921 he had captured bandits along the road to Colchester and had been given a medal for his heroism. In the fall of 1926 the *Macomb Journal* had referred to him as "a fearless and wide-awake enforcer of the law," and he had trounced his opponent in the November election.

Immediately afterward he had appointed the capable and popular Macomb chief of police, Cliff Leighty, as his deputy, indicating that he was determined to lift the sheriff's office to a new high level of performance. The public was impressed with Eakle, and Kelly probably admired him too.

Because the old jail's interior was dingy, Kelly offered to paint it for the young sheriff, who lived there with his wife and was responsible for maintaining the building. Eakle was glad to let him do it.

While he was in jail Kelly also arranged to get rid of Jay Moon, whom he blamed for the raid that led to his arrest. Also, Moon had become his competitor, running alcohol into the area from suppliers in Peoria and elsewhere. No one knows how or with whom Kelly made the arrangement to have his former partner eliminated, but sometime during the first few months of his jail term he must have realized that his incarceration was the perfect alibi.

On the morning of April 19, 1927, a bomb demolished Jay Moon's car and narrowly missed killing him. Naturally it was the headline story in the *Macomb Journal,* and two days later Harry Todd even put it on the front page of the *Independent:*

ATTEMPT MADE ON THE LIFE OF JAY MOON

Tuesday morning a cowardly attempt was made to murder Jay Moon, son of Mr. and Mrs. J. O. Moon, of this city. Mr. Moon had parked his car in the driveway of the Earl Rhodes home, which is directly across the street from the Moon home. It has been his practice to leave the car at this place. . . . At about ten o'clock Tuesday morning he had gone to his car, which is a new Buick coupe, to drive to the business section when the explosion took place.

He had seated himself in the car, and when he stepped on the starter there was an explosion which wrecked the car and broke several windows in the Rhodes house which stood about fifty feet away. Neighbors hearing the report rushed to the injured man's assistance and pulled him from the wrecked car, which had caught fire and would have burned but for the presence of mind of James A. Branson, who secured water and extinguished the blaze.

It is a miracle that Mr. Moon was not instantly killed, for the front part of his car was demolished, the windshield and rear window of the coupe were blown to bits, and one-half of the hood landed about one hundred feet away. A large hole was made in the upper part of the crankcase on the left hand side, the radiator almost torn from the car, and numerous small parts of the motor demolished. Appearances were that the explosive was placed near the starter switch so that the minute an attempt was made to start the motor, the driver would be killed. . . .

The young man was taken to Macomb, where during the afternoon Dr. J. B. Holmes operated upon both of his feet. One toe was dislocated, and bones in both feet were broken. He will be forced to remain in the Holmes hospital for several weeks, and it is feared that he will be left permanently crippled. . . .

Ironically, the same issue of the *Independent* also carried the news that John O. Moon had been elected mayor once again, so the townspeople could not avoid reflecting that their city government again had strong connections to the bootleggers.

Although Sheriff Eakle made a thorough investigation of the car bombing and determined that dynamite had been used, no leads turned up. Moon refused to say anything, of course, because accusing Kelly would have prompted an investigation into their bootlegging. Privately, however, he told friends that he knew Kelly was responsible, and at one point he reportedly said, "I'm going to get even with that son of a bitch if I have to go to Omaha and dig up the body of his dead wife." If that comment is accurate, he knew about Beulah's murder, but he recognized that he didn't have the evidence to pin it on Kelly.

Blanche Wagle was among those who rejoiced that Kelly was in jail— and not just because of his domineering character and explosive temper. She had a lover, a tall, slim, handsome fellow named Cecil Underhill. He was a butcher at the Terrill and Hulson store on Depot Street, and everybody said he made the best sausage in town. Cecil was as friendly as Kelly, but he was a mild-mannered, polite man who was always in a good mood. He often whistled when he walked down the street. Everybody called him "Ceese."

Underhill had chiseled good looks and reddish, wavy hair, and the townspeople regarded him as a ladies' man. Still a bachelor at thirty-six, he was the heartthrob of many a frustrated housewife. Blanche had undoubtedly met him where everyone else did, at the meat counter of Terrill and Hulson's store, but when Kelly started racing thoroughbreds, he hired Underhill to look after them while he was out of town, and that eventually brought the handsome bachelor into close contact with Blanche. By the time Kelly was arrested, they were in love, and Underhill was carrying a photograph of Blanche in his wallet.

The lovers were frequently together at the Wagle house while Kelly was in jail, and by the time he was released in June 1927, most of the townspeople had heard rumors about their affair. It wasn't long before Kelly heard the rumors too. No one knows what he said to Blanche, or did to her, but he ended his friendship with Underhill and warned him to stay away from her. For the rest of his life Kelly worried about what Blanche did when he was away.

Later that summer he got wind of some contact between them while he was out of town, and that led to a fight at Foster's restaurant, a small cafe with a soda fountain just off the west end of Macomb Street. Underhill was sitting at a table when Kelly walked in and spoke briefly to his young friend Alfred Kipling, who managed his pool hall. When Underhill got up to approach the soda fountain, Kelly suddenly stepped forward him and slugged him, knocking him down, and then said, "I told you to leave my wife alone." As Underhill started to get up, Kelly threw more punches, and the two men fought among the tables and chairs and wrestled on the floor while the horrified owner yelled for them to stop. When they finally did, Kelly stood over the beaten man and warned him again to leave Blanche alone. Then he left.

In twenty-four hours the story was all over town.

Of course, after his release from jail Kelly went right back to bootlegging. In fact, during that summer he bought two new cars largely for that purpose, a Chevrolet cabriolet and a Buick sedan. Both were sleek, roomy cars with big engines.

Despite increasingly tough laws against bootlegging, transporting liquor was still relatively safe and thus an easy way to make money. As Kelly knew and told his close friends, there were two main rules for a bootlegger: try to avoid attracting any attention and, if the police do try to stop you, be prepared to run for it. Kelly had never been caught on the road by the police, although he had run through stoplights and raced down country roads to avoid arrest.

As his own recent experience showed, storing the liquor was far more risky. For that reason, he became more inventive after his release. One of his favorite hiding places in the late Twenties was a two-room shack by an old sawmill northwest of town.

Also, Kelly did less selling to individuals and more selling to small-time bootleggers. It was simply safer to deal with men who had the same interest in avoiding the authorities.

As usual, the Colchester police were no problem. The marshal in the late 1920s was Cat Kipling, the former baseball hero, who had been a coal miner for twenty years and who was himself a drinker. Although he had participated in the raid that had resulted in Kelly's jail term, he had no personal interest in enforcing Prohibition, and after John O. Moon was elected mayor, he must have realized that the city government would not support strict enforcement anyway.

But the county sheriff, Paul Eakle, was another matter. Backed by State's Attorney William Harris, he was determined to stop the bootlegging, as well as the gambling. Often conducting multiple raids on a Saturday night, he soon had as many as twenty prisoners in the county jail at one time, primarily for liquor violations. By the close of 1927 the *Macomb Journal* reported that Eakle and his deputy had made 202 arrests that year—"a record . . . that has never been outdone in the history of the county."

Early in 1928 they raided an upper room on the east side of the Macomb square one Saturday night and arrested Everett ("Pete") Wells and Jay Moon, who were charged with running a gambling house. Wells, a forty-two-year-old, brown-haired, brown-eyed man who was a small-time bootlegger from Littleton, pleaded guilty and paid a fine. Moon, who was running a crap game, managed to beat the charge by claiming that he was just another player. He then moved his game to a more secure location—at the east end of Depot Street in Colchester.

Nevertheless, Eakle's campaign to dry up McDonough County had some real success in 1928. His most spectacular raid came on a Saturday night in early June when he arrested ten people, according to a *Macomb Journal* report:

ARREST TEN ON LIQUOR CHARGES
Sheriff's Office Conducts
Saturday Night Raids

Armed with search warrants based on evidence that liquor sales had been made at various places, Sheriff Paul Eakle and Deputy Cliff Leighty conducted a series of liquor raids in Macomb, Colchester, and Bushnell Saturday night, seized large quantities of home brew and some alcohol, and today ten were faced with charges of liquor violations.

Although Kelly's home was raided that night, no liquor was found, but charges were placed against him anyway, and when the grand jury met in September, he was indicted for "Illegal possession of liquor (second offense) and illegal sale of liquor (first offense)." He had gotten careless and had sold a pint of whisky to a man he didn't know—a man who turned out to be a liquor investigator. Kelly refused to plead guilty, however, so he posted bond and planned to fight the charges.

His bootlegging business may have been declining because of competition from Jay Moon and surveillance by the authorities, but Kelly's success at the racetrack was making up for it. In the summer of 1926 he had purchased a stallion named Mussolini from a breeder in eastern Tennessee, and the following season it finished in the money at Mt. Sterling, Burlington, Kahokia, Carthage, and other nearby places.

In July of that year he went to Kentucky and purchased another thoroughbred, a bay filly named Flossy Hare, which turned out to be the finest racehorse he ever owned. After being trained by Hockenbury in Bushnell, Flossy Hare won a series of races in Illinois during the summer of 1928 and then won purses in Missouri, Arkansas, and Louisiana. A race in New Orleans in early December brought the biggest purse that Kelly's horses ever won, plus an amazing return on bets, as Harry Todd proudly reported in the *Independent*:

COLCHESTER ENTRY AT NEW ORLEANS COPS
$700 PURSE FOR OWNER HENRY WAGLE

Nosing out a field of promising two-year-old maidens at New Orleans recently, Flossy Hare, Henry (Kelly) Wagle's entry, carried the Colchester horse fancier's colors to victory and brought down a $700 purse for the owner in one of the prettiest races of the current Jefferson Park program. . . .

While Banbrick and Kirby were fighting for the lead, Flossy Hare gained easily with T. Malley rein-riding her up to the finish. From fifth at the first quarter to fourth at the half, Flossy Hare, with an early spurt, passed Kirby as they raced to the stretch, and caught Bambrick under the wire, winning by a nose. . . .

Two dollar certificates on Flossy Hare paid $108, the biggest premium up to the present time at the New Orleans track.

Wagle paid $575 for Flossy Hare at Lexington, Kentucky in July, 1927. Recently he purchased another promising filly, Miss Fairmount. . . .

Wagle plans to go south after the first of the year, to devote all of his time to the development of his two mares.

As this well-informed article suggests, Kelly was increasingly drawn to racing, which provided him with an exciting, legitimate way to make money and to get the attention that he always craved. For the notorious bootlegger, success was measured not by achievement but by adulation, and nothing aroused that public response more dramatically than a victory at the racetrack.

By the time he won that purse at New Orleans, Kelly was lionized by many local residents, who saw in him only what they wanted to see. During 1928 Todd published eight articles on aspects of Kelly's racing career but never reported his arrest for bootlegging. Like many others, he was willing to overlook Kelly's persistent lawbreaking and apparent brutality, and simply regard him as a Colchester success story. In his later years Kelly welcomed that view, for he thought of himself as a person worthy of the town's respect—a self-made man.

But there was more to the townspeople's admiration for Kelly than just his rise to economic and social prominence in an era when success in Colchester was hard to achieve. Because of his numerous good deeds and neighborly dependability, he seemed to epitomize the old high-trust culture that everyone felt was fading. A writer for the *Quincy Herald Whig* said as much shortly after his murder: "True, many regarded him as mean, and sometimes brutal, but he was honest, kept his promises, and paid his debts. 'If Kelly says he'll do a thing [for you], he'll do it,' Colchester folks said of him, and forgot his faults."

Of course, some did not forget, and they put a different spin on the same blend of social concern and violent animosity. "Kelly would do anything for you," they said, "or anything to you."

Many of the townspeople felt sure that he was responsible for the car bombing that had crippled Jay Moon, and some even suspected that he was behind the mysterious disappearance of Howard Vance in mid-July. Kelly had known the twenty-seven-year-old Vance and had often stopped at his hardware store on Macomb Street. Rumors circulated that Vance had owed Kelly some money, perhaps for the new Chevrolet that had vanished along with him, but no one knew anything for certain. The only clue was the young man's car keys, found along the road to Macomb.

The Vance case was never solved.

Like Al Capone, Kelly Wagle symbolized the public's ambivalence toward the new individualism that had emerged since the war. By 1928 he had become the most well known figure in McDonough County, a much-admired success and the basis for a burgeoning legend that portrayed him as a hero, yet he was a lawbreaker and a violent man. Perhaps the townspeople and others in the county figured that it took that kind of a man to succeed in a fast-moving, uncaring, twentieth-century world. Or perhaps, in an era of corruption and fearful change, they simply wanted to believe in somebody.

It is not surprising that the most talked-about movie at the Princess Theatre that year was Paramount's *Jesse James,* the romanticized story of an outlaw hero.

The Killing That Finally Came

By the late 1920s the townspeople knew that the hard road was not going to help Colchester. Instead it took local shoppers away from town, especially to the county seat, which had so much more to offer. The merchants resorted to special contests and promotions, but the Saturday night trade was often disappointing.

Even the marvelous Princess Theatre was not doing as well as Tommy Smith had hoped. Despite the fact that it was the first theater in McDonough County to install sound equipment and show "talkies," the Princess often had many vacant seats, and Harry Todd upbraided the townspeople for not attending "more loyally."

The old ethic of community support was slowly losing ground to the new drive for self-fulfillment, and Macomb, which had two theaters, a bowling alley, a nightclub, an amusement park, and several chain stores, was a powerful attraction. As the townspeople used their automobiles to shop and seek entertainment when and where they pleased, the business district in Colchester declined as a social center.

Nearby villagers and farmers were also starting to shop at Macomb, especially when the Colchester streets were muddy. Late in 1928 Todd urged the townspeople to pave the business district for that reason:

LET'S TALK ABOUT PAVEMENT

Colchester is a shopping center. Its retail stores are dependent on the farm trade. . . . Merchants must realize that they are losing the "muddy weather" trade because of the mud and slush underfoot.

A limited amount of pavement in the business district would be an investment well worthwhile.

Of course, Macomb already had a completely paved business district, not to mention extensive cement sidewalks.

In the same editorial Todd asserted that street paving would have been underway already "had it not been for the untimely death of the mayor, who was an ardent advocate of progressivism." He was talking about John O. Moon, who had died in office the previous spring. Not since Van Hampton had left town for good in 1905 had Colchester lost such a talented civic leader.

But economic and demographic trends, not lost leaders or unpaved streets, were the underlying problem. The farmers were already in a depression, and many were leaving agriculture. The rural population was declining. In 1929, for example, the Cumberland Presbyterian Church, several miles south of town, closed its doors because of decreasing attendance. At about the same time, the Independence School, a few miles north of town, closed because of dwindling enrollment. Young people were also leaving Colchester for larger towns, which held greater promise. The townspeople would not learn the new census figure (1,342) until 1930, but they surely knew that, despite all their efforts, the local population had not grown and was probably still declining.

The most hopeful business development of the late 1920s was the rebuilding of the great Walty Hardware Store, which had been destroyed by fire in October 1927. For many months it looked as if Colchester might lose forever its finest store and foremost merchant leader because A. M. Walty was not sure that he wanted to rebuild in a town that was apparently losing the battle against decline. But local leaders finally convinced him, and in September 1928 the *Independent* carried the news in a two-inch headline story:

WALTY HDW. CO. ERECTING $12,500 BUILDING

The Walty Hardware Company is fully convinced that Colchester has a brilliant future, and to prove that a large force of workmen under John Haskins began work on a $12,500 building Monday morning. . . .

Although this is the age of chain stores and hard roads, an interview with A. M. Walty and his two sons, Glen and Elmer, has proven to us that they believe in Colchester's future and are ready to compare price and quality with any competition they meet. . . .

The Waltys have always been hustlers for business and draw trade to Colchester from a radius of many miles in every direction, and with the opening of their new store, with a complete stock of furniture, rugs, stoves, hardware, etc., every business located here will profit.

The new store did fairly well for several months after it opened, but slowly the crowds declined as more and more shoppers drove to Macomb.

The Exchange Club, an organization of businessmen formed by Harry Todd in 1927, was determined "to keep our town on the map," as one of the leaders put it in a 1929 article for the *McDonough County News*. To fulfill that aim, they promoted Colchester as a wholesome, friendly, caring sort of place. It was an ideal small town, they said, "free from all the immoral and unhealthy conditions of larger cities" and led by "good, religious, energetic, cooperative, and unselfish businessmen."

The club even developed an "Official Poem of the City of Colchester," which was approved by the city council. Inspired by Walter Foss's famous "House by the Side of the Road," the Colchester poem emphasizes old-fashioned community values:

COLCHESTER:
The Town by the Side of the Road
We live in the town by the side of the road,
By the side of the highway of life,
To serve all men with the ardour of hope,
The men who are faint with strife.

The poem gets even more sentimental, but it ends by extending a warm welcome to those who might visit or live in Colchester. Although the "Official Poem" was a product of small-town boosterism, it also reflected the local need to see Colchester as a neighborly place, where ideals still mattered and hope for a better life was available—at a time when the townspeople wondered about those very things.

The most notable new business of the late 1920s was indeed "by the side of the road," but it served something other than "the ardour of hope." It was a roadhouse called the Cottonwood Inn.

As paved roads spread throughout the state and more than one and a half million Illinois automobiles ran on them, roadhouses sprang up everywhere. They were not just eating places for motorists but amusement centers that commonly offered music, dancing, drinking, and gambling. The Cottonwood Inn was no exception.

Located one mile east of Colchester on the north side of Route 9, it was built in 1928 by Turk Stephens, a former coal miner who also harvested ice from the Ballast every winter. He was a short, stocky, broad-shouldered man who liked to drink and gamble.

The Cottonwood Inn consisted of a brick restaurant building that had a gas pump in front and an open-air dance pavilion, complete with a jukebox, in back. Stephens also had a dozen small cottages to rent, making the place a kind of early motel too.

The roadhouse got its name from a huge cottonwood tree that stood in front, shading the building. Like a gigantic Christmas tree, it was hung with hundreds of colored lights, and after nightfall it was the brightest spot in McDonough County.

Inside the restaurant there was a counter lined with stools where travelers could buy sandwiches, soda pop, ice cream—and booze. Turk Stephens was a bootlegger. Like many others, he made his own home brew, often storing it in the crawl space underneath his house, but he got his hard liquor from Kelly Wagle. One of his most popular concoctions was made by uncapping a bottle of legal "near beer" and pouring some 198-proof alcohol into it, to create a sort of boilermaker. Stephens kept his alcohol in a big pitcher so that he could rapidly pour it down a drain in case of a raid. And the Cottonwood Inn *was* raided, without success, shortly after it opened.

Some of the Colchester men, including Kelly Wagle, also gambled at the Cottonwood, playing craps on the counter late at night. It was not uncommon to see more than $100—two or three weeks' wages—won or lost on a single throw of the dice.

Kelly had known Turk Stephens for years. They had played poker from time to time since the war. Moreover, his son, John Stephens, whom Kelly always called "Young Turk," had ridden Sparkle in some county fair races a few years earlier. So the bootlegger must have felt that providing liquor for the Cottonwood Inn was a safe transaction.

But the world was no longer safe for Kelly Wagle. It hadn't been since Jay Moon had recovered from the car bombing that had shattered his legs. For the rest of Kelly's life, it was Moon, not Sheriff Eakle, who was his biggest concern. He knew that it was just a matter of time until his former partner, who now walked with a limp like he did, would try to get even. A few months after he got out of jail, Kelly went to a lawyer in Macomb and made out a will, and during the last two years of his life he often remarked to friends that Jay Moon was out to get him.

As a precaution he invited a young relative to live with him and act as an errand boy and bodyguard. It was Dean Walley, the youngest son of his uncle John. Dean was only four years old when John Walley died, after which he lived with his impoverished mother, who washed dishes at a local restaurant. In the early 1920s he was taken in by his divorced sister, Neva, who lived in Chicago, worked at a speakeasy, and dated Al Capone's bodyguard. The youth, who was only nineteen in 1928, was familiar with the world of gangsters, and like many other young men, he admired his cousin the bootlegger. Dean Walley was also a stocky six-footer who weighed well over 200 pounds, and he knew how to take orders. By the summer of 1928 he was living in the small building behind the Wagle house that Kelly always called "Monte Carlo."

By 1928 Moon had several reasons for wanting to get rid of Kelly. Revenge for the car bombing was one of them, but so was self-preservation. He couldn't be sure that Kelly would not try to kill him again. After his recovery Moon became extremely cautious about what he did, especially after dark. He always carried a gun, a .45 caliber Colt automatic. And he must have realized that if Kelly was eliminated, he could take over the distribution of liquor in McDonough County and nearby towns.

Like Kelly, he had not worked at a regular job for some time, and his income was entirely derived from illegal activities, especially bootlegging and gambling. Because Kelly had forged connections with the Capone gang in Chicago, Moon dealt instead with Peoria liquor suppliers, especially John Lipkin, who had a still across the Illinois River, near Pekin.

Moon also turned to theft. The extent of his stealing is hard to determine, but it included the burglary, carried out with an associate, of at least one clothing store in McDonough County. In February 1927 the *Macomb Journal* carried the following headline story:

GET $2,000 IN SUITS FROM INDUSTRY STORE
Burglars Smooth in Job Last Night

Only a few days ago Industry abandoned the policy of having a fulltime watchman for the business section, and last night burglars picked the locks on the H. A. Hoffman clothing store and, while the town was sleeping, hauled out more than $2,000 worth of men's suits and made a clean getaway.

Both doors of the store were left unlocked by the burglars. So far as could be learned today by Sheriff Eakle and Deputy Leighty, who investigated, no one heard them at work during the night, and they left no trace of their identity.

The *Industry Press* also reported that an unspecified sum of money was stolen from the store's safe.

The burglars were never caught, and many assumed that criminals from outside the county were responsible. However, Geneva Wagle later told close friends that Moon and another man from McDonough County had pulled that robbery. They apparently fenced the 106 men's suits in Chicago.

During that same month the P. D. Archer store in Bardolph, east of Macomb, was also burglarized. Rumor had it that Moon was responsible—and that Geneva's dresser drawers were the final resting place of the shoes, silk hose, and other women's clothes that were taken.

Later in the year Moon and a man named Charles ("Junk") Stewart, who lived in Macomb, burglarized the old Popel and Giller brewery in Warsaw, on the Mississippi River, and stole dozens of gallons of liquor that had been confiscated by federal agents and was being held as evidence. Moon later told friends about that job, which he apparently regarded as a clever stunt.

He may have been involved in other robberies as well.

Toward the end of 1928 Moon decided to make his move on Kelly Wagle. The attempt took place on Christmas Eve, and because of the holiday, the *Macomb Journal* did not carry the headline story until December 26:

SHOTGUN CHARGE BARELY MISSES K. WAGLE
Shoot into Auto Near Colchester

A shotgun charge fired from behind a tree into the Ford sedan of Henry "Kelly" Wagle of Colchester, at the east end of Colchester shortly after 8 o'clock Monday evening, shattered the glass in the rear left window of the car and barely missed Wagle, who was alone at the wheel.

He escaped the ambush unhurt, except for slight cuts about the face and neck inflicted by pieces of broken glass.

Following the shooting, Wagle openly charged that his assailant was Jay Moon of Colchester.

Kelly had been at the Cottonwood Inn and was driving to Dewey Hocker's home, on the east edge of town, when he turned off Route 9 and onto a dirt road. Just as he made the turn, he saw two men standing behind a tree, and beyond them was Jay Moon's Buick. Sensing an ambush, Kelly shoved the car into reverse and started rapidly backing up as one of the men fired a shotgun that shattered the backseat window. With the accelerator crammed to the floor, Kelly backed across Route 9 and onto another dirt road, where he wheeled the car into a ditch, jumped out, and ran to a nearby house as his assailants took off in the Buick. Then he telephoned Sheriff Eakle, who launched an investigation.

About an hour later Kelly showed up at his pool hall on Depot Street with holstered handguns strapped on his hips. "Now let the sonofabitches come and get me," he said, and he described the attack to young Alfred Kipling, who worked for him.

In the days that followed he often carried a gun.

At the close of 1928 McDonough County had a new state's attorney, elected in November. He was Wallace Walker, a stocky, bespectacled man with a long face and an affable, easygoing manner. A McDonough County native who had been raised on a farm, he had practiced law in Chicago for several years before returning to Macomb in 1907. Since then he had served as master in chancery of the circuit court for eight years and had been the law partner of two previous state's attorneys, T. H. Miller and Les Hainline. An avid storyteller and dedicated community leader, Walker was also a two-term past president of the McDonough County Bar Association. No one in the county's legal community was more widely admired or well liked. At fifty-two, he brought more legal experience to the state's attorney's office than anyone before him, and he was determined to curb the lawlessness in McDonough County.

Walker worked furiously on the Wagle-Moon case, supervising the investigation, going through police records on the two men, and phoning people from his office above the Ford-Hopkins drug store on the Macomb square. Soon he and Sheriff Eakle located witnesses who knew about the feud between the two bootleggers and who could place Jay Moon and his Buick at the edge of town that Christmas Eve, when the shotgun was fired into Wagle's car. In late January Walker took his case to the McDonough County grand jury, which indicted Moon, asserting that "on the 24th day of December, in the year of our Lord 1928 . . . with a certain gun then and there held in his hands and loaded . . . he did discharge the said loaded gun at Henry Wagle, with the intent . . . to commit murder."

Moon was arrested and then released on bond. The trial was slated for the May term of the circuit court.

Kelly could not identify the other man who participated in the ambush, but he suspected that it was Loren ("Ham") Burford, a twenty-eight-year-old carpenter and brick mason who was a notorious drunkard. He was the son of Harry Burford, a well-respected, ambitious barber who had become the leader of the Building and Loan Association. But young Burford was not at all like his father. Crude and stupid, he seemed to enjoy shocking people with his insensitivity. One time he and his drinking buddy Cody Boyd amused themselves by tying sticks of dynamite to a neighbor's dog, lighting a short fuse, and throwing a ball for it to fetch. A tall, stocky, unkempt-looking man, Burford had several scars on his face, the result of auto accidents when he was drunk.

The exact cause of Burford's hatred for Kelly Wagle is unknown, but he was convicted of transporting liquor in 1926 and spent two months in jail, so the problem may have been related to bootlegging. He was also a good friend of Jay Moon, whose brother's sister-in-law was married to Burford's brother. The two men often hunted duck and quail together. More outspoken than Moon, Burford reportedly told his friends that Kelly Wagle ought to be killed.

After the attempted murder, Kelly felt that he was a marked man. He was always cautious about where he went and what he did. According to a 1929 article in the *Peoria Journal Transcript,* "he slept in a bed placed in the middle of his room and surrounded by a screen" so that no one could easily shoot him at night. He also bought a lot at Mt. Auburn, next to the grave of his grandfather, Henry Walley, and he apparently made arrangements for his funeral.

Kelly occasionally talked to his friends about the threat from Moon and Burford. He once told Chick and Dewey Hocker, "They're out to get me, and they'll do it too. It's just a matter of time." To Theron ("Smut") Haines he remarked, "If Moon and Burford don't kill me, they'll have someone do it."

Four days after the ambush, Kelly went to the Godfrey Studio in Macomb to have his picture taken. With his cap on, his mouth closed, and his eyes staring straight ahead, he struck a solemn, almost frightened-looking pose. His mother had wanted a photograph of him anyway, so he ordered a few eight-by-tens and left one at her house. It later ended up in the newspaper.

Alice was not in town. On November 28, after six years as a widow, she had married John Terrill, a small, friendly, easygoing man who had been a rural mail carrier since 1903 and had recently retired. Soon after the wedding, they left to spend the winter in North Carolina.

In the years following Arch's death, Kelly had remained close to his mother, often taking her to shop in Macomb or to visit relatives in Keokuk, Iowa, or Louisiana, Missouri. He regarded her welfare as his responsibility, and as she later said, he saw to it that she never wanted for anything. In a certain sense, he was a good son.

Kelly apparently thought of himself as a fine guy in a hard and hypocritical world. His manifold good deeds were perhaps an attempt to prove that to himself. In the same way, his outrage at any real or imagined betrayal suggests that he regarded himself as a good person who deserved the loyalty of those around him.

Late in his life he bought a gold ring that he liked very much and wore all the time. Set with small diamonds and rubies, it bore an image of Christ with a crown of thorns.

By the winter of 1929 there was a growing sense that the era of bootlegging and lawlessness was reaching some kind of a climax. In Chicago the St. Valentine's Day Massacre brought renewed attention to the gang war that had killed more than a thousand men since the mid-1920s. Macomb newspaper headlines conveyed the public perception of the violence:

GANG WAR FLARES ANEW IN CHICAGO

CHICAGO GANGSTERS SHOOT SEVEN TO DEATH

CAPONE GANG IS LINKED TO KILLING

POLICE IN MOVE AGAINST CAPONE

CHICAGO IN DEATH GRIP WITH GANGLAND

There was also evidence that Chicago killers were starting to operate downstate. In the early spring, for example, two Macoupin County rumrunners were shot to death by men with machine guns, and local authorities linked those killings to the Chicago gang war.

Public outrage was also aroused over poisonous liquor. Deaths from poorly redistilled industrial alcohol had been occurring throughout the decade, but by the late 1920s alcohol poisoning was a kind of illicit epidemic. In Illinois alone 421 people died from poisonous liquor in 1928. Then, early in March 1929, downstate suffered a major catastrophe. Twenty people died in Peoria and nearby Knox County in a single incident, after drinking booze that was 10 to 15 percent wood alcohol. Others were crippled or went blind. Several bootleggers were arrested and charged with manslaughter.

By that time people across the country were calling for the repeal of Prohibition. In March the editor of the *McDonough County News* summarized the most common arguments when he said that "the 18th Amendment has created twenty-five million lawbreakers," and "the weak attempt to enforce it has cost billions of dollars." Alluding to the poisonous liquor catastrophe, he added, "Assuredly twenty new headstones in Illinois cemeteries can be attributed to the failure of enforcement— or the failure to repeal the amendment."

Although the end of Prohibition was still four years away, some states were starting to take individual action, passing legislation that put an end to their support for dry enforcement. In April a bill to rescind the Illinois prohibition laws was passed by the state legislature, even though all the representatives from the rural and small-town world of western Illinois voted against it.

Like the days of Kelly Wagle, the days of Prohibition were clearly numbered.

Kelly's last known fight occurred one evening in early March when Ham Burford came to his house looking for him. The big disheveled-looking boozer had been drinking most of the day, and he had a gun.

Kelly saw him coming, and he managed to sneak up behind him and hit him with a board. The big man dropped his gun, staggered, and fell down as Kelly hit him again. Then he got up and ran across the hard road, heading for town, with Kelly yelling and swearing behind him.

Kelly caught up with him behind the city building, where workmen had left a pile of bricks. He started throwing bricks at his frightened enemy, hitting him at least twice. His face covered with blood, Burford ran to Depot Street and hid in his father's barber shop.

Some of the townspeople suspected that Moon had prompted Burford to go after Kelly. After all, Moon had been identified at the Christmas Eve ambush and was under indictment for attempted murder, so he couldn't afford to attack Kelly himself, and Burford was easily manipulated.

Whatever the case, after Burford's clumsy effort failed, Moon surely realized that any future attempt to get Kelly would have to involve a third party, an outsider whom no one in Colchester would recognize. And he and Burford would need an airtight alibi when the police came looking for them.

As the conflict with Moon and Burford continued, Kelly became extremely nervous. He sometimes had chest pains and was unable to sleep. Eventually he went to see Dr. Bruce Harrison, whose office was upstairs at the Fraternity Building. "Nervous indigestion," the doctor said. "Nothing to worry about. Try to relax." Under the circumstances, it was difficult advice to take.

Kelly felt best when he was surrounded by his close friends—George and John Rundle; Chick, Bill, and Dewey Hocker; Smut Haines; Dean Walley; Chiny Rhodes; Fred Wayland, and a few others. They frequently met in the evening at George Rundle's garage on Macomb Street, just east of the city building. It was a brick service station with a big white door facing the street, and it had a pit inside, toward the back, where

Rundle could get underneath a car to work on it. The front of the building was an office, containing a desk and several chairs, where Kelly and his friends talked and sometimes played craps.

On one occasion early that spring, when Kelly and his crowd were there, the talk turned to Moon and Burford, and he told the group, "They're going to get me. But give me an even break and I'll shoot it out with them. I'll die with my boots on." He embraced his doom like a western gunfighter—but he never got that break.

Typically Kelly walked across the road from his house and came into Rundle's garage through the back door. On the evening of April 8, that's what he did, and he had Dean Walley with him, as usual.

After talking awhile with George and John Rundle and others, Kelly said he was going to walk down the street to William ("Winker") Brent's restaurant, to get something to drink at the soda fountain, and he invited the others to go with him. None of them did, not even Dean Walley.

It was almost nine o'clock when Kelly stepped through the big front door into the dark street. It was Monday evening and the town was quiet. The temperature had already dropped below fifty degrees, cool enough to feel chilly after a near-record heat wave the previous week.

As Kelly emerged from Rundle's, a friend named Ed Carpenter happened to come along, so they walked together, past the city hall and the Chevrolet dealership; past the tin coal shed owned by the public service company; past a paint store, a barber shop, and a drug store; and finally to Brent's restaurant, shining in the dark next to the huge Fraternity Building. Except for Rundle's, it was the only place still open on Macomb Street.

As Carpenter went his own way, striding toward Coal Street, Kelly entered the familiar cafe, which was empty except for the proprietor, who was getting ready to close.

While Kelly was inside, having a fountain drink and ordering cigars for the Rundle brothers, an outsider in a green Ford roadster waited down the street. He was parked across from the tin shed, facing east, with his engine off, his lights out, and his side curtains drawn.

The street was deserted at ten minutes after nine, when Kelly started back to Rundle's. Behind him the lights were switched off in the restaurant, so that only the streetlight at the corner cast a dim glow down the block. The outsider apparently got out of his car on the passenger side, stood by the right front fender, leveled an automatic shotgun across the hood, and waited.

As Kelly stepped in front of the shed, where he was clearly visible against the galvanized tin, BLAM!, the outsider fired, hitting him on the right side, stopping his forward motion, and turning him slightly toward the street; then BLAM!, the man fired again, hitting Kelly squarely in the chest and throwing him backward onto the sidewalk, with his hands above his head; then BLAM!, he fired a third time at the fallen body, one of the No. 0 buckshot ripping through the sole of Kelly's shoe.

The outsider got into his car before anyone could see him. Setting his gun down, he tramped on the starter, but the engine cranked loudly without turning over. Still, no one came running; no one saw him. He tramped on the starter a second time, but again the new car failed to fire. When he tried a third time, no doubt pulling on the choke as his foot pushed down, the engine finally sputtered to life. In a second he pulled forward, quickly turning south to Depot Street to avoid driving past Rundle's garage; then he went east for a block and turned back north to the hard road.

The eyewitnesses who soon appeared on the street saw nothing but a green Model A roadster with a black top and no license plates heading toward Macomb.

Accounts of the crime that were soon reported to the police centered on the discovery of the dying bootlegger, and most of them appeared in the April 13 *Macomb Journal*. Dean Walley was the first of Kelly's group to learn what had happened:

> I was inside the garage when I heard three shots fired. All of us got up and went to the door and looked west. Cecil Kipling said, "That was a car backfiring." After the car started and left, George Rundle said, "That fellow must have done something." I started walking on down the street and met Mr. Hotten and then Mr. Tones. Mr. Tones said, "What was that?" I said, "I don't know. Let's go and see." I hadn't gone very far when I could see Henry's feet on the sidewalk, so I ran up to him and turned around and hollered back, "They have shot Kelly!"

Chiny Rhodes happened to be uptown, and he was among the small crowd that soon gathered around Kelly, who was still alive but only semiconscious, bleeding in thirty-six places:

I heard three shots. I cranked up my car and turned east, and stopped at the place where Wagle was lying. George Hotten and Reuben Tones were there. I got out of the car, went over where he was, and recognized it was Henry Wagle. I leaned over him and raised up his head and asked him if he was alive. He said, "Doctor." By that time there were possibly eight or ten there. I helped carry him to the doctor's office. The doctor was not in his office, so we put him in the receiving room of the lodge hall. Going up the stairs, he said, "Don't raise my arm too high." Dr. Harrison came in a few minutes. Then we noticed Kelly's eyes turning back. Dr. Harrison said he was dead.

The receiving room of the lodge was next to Dr. Harrison's office. That's where Blanche came when she got the news. She was accompanied by Geneva, who had just returned from taking fifteen-year-old Elinora to a movie at the Princess Theatre. Despite the lingering bitterness between Kelly and his sister, Blanche and Geneva tried to be civil to each other for the sake of the family. They sat together on wooden chairs and wept quietly over Kelly's body until the undertaker came.

The investigation was headed by Sheriff Eakle, who already had his hands full with another major crime. Three days earlier burglars had robbed the Macomb Post Office, taking $21,000 in stamps and at least $200 in cash. It was the biggest theft in the history of Macomb, and it was clearly a professional job, done by safecrackers who had used acetylene torches and nitroglycerine. Federal investigators were in town, and Eakle was immersed in the case when he got the call about Kelly Wagle's murder. There was apparently no connection between the two cases, yet "big city gangsters" had done them both.

Kelly's murder had been carefully planned. The outsider was evidently in town by Saturday night, for on Sunday morning Sheriff Eakle went to his car and discovered that all four tires were flat. On Monday morning he found that his ignition wires had been pulled. Apparently someone had been stalking Kelly and had expected to kill him on Saturday night, then on Sunday night, and had finally done it on Monday evening.

As it turned out, the outsider didn't need to tamper with Sheriff Eakle's car a third time. He made a clean getaway, driving toward Macomb for a short distance and then south on a dirt road.

Pete Wells, Jay Moon's partner in the ill-fated gambling room on the square, owned a car identical to the one used in the killing, so he was questioned, but he had been in Macomb that night and could prove it. He claimed that he had parked his green Ford roadster near the La-moine Hotel that evening. If it had been used in the killing, he didn't know anything about it. The sheriff suspected that he knew more than he was saying, especially since the outsider had driven down muddy roads to avoid the police, and the first thing Wells did on Tuesday morning was wash his car.

Of course, immediate suspicion fell on Kelly's avowed enemies, Jay Moon and Ham Burford, who were the first men to be questioned, but on the night of the killing they were together in Burlington. In fact, they had been arrested there for disorderly conduct, which gave them an airtight alibi. But no one suspected them of pulling the trigger anyway. The gangland-style slaying had been a murder for hire, done by an outsider who knew what he was doing.

Sheriff Eakle soon reported that he had no leads, so on the day of Kelly's funeral, under the headline "WAGLE IS BURIED: MURDER STILL MYSTERY," the *Macomb Journal* concluded that "the murder will probably go down in local history as an unsolved crime."

Two days later, on Friday evening, an inquest was held in Colches-ter at Frank Williams's funeral home. So many townspeople came, hop-ing to hear the details of the crime, that before eight o'clock the build-ing was packed, and some had to stand outside and wait in the dark to learn what had been said. Inside, the jury of six men, including former editor J. H. Bayless, listened to seven witnesses who had heard the shots and seen the body. None of them had seen the killer.

Sheriff Eakle reported that the lead balls found in Kelly's body and the coal shed were very large—the kind often used by duck hunters and known as "bird shot." They had apparently come from an automatic shotgun, fired three times in rapid succession. There were no other clues except the green Ford roadster that a few people had seen after the killing. It was not a local car.

After three hours the jury reached the only possible conclusion under the circumstances: "The deceased came to his death by gunshot wounds, inflicted with murderous intent, by parties unknown to the jury."

Still, the townspeople in Colchester, especially those who had known Kelly, were convinced that Jay Moon and his buddy Ham Burford were responsible. Their hatred of the bootlegger was too deep; their alibi was too convenient. And Kelly had predicted his death at their hands several times. Two days after the killing, Blanche summed up the feeling of the townspeople when she told a reporter for the *Quincy Herald Whig,* "Everyone knows who did it."

The End
of It All

The 1930s were hard on the people of Colchester, as they were on most Americans. The coming of a world-wide economic collapse, signaled in the United States by the stock market crash of 1929, damaged most local businesses and caused soaring unemployment. By the end of 1930 the Gates Fire Clay Company, which had employed fifty men, and the Northwestern Terra Cotta Company, which had employed twenty, were closed, and they never reopened. Production also declined at the King brickyard, the Baird and Myers clay mines, and the Colchester Milling Company. Although two dozen coal banks still operated in 1930, that number gradually decreased too.

To make matters worse, Saturday night shopping crowds steadily diminished, despite the slow paving of the business district. That eventually had enormous consequences. In 1931 the commercial pride of Colchester, the great Walty Hardware Store, was closed, and as the decade continued, several other stores failed as well.

Although one promising agricultural equipment company, Yetter Manufacturing, was launched in 1930, no one referred to Colchester as a town with a bright future.

Concerned about the local breakdown of law and order and the apparent lack of civic commitment in Colchester, Harry Todd finally spoke out in his own way for the revitalization of community life. Early in 1930 he printed the Athenian Oath, developed in the Age of Pericles, and recommended it to his readers:

THE SPIRIT OF COLCHESTER

"We will never bring disgrace to this our city, by any act of dishonesty or cowardice . . . and we will fight for the ideals and sacred things of the city, both alone and with many; we will revere and obey the city laws, and do our best to incite a like respect and reverence in others; and we will strive unceasingly to quicken the public's sense of civic duty; that thus in all these ways we may transmit this city, greater, better, and more beautiful than it was transmitted to us."

The Athenian Oath needs no comment, except to remark that it was taken seriously.

The spirit exemplified in the oath played its part in creating the Athens of history. The same spirit in our community might do likewise [i.e., create a great city], but whether it did or not, it would certainly result in making Colchester a better place in which to live.

Although he was not a moral crusader, the anxious editor urged responsibility to the social order, hoping that words of commitment from an ancient culture would inspire the town.

Despite his concern about the spirit of Colchester, however, Todd continued to promote the community. He even idealized it now and again, and proclaimed its enormous significance for local residents, as in this remarkable 1930 editorial, which reflects the communal vision of the townspeople:

COLCHESTER

We love Colchester. It is everything to us. It is our home, our universe. We love its people—the ministers, the businessmen, the laboring men; its beautiful houses, its schools, its churches, its factories. In fact, we love everything in and around Colchester. To us, it is the whole world.

Our laboring men give full services for the pay they receive; our factories give honest products to the consumer. Our ministers preach a true gospel, and our leaders live the lives of Christian gentlemen. . . .

Colchester is the best place on earth in which to live and rear a family.

Unfortunately Todd could not quite convince himself that his closing comment was true. In the spring of 1931 he sold the newspaper and moved away.

Whatever its prospects, Colchester in the Thirties was a town with a distinctive past, centered on the rise and fall of a coal-mining enterprise that once gave purpose and hope to the people there. Despite the town's failure to recover its economic momentum and spiritual cohesion, the mining heritage, winding through local life like the water of the creek, was a source of community pride and self-understanding.

The bootlegger's career was another matter. It was a troubling episode that reflected the dark side of life in Colchester, and like a crime in a close family, there was no easy way for the townspeople to regard it. Nevertheless, it was the most well known aspect of the town in the twentieth century, as Al Capone's career was in Chicago.

And the Kelly Wagle story still wasn't over. In August 1930 that part of the local past suddenly erupted in a completely unexpected way: the Omaha Mystery Girl was identified as Beulah Wagle.

That breakthrough was achieved not by the police but by persistent newspapermen who had never stopped working on the case. Allen Kohan and Reid Zimmerman, of the *Omaha World-Herald,* were young police reporters in 1919, when they covered the most talked-about murder in the history of their city, and they became personally committed to identifying the Mystery Girl. *World-Herald* city editor Benjamin Sylvester also crusaded to solve the case and encouraged the younger men to stay with it. Although the police investigation was fruitless, Sylvester and the reporters continued to follow leads. Eleven years after the body was discovered, Zimmerman, who was then the night editor, chanced to hear that a woman in Chicago knew something about the Mystery Girl, so he contacted J. Loy Maloney, the city editor at the *Chicago Tribune,* who dispatched a man named Harris to question her. That woman turned out to be Kelly's first wife, Ruth.

At the time of her divorce, while living with her sister in Kewanee, Ruth had met a young man named Orlie Ewing. As Kelly had been a few years earlier, Ewing was a potter. By 1909 they had married and moved to Monmouth, where he worked for the Western Stoneware Company. A few years later they moved to Chicago, where they operated a series of restaurants on the South Side. They had no children of their own, but Orlie Ewing was a good stepfather to Archie, who eventually changed his name to Ewing and managed the family's restaurant on South Halsted Street. When Harris, whose first name is unknown, located Ruth, she and her husband were living on West Garfield Boulevard.

On August 19, 1930, Maloney sent Zimmerman a confidential report of the Harris interview with Ruth Ewing, which broke the Mystery Girl murder case:

> Maloney:
> FYI—Here's what Mrs. Ruth Ewing, formerly Mrs. Ruth Wagle, has to say, very confidentially, about the purported murder of her former husband's second wife. I persuaded her to tell her story only after assuring her that her name would in no way be connected with subsequent developments, if any.
>
> About 26 years ago, the present Mrs. Ewing, then Miss Jones of Colchester, Ill., married Henry Wagle, of Colchester. She said Henry turned out wrong and she divorced him more than 20 years ago. They had one son, Archie, who is now about 25. Shortly after her divorce she married her present husband, Orlie Ewing, a prospering restauranteur, and since they have remained happily married, her first affair has been regarded as a closed incident in their life.
>
> Wagle later married again, a young Colchester woman about 25 or 30, named Bertha. Mrs. Ewing was unable to recall Bertha's maiden name, although she said Bertha's parents and sister still reside in Colchester. Bertha died or disappeared, and is the probable "unknown stranger" slain and buried in Omaha. Wagle married a third time, and according to Mrs. Ewing, was forced into his third marriage because his third wife "knew too much and had him under her fingers." This third wife, whose name I could not learn, still resides in Wagle's home in Colchester.
>
> According to Mrs. Ewing, after Wagle was slain in Colchester early in the spring of 1929, his will was probated, and it left his home to his widow, $50 to his mother who resides in Colchester, $5 to his brother Glen Wagle, some race horses to another brother, and only $5 to his son, who has always been with his mother, the present Mrs. Ewing.
>
> After the will was filed, cutting off his close relatives, Mrs. Ewing said Glen Wagle, who she said is a brakeman on the Santa Fe

out of Des Moines, came to Chicago and talked to her in an effort to get her to start suit to break the will in order to get a bigger share of Wagle's estate, thought to have been considerable, for his son. Glen, she says strictly in confidence, at that time told her that Henry had murdered his second wife, because she had left him, taking a quantity of his liquor, his car, and his favorite pistol. Mrs. Ewing said Glen was positive that Henry had slain Bertha, but she was unable to say why or how Glen knew. She said she decided not to start any proceedings against the will, it appearing that the estate largely had been disposed of prior to Wagle's death. . . .

Mrs. Ewing said Wagle kept no bank accounts, but instead had a vault built into his Colchester home where he was supposed to have kept fabulous sums, as well as his liquor stores. He sported a string of race horses and was quite affluent in his prime. Of course, he is dead now, and even if it should develop that he killed his second wife, there is little that could be done, although the possibilities seem worth further investigation.

Harris

Ruth, who had never known Beulah or her family, had misremembered as "Bertha" the name that Glenn had mentioned, but the interview makes it clear that Kelly's younger brother knew about the killing. Glenn also obviously disliked Blanche and was surely the source of Ruth's comment that Blanche had forced Kelly to marry her after the murder, which may have been just speculation on his part.

On the strength of that interview, which was never made public, Zimmerman sent Kohan to Colchester, where he discovered that Wagle's second wife was named Beulah, not Bertha, and that her family still lived in nearby Carthage. Kohan looked them up, and they identified the morgue photographs of the Mystery Girl. Dental records later confirmed the identification.

In late August the Omaha newspapers ran a compelling series of headline stories as the Mystery Girl case again captured the front page:

"MYSTERY GIRL" REVEALED;
IDENTITY PROVED BY TEETH
Exhumed Body Reveals
Victim Gangster's Wife

MYSTERY GIRL FLED WITH OMAHAN
*Family Asserts She Left
Home with $1400 and Man*

FATHER CLAIMS "MYSTERY GIRL,"
WEEPS AT GRAVE
Believes Murderer Will Yet Be Found

The Omaha police questioned Earl Harper, but they discovered that he was a mild-mannered, law-abiding citizen, still married to the woman he had apparently considered leaving in 1919, and there was no evidence to link him with the crime. Also, Beulah had been beaten before she was killed, and Harper was not hot-tempered, vengeful, or abusive.

By that time the McConnell family was convinced that Kelly had killed her or had arranged to have her killed. According to the *Omaha News,* which interviewed Beulah's sister, "The relatives believe that 'Kelly' Wagle, the rough and tumble rum boss, had his wife done away with because she had double-crossed him."

Back in western Illinois, the Mystery Girl case was also front-page news. In an August 24 headline story, "SLAIN WOMAN KELLY WAGLE'S WIFE," the *Quincy Herald-Whig* flatly asserted what many of the townspeople believed—"that Wagle followed the girl to Omaha and murdered her." The *Macomb Journal* ran a series of articles about the case, including one, "Learn Wagle Had Contacts in Omaha," that implied he had the opportunity to kill Beulah or have her killed.

Despite all the coverage in larger newspapers, the *Colchester Independent* simply carried a short piece at the bottom of page one, reporting that Beulah Wagle's body had been identified and expressing the hope that "her murderer may be apprehended." It deliberately avoided any reference to the long-held suspicion that Kelly had killed her.

Because the chief suspect was dead, and the murder had not occurred in McDonough County anyway, State's Attorney Walker and Sheriff Eakle did not launch an investigation. They did not know about the Ruth Ewing interview or Glenn Wagle's knowledge of the crime.

On August 31 a funeral was held at the McConnell home in Carthage. So many people attended that scores of them had to stand outside on the lawn. Afterward, in a procession stretching for more than a mile,

Beulah's body was taken to the McConnell Cemetery in the countryside near Fountain Green, where some four hundred people attended the graveside service.

A few days later a reporter for the *Carthage Republican* remembered her as "warm-hearted, generous, and kind, devoted to the family circle, and popular with relatives and friends." In the same issue a stringer from nearby Webster summed up the response of her old friends and neighbors, who had crowded into the little cemetery for the long overdue burial service: "There have been many sad things happen in our lifetime, but nothing has been worse than the sad ending of our friend, Beulah McConnell Wagle. . . . It was one of the largest funerals ever held in that cemetery. The lovely floral tributes completely covered her grave. . . . Words fail to express our love."

Few people from Colchester attended the services for Beulah, which were never reported in the pages of the *Independent*. It was less troubling, perhaps, to maintain some distance from the whole affair. After all, the townspeople should have pressed for a thorough investigation of her disappearance, but they never did. Now it was too late.

Likewise, those who knew that Kelly had trailed Beulah to Omaha and perhaps had killed her there—surely Joe and Blanche, probably Geneva, and maybe Alice and Glenn—had said nothing, and now that the body was identified, they may have felt guilty of a certain callous disregard for Beulah and her family. (Of course, by 1930 Glenn, who did not live in Colchester and was not close to Kelly, definitely knew that his brother had killed Beulah, as he told Ruth, but he may not have learned that, from Joe or Geneva, until after Kelly's death.) In any case, no member of the Wagle family attended the services for Beulah.

That murder remained officially unsolved, and so did the Wagle case. As the months went by, there was no real progress in the latter investigation, and some of the townspeople felt that county authorities were not putting forth much effort, that they were simply glad the bootlegger was gone.

But they were wrong. State's Attorney Wallace Walker was anxious to resolve the case, and he conducted a thorough investigation. He always regarded Jay Moon as the chief suspect, but since the hit man had escaped and Moon had an alibi, there was nothing that he could take to court.

At the same time, Walker was making an enormous personal effort to enforce the unpopular Prohibition law, which had mounting opposition everywhere, and that brought him into continual conflict with Moon. Early in 1930 he worked with federal agents to have Moon arrested for possession and transportation of liquor. In a sting operation they caught him in the act of delivering three gallons of alcohol to a place on the Macomb square. Moon eventually pleaded guilty to charges of transporting and selling liquor and served a four-month prison term in Peoria. He also paid a $500 fine and, under a new regulation, had his car confiscated. Nevertheless, when he was released in the spring, he went right back to bootlegging.

On July 2, 1931, Walker sent to Deputy Prohibition Administrator James Eaton, of the U.S. Department of Justice, an extensive report on the illegal liquor traffic in McDonough County, which by that time involved dozens of small-time bootleggers as well as the corruption of local officials. Moon was apparently behind it all, as Walker pointed out in the "Jay Moon" section of his report, which includes comments on the Wagle murder case:

JOHN W. MOON, ALIAS JAY MOON, COLCHESTER, ILL.

Moon was the rival of Henry Wagle, alias Kelly Wagle, who was murdered in Colchester, Illinois, two years ago this spring. There was an attempt to murder Wagle on the 24th of December, 1928, and Wagle positively identified Moon as the man who shot at him, as he was only about thirty feet from him at the time the shot was fired and it was bright moonlight. Moon was indicted for assault with intent to commit murder at the January term, 1929, of the circuit court of McDonough County. He secured a continuance, which was unopposed at that time as the State wished to secure further corroborating evidence, but at the time the continuance was granted it was understood that the case would be set down for trial at the May term, 1929, which was the next term of the circuit court. Before the May term of the court convened, Wagle was murdered on the streets of Colchester about nine o'clock at night, and although a great deal of work was done endeavoring to get some evidence as to who committed the crime, no evidence that would justify any action has ever been secured. One significant circumstance is the fact that when Wagle was removed, there was no one left to identify Moon as the man who attempted to kill

Wagle on the preceding December 24, so Wagle's death absolutely blocked the prosecution of Moon on that charge.

Since Wagle's death Moon has had no serious competitor. It is generally believed that he is one of the closest friends of our present sheriff. It is known that he and the sheriff hunted together last fall almost continuously from the time of the election until the sheriff took office in December. For a time he visited the sheriff's office quite often and was closeted with him on numerous occasions.

It is reported that Moon served notice on Leo Parish to cease selling alcohol. (See report on Leo Parish.) It is reported that he is the one who collects protection money. (See report on Lawrence Fosdyck.) It is reported that he notified Elmer Janes to quit delivering alcohol in this county, and other reports are to the effect that he and Janes have a working agreement. (See report on Elmer Janes.)

It was reported to me, and the report could be verified, that Homer Bolling, otherwise known as Doc Bolling, of Bushnell, Illinois, was warned by Moon to quit selling liquor in this county; that Bolling paid no attention to the warning, and that one night Moon shot the spotlight off of Bolling's car on the hard road east of Macomb; that when the sheriff of this county and the deputy went to Bushnell during the past winter to arrest Bolling on a peace bond warrant, that Moon accompanied them in his car, for the purpose, as Bolling believed, to get an opportunity to shoot him in the case Bolling should show any resistance whatever to the arrest. . . .

As you probably know, Moon is a very hard man to get any information from. His face is expressionless, and it is believed that he will go to any length that he may consider necessary to protect himself and his interests. It is commonly believed and is common street talk that Moon has the alcohol concession for this county.

The sheriff who was Moon's close friend, and who was in fact paid off by Moon to ignore his bootlegging, was Guy Hardisty, a stocky, outgoing, forty-year-old man from Blandinsville who had been elected in November 1930. He was an untrained day laborer with no police experience, and he was poor—an easy mark for a bootlegger with a sizable income. It is likely that Moon had encouraged him to seek the office.

The crusading Paul Eakle had not run for reelection because McDonough County law prohibited the sheriff from succeeding himself in office, but he would not have been much help anyway. Ironically, by the close of his four-year term he had become an alcoholic, so he was dependent on the illegal trade he had once combated with such vigor. After an arrest for drunken behavior, which landed him in the jail he used to manage, he left town for Chicago, where he worked for a time with federal agent Eliot Ness, who was trying to stop Al Capone. He eventually drifted back to Macomb, where he worked as a police detective, but he never conquered his addiction to alcohol.

Eakle's deputy, Cliff Leighty, could have carried on the vigorous dry law enforcement, but by 1930 most of the voters didn't want him or anyone else who was seriously committed to Prohibition. Sheriff Hardisty, who was himself a drinker and who often patronized the bootleggers, was a perfect example of the moral ambivalence and local corruption that had swept the country.

The mayor of Macomb, John Graves, a distinguished-looking, gray-haired man with a reputation for social activism, had also cut himself in on the payoffs. In 1932 an undercover investigator reported to Walker that "Mayor Graves makes regular collections, it seems, from the numerous local joints he is backing up."

As Walker's report and other documents reveal, Moon developed an extensive protection racket whereby the county's bootleggers avoided arrest by making payments either to Moon or directly to local officials. That arrangement necessarily involved close cooperation among Moon, Hardisty, Graves, and others.

At the same time, Moon used intimidation (threats and beatings) as well as the corrupt officials to gain control of the liquor traffic in the county, which is exactly what Al Capone had accomplished, with much greater violence, in Chicago.

Because of the situation in McDonough County, Walker reported to Deputy Prohibition Administrator Eaton that "it would be useless to ask any assistance from the sheriff's office or from the police department in Macomb," and he suspected that police in the county's smaller towns were also paid off. Feeling that he may have been the only uncorrupted law enforcement official left in McDonough County, Walker nevertheless refused to give up and worked exclusively with federal agents, often making trips to Springfield to confer with Eaton. That effort led to the arrest and conviction of fifteen bootleggers (thirteen men and two women) in the fall of 1931. All of them were sent to prison, and Walker was commended by the Justice Department.

Nevertheless, Moon remained at large, and the widespread bootlegging and corruption continued. To make matters worse, by 1932 the depression had taken its toll: McDonough County was broke, and there was no money available for jury trials, much less undercover investigators. The bootleggers had won.

When his term expired later that year, Wallace Walker did not run for reelection.

What finally defeated Moon, of course, was the repeal of Prohibition in 1933. He and the other bootleggers were suddenly out of business.

The following year Moon launched a wholesale liquor company, J. W. Moon Distributing, which he operated on North Randolph Street in Macomb for thirty years. Although he was engaged to Geneva Wagle shortly after her brother's death, he eventually broke with her and, in 1937, married someone else. Then he moved to Macomb.

Moon slowly became a respected businessman, although for a number of years he carried a gun and lived in fear that some enemy from his criminal days would try to get him. Rumor had it that some windows in his home on Ward Street had been fitted with bullet-proof glass.

Throughout his life Moon said little about his notorious past, but if the recollections of certain old men are true, he eventually admitted to a few of his gambling cronies that he had gotten rid of Kelly Wagle. He died in 1984 at the age of eighty-seven.

Moon's accomplice in the plan to kill Wagle did not fare as well. Ham Burford remained an uncouth slob who worked irregularly and drank continually. Some of his drunken exploits—such as the time he missed the iron bridge north of Colchester and drove his car into the creek—became well-circulated stories among the townspeople.

In the mid-1930s, when he was out of work and desperate, Burford offered to sell his sixteen-gauge shotgun to roadhouse owner Turk Stephens, telling him flatly, "This is the gun that killed Kelly Wagle." It probably was.

Late in 1938 a drunken binge in cold weather led to double pneumonia, and Burford died on New Year's Day 1939. He was thirty-eight.

In many ways the most fascinating figure of the Wagle era in Colchester was Geneva, and the most difficult question about her is this: did she know in April 1929 that her long-time lover had arranged to have her brother killed? More to the point: was she in on it?

There is no doubt that by the mid-1930s Geneva knew that Moon was responsible. She told a number of people, then and later, that he had hired someone to kill her brother and that she hated him for it. In fact, she told close friends that for a few years she had sent red roses to Moon on the anniversary of her brother's death, to remind him that she remembered what he had done. Of course, because of her own involvement in criminal activities, she was in no position to go to the police.

Geneva turned against Moon either because she discovered the truth about Kelly's murder or because he broke their engagement, after which she revealed to others what she had known all along. The latter is more likely, for after Kelly had beaten up Moon and pistol-whipped her following the hijacking, she hated her brother—or at least, part of her did—and long after Moon was indicted for attempting to murder Kelly on Christmas Eve 1928, she continued her relationship with him. That doesn't mean that she conspired in the murder, but as Blanche said afterward, "Everyone knows who did it," and except for Moon and Burford, no one knew more than Geneva.

It is likely that Geneva was the figure from his past whom Jay Moon feared the most. She owned a handgun, knew how to use it, and had gangster friends in Chicago, where she worked for a few years in the mid-1930s. One of those friends was a former Capone bodyguard named Tony Accardo, who later headed the Chicago mob.

After a series of love affairs and casual sexual relationships, which gave her a scandalous reputation in Colchester, Geneva was married in 1939 to a traveling salesman named Wayne Campbell, who died six years later. For a time she also lived with a man named Ernie Cotton, who owned a bar in Blandinsville where she often drank on weekend nights. Always wild, she once drove her car on the sidewalk beneath the wooden awning of another tavern (The Bloody Bucket, in nearby Plymouth) just to show that she could do it. Hot-tempered and vengeful, like her dead brother, she once got mad at a local man in Colchester, followed him out of town, and ran his car off the road. On another occasion, after she had moved to Macomb, she got in trouble with the police for brandishing a gun at her neighbors.

After her mother died in 1943, Geneva had little contact with people in Colchester. She regarded most of them as too staid and conventional. But as she got older she was often nostalgic about the 1920s and sometimes told a few close friends quite frankly about the criminal activities of Kelly Wagle and Jay Moon. She even showed them a Thompson submachine gun that she had acquired back in the good old bootlegging days. She seemed to long for the excitement of that time when she was young, and she viewed it all through a permanent romantic haze. One of her most cherished mementos was a photograph of Kelly and herself with Al Capone, taken at Chicago's Lexington Hotel, where Capone had his headquarters.

She died in 1984 at the age of eighty-six.

Geneva was not the only one who both loved and hated Kelly; Blanche was also ambivalent toward him, and she must have had a mixed reaction to his death. On the one hand, he had rescued her from poverty and frustration and had provided her with nice clothes, a new house, and good times. He also had been a doting, if erratic, stepfather for Elinora. But the strain of living with a demanding, volatile man who constantly broke the law and frequently saw other women surely made her long to escape that marriage. More than anything else, her affair with Underhill revealed the depth of her unhappiness. While shocked and saddened by Kelly's murder, she was also relieved that he was gone.

Although she had apparently persuaded Kelly to change his will, completely cutting off his son Archie and leaving everything to her, she was surprised to find that his estate was small, a mere $7,000. Kelly had always been secretive about his business affairs, and he had often spent so lavishly that she thought he was wealthy. (So did the rest of the town.) Blanche checked his vault, of course, but supposedly found only some empty liquor cans and his records, which she burned. For years she was convinced that he had hidden some money that simply had not been located.

Although she was not poor, Blanche needed to get a job. For many years she was a clerk at Terrill and Hulson's Store, where Underhill was also employed, and later she worked at other places. Although she was cordial to neighbors and old friends, Blanche was reserved, if not reclusive, spending most of her time in the house that Kelly had built for her.

She and Underhill must have realized that some of the townspeople suspected them of being involved in the murder, both because her marriage to Kelly had been keeping them apart and because Kelly had fought with Underhill at Foster's Restaurant. That was surely one reason they were discreet in pursuing their relationship after the killing. They did eventually marry, but not until more than ten years later, in 1940, and not in Colchester, but in Missouri.

Afterward Underhill finally moved in with her, and they lived together very happily for almost half a century. Virtually everyone in town who knew them, liked them.

During all that time Blanche tried to forget her past with Kelly Wagle, as if by disregarding it she could separate herself from it. She resented any reference to him that was made in her presence, in the newspaper, or otherwise in the community. She wanted the townspeople to forget about him too. When the 1956 Colchester Centennial Pageant referred to the bootlegger's career, she was offended.

In 1988, after they had been married forty-eight years, Underhill died, and Blanche was again alone. By then she was an elderly, but still erect, white-haired woman who seldom went anywhere, and she had outlived almost everyone of her generation. In those final years the townspeople occasionally saw her sitting on her front porch, looking out at the town, right across from the spot where gunshots had brought the most turbulent part of her life to an end more than sixty years earlier.

She died in 1990, at the age of ninety-five.

Long before then, the old town itself was dead. Colchester had ceased to resemble the community in which the bootlegger had flourished.

When Prohibition was repealed in 1933, Colchester had legal drinking places again, after more than two decades, but they were called "taverns" rather than "saloons," and all six of them sold food as well as drinks. Some women patronized them too, especially when escorted by a man, for things were different then.

Nevertheless, the taverns didn't last very long. The town's newly formed Dry League for Moral and Civic Righteousness regalvanized the local anti-liquor sentiment, and in the spring of 1937 the townspeople voted against liquor selling once again.

Colchester has been dry ever since.

But the town's recent past was so different from its present that the legend of Kelly Wagle, who symbolized both the old commitment and the new individualism, could not help but grow. As the years went by, his story echoed through the minds of the townspeople, who held on to what they most needed to remember and reshaped it without intending to. In general, Kelly's crimes and brutality were slowly forgotten—except for the "harmless crime" of bootlegging—but his daring exploits and good deeds were recalled, retold, and simply invented.

As time went by, rumors and stories arose that depicted him as the preeminent rumrunner for Al Capone and the head of a vast bootlegging organization, which he controlled with an iron hand. Because the townspeople knew little about Kelly's youth, they even developed stories like the following one to explain how the bootlegger had arisen in their community: "The Wagles were poor, so Kelly bootlegged even when he was a kid. They lived down the road to Vinegar Knob then. When he was only nine or ten years old, people would see him carrying a tin bucket in his hand, walking towards town. They thought it was milk or butter, but it was booze. Kelly was making a delivery."

Continuing a process that had begun while he was still alive, the townspeople and others in the county created a small-town version of the gangster-hero, and his widely reported gangland-style slaying put the seal of truth on it all.

For many years after the bootlegger's death, the tin coal shed stood on Macomb Street, like a shrine to a mysterious and turbulent era, or to the man who symbolized it, and many McDonough County residents, especially young people, made a journey to Colchester just to see it and to put their fingers into the holes.

The coming of strip mining to other downstate Illinois counties in the 1930s made Colchester coal even less competitive in price, so the remaining drift mines were closed during the depression and World War II. The clay mines slowly petered out over the next twenty-five years, and the last old industrial company, the King brickyard, finally ceased operation in 1970. Increasingly the townspeople sought jobs in Macomb.

While that process was going on, the business district slowly declined. Fewer and fewer people shopped in Colchester unless they lived there and couldn't get away.

The People's State Bank went into receivership in 1932, and many of the townspeople lost money. Nine years later the National Bank was closed too. Its assets were purchased by the Union National Bank in Macomb, a move that further oriented Colchester to the county seat.

So, too, with the newspaper. Between 1931 and 1943 the *Independent* was owned and edited by three different families from other towns who moved to Colchester to operate it, and then C. R. Crabb of Macomb bought it and managed it from his office at the county seat. The intense focus on the culture and future of the town that had characterized the *Independent* from Van Hampton to Harry Todd slowly dissipated.

The Princess Theatre, once the cultural center and chief attraction of the business district, slowly deteriorated, and it finally closed in 1954. It still sits at the corner of Fulton and Market Streets, its doors boarded up and its marquee rusting—an image of Colchester's faded glory.

The huge Fraternity Building, which had symbolized the town's determination to thrive in the twentieth century and the community spirit of local residents, gradually fell into disuse as the lodges were dissolved for lack of participation. The once-elegant structure slowly became an old-fashioned, decaying, and empty hulk that no one wanted to occupy. It was demolished in 1972, and nothing took its place.

As the town declined, railroad service steadily diminished too. By World War II only three eastbound and three westbound trains stopped in Colchester, and that number went down until the spring of 1957, when the trains quit taking passengers altogether and freight service was all but discontinued. In July 1969 an unidentified arsonist—perhaps someone who couldn't stand the irony—set fire to the unused depot. It was half-gutted before the blaze was extinguished, and shortly afterward, what remained of it was torn down.

Colchester was adrift in the land of promise.

Now no one in town can remember when mining really mattered and coal was shipped out by rail, and few can recall when the streets were crowded on Saturday nights. Colchester is a bedroom community for the county seat, a place to retire where nothing much happens, and a gasoline stop for drivers on the hard road, known for half a century as Route 136. The last of the old townspeople, those who knew Colchester in the 1920s, are almost gone. But the story of the bootlegger remains, and it gets better all the time.

SOURCES AND
ACKNOWLEDGMENTS

Although it is focused on one community and one individual, *The Bootlegger* is indebted to a wide range of broader studies that illuminate the cultural context of the town and the man, as well as to a myriad of local records, accounts, and residents.

Among the many fine books on the history of Illinois, John H. Keiser's *Building for the Centuries: Illinois, 1865 to 1898* (1977) and Donald F. Tingley's *The Structuring of a State: The History of Illinois, 1899–1928* (1980) are the most helpful for the time period covered by my account. The most thorough study of lawlessness in Illinois during the 1920s is the massive *Illinois Crime Survey* (1929), produced by the Illinois Association for Criminal Justice, and two of the finest historical accounts with a more narrow focus are Paul Angle's *Bloody Williamson: A Chapter in American Lawlessness* (1952) and Kenneth Allsop's *The Bootleggers: The Story of Chicago's Prohibition Era* (1961).

There are also a number of good books on American culture in the 1920s, including Frederick Lewis Allen's classic *Only Yesterday: An Informal History of the 1920s* (1931), Paul Sann's pictorial volume *The Lawless Decade* (1957), George E. Mowry's collection of documents *The Twenties: Fords, Flappers, and Fanatics* (1963), and Geoffrey Perrett's study *America in the Twenties: A History* (1983), to name a few. The drinking issue in that decade has been separately discussed in several important works, the best of which are Andrew Sinclair's *Prohibition:*

The Era of Excess (1962) and Sean Dennis Cashman's *Prohibition: The Lie of the Land* (1981). Also useful for understanding the development of the temperance movement was the *Standard Encyclopedia of the Alcohol Problem* (1924), edited by Ernest Hurst Cherrington and others.

Various studies of the American small town also contributed to my understanding of Colchester, and among the most important are Albert Blumenthal's *Small-Town Stuff* (1932), Lewis Atherton's *Main Street on the Middle Border* (1954), W. Lloyd Warner's *The Living and the Dead: A Study of the Symbolic Life of Americans* (1959), Thomas Bender's *Community and Social Change in America* (1978), Richard Lingeman's *Small Town America: A Narrative History, 1620–the Present* (1980), and John A. Jakle's *The American Small Town: Twentieth-Century Place Images* (1982).

An excellent overview of some Illinois coal-mining communities is Daniel J. Prosser's *Coal Towns in Egypt: Portrait of an Illinois Mining Region, 1890–1930* (1973), and a similar account from a nearby state is Dorothy Schwieder's *Black Diamonds: Life and Work in Iowa's Coal Mining Communities, 1895–1925* (1983). A relevant sociological study of one Illinois mining town is Herman R. Lantz's *People of Coal Town* (1958), but the community he analyzed (Zeigler) was very different from Colchester. John Benson's fine study *British Coal Miners in the Nineteenth Century: A Social History* (1980) is a helpful depiction of the cultural background of the Colchester mining families.

Among the many studies that shed light on the problem of individualism and community in America, the most enlightening for me were Roy F. Baumeister's *Identity: Cultural Change and the Struggle for Self* (1986) and John P. Hewitt's *Dilemmas of the American Self* (1989).

My approach to writing history was influenced by a number of fine works, including *American Historical Explanations: A Strategy for Grounded Inquiry* (2d ed., 1980), by Gene Wise; *The Past Is a Foreign Country* (1985), by David Lowenthal; and *The Content of the Form: Narrative Discourse and Historical Representation* (1987), by Hayden V. White.

Anyone interested in the history of Colchester or McDonough County should contact the Archives and Special Collections unit at Western Illinois University Library, which has an array of county histories, atlases, maps, directories, photographs, public records, newspapers on microfilm, and other materials. Of particular value for this book were June Moon's *"Multum in Parvo": A History of Colchester, Illinois* (1956), Dean Duane Monteith's "The Changing Situation and Function of Colchester, Illinois, the Nineteenth Century to the Present" (master's thesis, 1976), and Vera Cordell's *Mt. Auburn Cemetery, Colchester, Illinois* (1983). One of my own books, *McDonough County Heritage* (1984), includes several short articles on Colchester as well as a discussion of McDonough County historical materials; another one, *Macomb: A Pictorial History* (1990), reflects cultural change at the county seat and includes a short section on bootlegging and corruption during the Prohibition era.

The essential sources for *The Bootlegger* were the back issues of the *Colchester Independent* (1880–1977) and the *Macomb Journal* (1855–) as well as selected issues of the Omaha newspapers—all of which are available on microfilm—and the recollections of scores of people who live, or once lived, in Colchester or McDonough County.

It is doubtful that anyone could have written about Kelly Wagle before a few people who were close to him had died: his widow, his sister, and his rival, Jay Moon. They all had things to hide. As Geneva Wagle once said, "Nobody is going to write any damn history of my brother while I'm alive." The townspeople waited a long time, until the last of them was gone, and then confided what they knew to an outsider who was anxious to listen. I am particularly indebted to several older residents, in their nineties when I interviewed them, who could recall young Kelly, as well as his father, his mother, his uncle, his early wives, and others who died or left town long ago.

None of those who shared what they knew about Kelly Wagle or the town is identified in the history itself—an agreement that made very frank interviews possible. Colchester is, after all, a typical small town where people often know more than they are willing to say publicly.

The following 103 residents or former residents of McDonough County provided recollections, stories, and other information that, taken together, made the book possible: Geraldyne Baumgardner, Lily Beck, Larry Bland, John Bliven, Estelene Bodenhamer, Gerald Booth, Peggy Booth, Tom Brown, Albert Burgard, Dorothy Burgard, Marlin Burton, Opal Burton, Clair Butcher, Martin Calvert, Delbert Campbell, Elsie Carnahan, Hazel Carson, J. Cuyler ("Tink") Carson, Larry L. Carson,

Maxine Carson, Elva Hagan Clark, Pearl Cooper, James Cordell, Richard Cordell, Vera Cordell, Richard Crabb, Elizabeth Creasey, Howard Creasey, J. W. ("Bill") Day, John Denney, Arlin Fentem, Damon Fentem, Ruth Forner, James Foster, Marcia Foster, Jack Frost, Burdette Graham, Eloise Graham, Cecil Graves, Jim Haines, Ethel Hanks, Dorothy Harris, Jean Henderson, Viletta Hillery, Frank Hocker, Leland Hocker, Kenneth Hodges, Reynolds Hungerford, Charles ("Chick") Hunt, Dorothy Irish, Pat Irish, Bluford Jackson, James B. Jackson, Pam Johnson, Keith King, Alfred Kipling, Ray Kipling, Eva Lambert, Albert ("Swede") Larson, Ruby Larson, Alfred J. Lindsey, Jr., Clarence ("Mac") Maguire, Ralph McFadden, Russell McGrann, Doris McRaven, Joe McRaven, Harriet Measley, Everett Moon, June Moon, Richard Moon, Bennie Mordue, Vail Morgan, Leroy ("Stix") Morley, Charlotte Morrow, Helen Myers, Joe Myers, Frances Naylor, George Naylor, Orval ("Tenny") Nelson, Donald O'Harra, Laura O'Harra, Max Powell, Dean Reeverts, Morris E. Roark, Eleanor Rudolph, Marilyn Shelley, John Stephens, Stella Stewart, Raymond Stones, Nick Thompson, Eleanor Twaddle, Rollon ("Ozzie") Van Fleet, Robert Vawter, Alan Walker, John Walley, Cecil ("Buss") Wayland, George Webster, Frances Welch, Norm Welker, Leona Wetzel, Lloyd R. Williams, William Wyne, and Elinora Ziesler.

I am also indebted to the following people from other locations, who also supplied information: Mildred Blythe (Fountain Green), Kenneth Cutler (Carthage), Ida Jackson (Fountain Green), James H. Lawton (Plymouth), Don Metzler (Hinsdale), Carma J. Owens (Louisiana, Mo.), Irvin Pogue (Chillicothe), and Marilyn Richey (West Lafayette, Ind.).

I am particularly grateful to Donald O'Harra, a Colchester newspaper editor and historian who not only provided information and photographs over many years but also read and commented on the typescript. In his time, no one had been more important to the historical enterprise in Colchester.

Likewise, I greatly appreciate the contributions of Ray Kipling of Colchester and the late Rollon ("Ozzie") Van Fleet of Blandinsville, who also provided information and read the typescript. Their comments led to a number of changes.

My sincere thanks to my long-time friends and former colleagues at Western Illinois University, Kenneth D. Alley and Ray B. Blackwelder, as well as my friend James Hurt, of the University of Illinois at Urbana-Champaign, who also read and critiqued the typescript. I could not have asked for more talented, helpful commentators. Two scholars who evaluated the manuscript for University of Illinois Press, James Ballowe of Bradley University and Gerald Danzer of the University of Illinois at Chicago, also provided useful comments and much-appreciated enthusiasm for the book.

My thanks also to the staff at the University of Illinois Press, especially director and editor-in-chief Richard L. Wentworth and managing editor Theresa L. Sears, for their expertise in book production and contributions to the final form of *The Bootlegger.*

As always, I am indebted to three people with whom I have worked for many years at the Archives and Special Collections unit of Western Illinois University Library: Sally McPherson, Gordana Rezab, and Marla Vizdal. During the ten years when I was working on this project, they provided a variety of helpful information and suggestions. Also, the following Illinois Regional Archives Directory interns who worked at the library during those years occasionally tracked down information for me: Teresa Chapman, Bill Cook, Anne Pulley, Phil Reynolds, Hope Simmons, and Abigail Sutton.

The maps of Colchester in the 1870s and 1880s and of the street where Kelly Wagle was killed were adapted from McDonough County atlases and the *Macomb Journal,* respectively, by Scott Miner, the cartographer at Western Illinois University.

My thanks to the Library-Archives Center of the Douglas County Historical Society in Omaha, for permission to reprint the Harris report to J. Loy Maloney; to Joe McRaven, for permission to reprint Wallace Walker's report on Jay Moon; to the *Macomb Journal,* for permission to reprint the 1929 murder scene map as well as several articles from that newspaper; and to the *Omaha World-Herald,* for permission to reprint the photographs of Kelly and Beulah Wagle and the Omaha Mystery Girl's headstone, which appeared in 1930, and the morgue shot of Beulah, which appeared in 1919. Also, special thanks are due to Archives and Special Collections, Western Illinois University Library, for permission to print some two dozen photographs from the Colchester and McDonough County collections.

The following institutions also provided information: Burlington (Iowa) Public Library, Chicago Historical Society, Colchester Public Library, Drake Public Library (Centerville, Iowa), Galena (Kans.) Public Library, Galesburg Public Library, Historical Society of Douglas

County (Omaha), Illinois State Archives, Illinois State Historical Library, Joplin (Mo.) Public Library, Kenton County Public Library (Covington, Ky.), Macomb Latter Day Saints Family History Center, McDonough County Circuit Clerk's Office, McDonough County Clerk's Office, Missouri Historical Society (St. Louis), Quincy Public Library, and Warren County Public Library (Monmouth).

Finally, I would like to thank my son Darrin for putting the final draft of *The Bootlegger* onto the computer, and my wife Garnette for her patience and support during this long project.

John E. Hallwas is a professor of English and an archivist at Western Illinois University in Macomb, where he teaches courses in American literature and nonfictional creative writing. He has written or edited twenty books related to Illinois history and literature, including *Western Illinois Heritage* (1981) and *Spoon River Anthology: An Annotated Edition* (1992). He has also written dozens of articles for journals and magazines as well as hundreds of newspaper essays.